1 MONTH OF FREE READING

at

www.ForgottenBooks.com

By purchasing this book you are eligible for one month membership to ForgottenBooks.com, giving you unlimited access to our entire collection of over 1,000,000 titles via our web site and mobile apps.

To claim your free month visit: www.forgottenbooks.com/free1055426

* Offer is valid for 45 days from date of purchase. Terms and conditions apply.

ISBN 978-0-331-76476-5
PIBN 11055426

This book is a reproduction of an important historical work. Forgotten Books uses state-of-the-art technology to digitally reconstruct the work, preserving the original format whilst repairing imperfections present in the aged copy. In rare cases, an imperfection in the original, such as a blemish or missing page, may be replicated in our edition. We do, however, repair the vast majority of imperfections successfully; any imperfections that remain are intentionally left to preserve the state of such historical works.

Forgotten Books is a registered trademark of FB &c Ltd.
Copyright © 2018 FB &c Ltd.
FB &c Ltd, Dalton House, 60 Windsor Avenue, London, SW19 2RR.
Company number 08720141. Registered in England and Wales.

For support please visit www.forgottenbooks.com

THE FRATER

Official Organ of The Psi Omega Fraternity.

PUBLISHED BY
THE SUPREME CO
In November, January, March and
AT TIFFIN, OHIO.

SUPREME COUNCIL

Dr. EDW. H. STING,   91 E. Perry St., Tiffin, Ohio.
Dr. J. E. NYCE,   1001 Witherspoon Bldg., Philadelphia, Pa.
Dr. H. E. FRIESELL,   6000 Penn Ave., Pittsburg, Pa.

BUSINESS MANAGER.

Dr. J. E. NYCE,   1001 Witherspoon Bldg., Philadelphia, Pa.

EDITOR-IN-CHIEF.

Dr. EDW. H. STING,   Tiffin, Ohio.

SUBSCRIPTION.

One Dollar per year, payable in advance :: The Frater will be sent to all subscribers until ordered discontinued :: Send all communications to the Editor-in-Chief. :: Exchanges please send one copy to each of the Supreme Councilors.

Entered as second-class matter November 7, 1904, at the Post Office at Tiffin, Ohio.

FRATERNITY DIRECTORY.

Active Chapters.

ALPHA	Baltimore College of Dental Surgery.
BETA	New York College of Dentistry.
GAMMA	Pennsylvania Col. of Dental Surgery, Phila.
DELTA	Tufts Dental College, Boston, Mass.
EPSILON	Western Reserve University, Cleveland, O.
ZETA	University of Pennsylvania, Philadelphia.
ETA	Philadelphia Dental College.
THETA	University of Buffalo, Dental Department.
IOTA	Northwestern University, Chicago, Ill.
KAPPA	Chicago College of Dental Surgery.
LAMBDA	University of Minnesota, Minneapolis.
MU	University of Denver, Denver, Col.
NU	Pittsburg Dental College, Pittsburg, Pa.
XI	Milwaukee, Wis., Med. Col., Dental Dept.
MU DELTA	Harvard University, Dental Department.
OMICRON	Louisville College of Dental Surgery.
PI	Baltimore Medical College, Dental Dept.
BETA SIGMA	College of Physicians and Surgeons, Dental Department, San Francisco, Cal.
RHO	Ohio Col. of Dental Surgery, Cincinnati.
SIGMA	Medico-Chirurgical College, Philadelphia.
TAU	Atlanta Dental College, Atlanta, Ga.
UPSILON	University of Southern California, Dental Department, Los Angeles.
PHI	University of Maryland, Baltimore.
CHI	North Pacific Dental Col., Portland, Ore.
PSI	College of Dentistry, O. M. U., Columbus.
OMEGA	Indiana Dental College, Indianapolis, Ind.
BETA ALPHA	University of Illinois, Chicago.
BETA GAMMA	George Washington, Uni., Washington, D.C.
BETA DELTA	University of California, San Francisco.
BETA EPSILON	New Orleans College of Dentistry.
BETA ZETA	Marion-Sims Dental College, St. Louis, Mo.
BETA ETA	Keokuk Dental College Keokuk, Iowa.
BETA THETA	Georgetown University, Washington, D. C.
GAMMA IOTA	Southern Dental College, Atlanta, Ga.
GAMMA KAPPA	University of Michigan, Ann Arbor.
GAMMA LAMBDA	Col. of Dental and Oral Surg. of New York.
GAMMA MU	University of Iowa, Iowa City.

Alumni Chapters.

New York Alumni Chapter	New York City.
Duquesne Alumni Chapter	Pittsburg, Pa.
Minnesota Alumni Chapter	Minneapolis, Minn.
Chicago Alumni Chapter	Chicago, Ill.
Boston Alumni Chapter	Boston, Mass.
Philadelphia Alumni Chapter	Philadelphia, Pa.
New Orleans Alumni Chapter	New Orleans, La.
Los Angeles Alumni Chapter	Los Angeles, Cal.
Cleveland Alumni Chapter	Cleveland, Ohio.
Sealth Alumni Chapter	Seattle, Wash.
Portsmouth Alumni Chapter	Portsmouth, Ohio.

ALUMNI DIRECTORY.

Ada, O.—
C. W. Brecheisen, Psi, '02.
Aiken, S. C.—
G. A. Milner, Tau, '05.
Allegheny, Pa.—
F. H. Deterding, Nu, '05, Room 4, Sterrit Bldg.
Reynolds M. Sleppy, Nu, '04, 1915 Beaver avenue.
Altoona, Pa.—
Herbert R. Wehrle, Nu, '03, Altoona Trust Bldg.
Arkadelphia, Ark.—
J. C. Settles, Omicron, '04.
Augusta, Ga.—
R. H. Calhoun, Tau, '04, 936 Broad street.
Baltimore, Md.—
Prof. W. Simon, Alpha, 1348 Block street.
Brooklyn, N. Y.—
Ellison Hillyer, Beta, '93, 472 Greene avenue.
Winthrop W. Thompson, Beta, '02, 383 Hancock street.
Horace P. Gould, Beta, '95, 193 Joralemon street.
Walter S. Watson, Beta, '02, 270 Halsey street.
Bowling Green, O.—
E. J. Frowine, Psi, '04.
Buffalo, N. Y.—
Wes. M. Backus, Theta, '04, 485 Grant street.
Chihuahua, Mexico.—
M. F. Bauchert, Beta, '96.
Chico, Cal.—
J. R. Young, Beta Delta, '03. Box 515.
Columbus, O.—
H. M. Semans, Beta, '97, 289 East State street.
Delhi, La.—
T. K. McLemore, Gamma Iota, '06.
Edgefield, S. C.—
Augustus H. Corley, Tau, '04.
Florisant, Mo.—
G. S. Steinmesch, Beta Zeta, '04.
Fort Gaines, Ga.—
R. H. Saunders, Tau, '05.
Fort Leavenworth, Kan.—
J. D. Millikin, Beta Sigma, Dental Surgeon, U.S.A.

Fredericksburg, Tex.—
F. Keidel, Alpha, '04.
Gallitzin, Pa.—
J. L. Paul, Alpha, '01.
Gonzales, Tex.—
S. C. Patton, Tau, '03.
Hancock, Mich.—
Ralph W. DeMass, Beta Gamma, '05, Funkey Block.
Hull, Ill.—
L. H. Wolfe, Beta Eta, '05.
Iager, W. Va.—
G. E. Dennis, Phi, '05.
Ithaca, N. Y.—
A. M. MacGachen, Theta, '03, 218 East State street.
Johnsonburg, Pa.—
H. C. Coleman, Nu, '03.
Johnstown, Pa.—
Owen Morgan, Alpha, '95.
Kaufman, Tex.—
Henry Hoffer, Alpha, '95.
Lafayette, Ind.—
A. R. Ross, Gamma, '03.
Lake City, Cal.—
W. W. Shartel, Chi, '01.
Lewistown, Pa.—
Curtis H. Marsh, Gamma, '06. 14 E. Market street.
Liberty, N. Y.—
W. A. Buckley, Beta, '00.
Logansport, Ind.—
H. G. Stalnaker, Omega, '03.
Los Angeles, Cal.—
J. F. Curran, Kappa, '01, 1919 S. Grand avenue.
C. C. Jarvis, Upsilon, '04, 302 Severance Bldg.
Malone, N. Y.—
R. N. Porter, Gamma, '01.
Manila, P. I.—
O. M. Sorber, Nu, '97, Dental Surgeon, U. S. A.
Mansfield, La.—
G. J. Griffiths, Tau, '03.
McKeesport, Pa.—
W. D. Fawcett, Nu, '99, 508½ Fifth avenue.
Milwaukee, Wis.—
E. J. Schlief, Xi, '97, 417 Wells Bldg.

Morganfield, Ky.—
  W. S. Green, Omicron,' 04.

New York City.—
  A. S. Walker, Beta, '97,
    295 Central Park, West.
  E. W. Burckhardt, Beta,'04,
    Van Corlear Place,
    Kingsbridge.
  S. W. Van Saun, Beta, '00,
    Broadway and 74th St.,
    The Ansonia.

New Kensington, Pa.—
  A. J. Rose, Rho, '03,
    Logan Trust Bldg.

New Orleans, La.—
  A. J. Cohn, Alpha, '99,
    703 Morris Bldg.
  Leon Barnett, Beta
    Epsilon, '05,
    703 Macheca Bldg.
  Rene Esnard, Beta
    Epsilon, '05,
    612 Macheca Bldg.

Norristown, Pa.—
  D. H. Wetzel, Zeta, '02.

Oakland, Cal.—
  C. H. Merritt, Alpha, '98,
    308-9 Union Savings
    Bank Bldg.

Oroville, Cal.—
  L. H. Marks, B. Sigma, '04.

Paso Robles, Cal.—
  W. G. Gates, Kappa, '05.

Paterson, N. J.—
  A. Dewitt Payne, Beta, '99,
    160 Broadway.

Pikesville, Ky.—
  J. M. Williams, Rho, '05.

Pittsburg, Pa.—
  W. Emmory Ferree,
    Alpha, '00, 7138 Hamilton ave., East End.
  C. L. McChesney, Nu, '99,
    98 Washington avenue.
  H. E. Friesell, Gamma, '95,
    6000 Penn avenue.

Philadelphia, Pa.—
  A. F. Goddard, Gamma, '01,
    15th and Chestnut Sts.,
    1302 Pennsylvania Bldg.
  A. P. Lee, Eta, '00,
    3403 Chestnut street.
  J. E. Nyce, Gamma, '02,
    1001 Witherspoon Bldg.

Port Clinton, O.—
  John G. Yingling, Alpha,'97.

Raleigh, N. C.—
  R. G. Sherrill, Omicron, '04.

Roby, Tex.—
  J. N. Platt, Pi, '02.

Rowland, N. C.—
  C. H. Lennan, Tau, '03.

San Francisco, Cal.—
  C. W. Knowles, M.D., D.D.
    S., Beta Sigma, '99,
    Rooms 101-7 Spring
    Valley W. Works Bldg.
  Thos. R. Morffew, Beta
    Sigma, Examiner Bldg.

Seattle, Wash.—
  Geo. T. Williams, Nu, '04,
    Snoqualmie Hotel.
  F. W. Hergert, Chi, '03,
    651 Colman Block.
  C. P. Poston, Chi,
    218 Lumber Exchange.

Springfield, Mass.—
  H. Everton Hosley,
    Gamma, '95,
    Phoenix Bldg.

St. Joseph, Ill.—
  H. E. Davis, Rho, '03.

St. Louis, Mo.—
  H. J. Braun, Beta Zeta, '04,
    2850 St. Louis avenue.
  H. V. Pfaff, Iota, '99,
    2217 St. Louis avenue.

Tiffin, O.—
  W. H. Holtz, Rho, '03.
  E. H. Sting, Alpha, '95.
  E. C. West, Psi, '02.

Topsham, Maine.—
  H. Q. Mariner, Sigma, '05.

Tuscaloosa, Ala.—
  H. Clay Hassell,
    Omicron, '98.

Upland, Ind.—
  J. A. Loughry, Psi, '04.

Union, S. C.—
  Jas. M. Wallace, Phi, '04.

Vinton, Iowa.—
  B. F. Schwartz, Iota, '04.

Warren, Pa.—
  E. C. Thompson, Alpha,'02.

Washington, D. C.—
  Shirley W. Bowles, Eta,'98,
    1315 New York avenue.
  C. L. Constantini,
    Beta Gamma, '03,
    814 14th St., N. W.

Washington, Pa.—
  F. H. Magill, Nu, '04.
    Room 15, Hallam Block.
  Howard R. Smith, Nu, '03,
    17 West Chestnut street.

Waynesboro, Miss.—
  C. H. Gray, Tau, '04.

Winchester, Ky.—
  George S. Brooks, Rho, '02.

Westfield, N. J.—
  Theo. R. Harvey, Gamma,
    '94, 245 Broad street.

Williamson, W. Va.—
  Wm. S. Rosenheim, Pi, '05.

Wellsburg, W. Va.—
  K. C. Brashear, Psi, '02,

THE FRATER.

Vol. 6.   November, 1906.   No. 1.

PHILIPPINE EXPERIENCES.

O. M. Sorber, Nu, '97, Dental Surgeon, U. S. A.

My order to proceed to Manila was received as I was about to proceed, for temporary duty, to Fort Ringgold, one of the remote frontier posts on the Mexican border, about one hundred and thirty miles from the mouth of the Rio Grande river.

The trip to Ft. Ringgold was of course abandoned and instead I proceeded to San Francisco and embarked on the U. S. A. Transport Sherman which sailed from that port Nov. 1st, 1904.

We experienced rough weather from that day until we entered the strait between Luzon and Samar, P. I.

Two stops were made en route; one of twenty-eight hours at Honolulu, the other at Guam, one of the Ladrone Islands.

Honolulu was voted an earthly paradise, especially appreciated after eight days of stormy weather at sea.

Between Honolulu and Guam lonely little Wake Island was passed at a distance of several miles. It is simply a coral atoll about ten miles in diameter and only a few feet above sea level. It is covered with trees and is rich in guano but has no inhabitants.

Eventually we arrived at Guam which your readers will probably recall as the scene of the incident, during the Spanish-American war, where the "Commandante" of the fort mistook hostile shots from an American ship for a salute, and came on board to apologize for not returning the salute, explaining that he was out of powder. The transport stopped here for some time to unload some supplies, this being now a naval and also a cable station.

The harbor is behind a very dangerous reef, and, as we entered, occasional glimpses could be had of the wreck of the big cable ship "Scotia" of London, which was sunk by running on the reef. An opportunity to go ashore here was embraced by a large number of the passengers, the ship's boats being towed to the "hole in the wall," an opening in an inner reef, by launches from the navy collier "Alexander." From this point we were obliged to row several miles through a narrow and tortuous channel, frequently running aground on coral rock. From the landing at Piti, we proceeded to Agana, the capital, by means of two-wheeled vehicles drawn by small, humped, trotting bulls over a splendid road, bordered on both sides by thousands of cocoanut trees, as well as other varieties of trees, some of them covered by orchids.

Many native "shacks" are to be seen along the road; built of palm leaves and poles and elevated about four feet from the ground. Under the houses may generally be seen a family of pigs.

Agana is a quaint old place, not without beauty, built in the characteristic Spanish fashion, generally speaking, without sidewalks.

Some interesting photographs were obtained here including one of the old church much damaged by earthquakes, the Governor's "Palace" and the little old arsenal on top of the hill. The shallow waters of the bay have all the beautiful tints of an opal.

A blinding rain storm made our return to the ship very disagreeable, as we had great difficulty in keeping in the channel, and on arriving in deep water we found a heavy swell which caused some members of the party to "give up" the lunch they had enjoyed at the Governor's Palace. Two passengers fell into the sea in trying to get aboard but were promptly fished out of the "briny" by the ever watchful sailors. Some of the ladies, in ascending the gangway, could not keep ahead of the waves, with what result can be left to the imagination.

We got under headway after dark but almost ran on the reef because a sudden rain squall obscured the light sent out to mark the buoy at the channel. It became necessary to drop the anchor to avoid the fate of the "Scotia," but after the squall passed we got away without further incident and made good time for a few days. A typhoon was then encountered and for fourteen hours the ship was headed toward home while the storm blew itself out. The rest of the voyage was without particular interest except that Albay volcano was sighted while we were passing through San Bernardino strait; early on Nov. 30th we arrived in Manila.

The Oregon and the Wisconsin of the U. S. Navy were seen off Cavite as we passed in.

In Manila the most interesting features are the wall of the

old city, with its gates and moat, and the motley population which includes many races and nationalities, many of them dressed in gaily colored costumes. The wall is being demolished and the moat is being filled to make room for modern improvements. The city is very hot and a very expensive place in which to live. A modern street car line was approaching completion and is now in operation.

After a ten days' stay, I proceeded to Camp McGrath, Batangas province, for duty, arriving on Dec. 11th, '04· The buildings of this post are built of unplaned Oregon pine, roofed with boards, and covered with one of the patent roofing papers. The officers' quarters are lined with a woven bamboo fabric and are fairly comfortable.

The location of the post, upon a bluff overlooking the town and bay of Batangas, is very fine and a good breeze generally blows. A few miles to the northwest is Taal volcano, at present only mildly active. South, across the bay and intervening arm of the China sea, is the Island of Mindoro with mountains rising to an elevation of nearly nine thousand feet.

During my tour of duty at Batangas large bands of ladrones (robbers) raided the northern part of that province and visited terrible vengeance upon those natives whom they suspected of giving information about them by cutting off noses, lips, ears, and even removing the tongue.

While at this post a visit was made to a strip of woods in the neighborhood where thousands of fruit bats or flying foxes hang up by day. They resemble in shape the small bats with which we are all familiar, measuring about fifty-four inches from tip to tip of wings and weigh about as a leghorn hen. They are highly esteemed as an article of diet by the natives who carried away those that we killed. When alarmed by the firing of guns thousands of them rose and circled about, and when brought down by a charge of shot the twisting and flapping of great leathery wings called to mind some of Dore's illustrations of "Paradise Lost."

Another interesting "critter" here is a large lizard that often establishes himself under the eaves of the house or in the attic, where at intervals he emits a loud noise resembling the words "tuck boo," with a marked accent on the "tuck." He is usually most noisy when one is about to go to sleep. One of these chaps fell through an opening in the ceiling one night while we were at dinner and landed on the table, causing a stampede. About half an hour later an earthquake got busy and caused another hurried departure but no damage resulted. Next day we saw a great cloud of steam over Taal volcano.

Some time later a trip was made to the Island of Mindoro, for the purpose of shooting ducks. This expedition filled the full measure of the strenuous trip, commencing with a night ride on a launch and the ascent of a river for a distance of about three miles before daylight in canoes, called "bancas," which were about a foot wide and sixteen inches deep, steadied by bamboo outriggers, and seating two passengers besides the two natives who furnished the motive power. The one in which Captain B—— and I took passage promptly sank when shoved off the beach at the mouth of the river. Our guns and ammunition were quite moist when rescued but we were soon in another and larger boat and away, only to find that the second one was leaking badly and required to be constantly baled out with a cocoanut shell. At this point some ammunition fell overboard but one of the boatmen was induced to dive and bring it up, however, he appeared to be somewhat reluctant about going after it. Later, upon learning that there are crocodiles in the river, his reluctance was better understood.

The rendezvous, a plantation called "Chicago," owned by a trading company, was at last reached, where an opportunity presented for us to see hundreds of cocoanuts sprouting, preparatory to being set out; also abaca (hemp), one of the great products of the islands, scarcely to be distinguished from banana plants, except by those familiar with both. There were also a few cocoa trees. From the bean which grows on this tree chocolate is made.

Here our party was joined by several members of the Philippine Commission, the Governor of Mindoro, and a number of others.

As no ducks could be found, attention was then turned to other game and your correspondent secured a large monkey, a lizard four feet, ten inches long (said to be an iguana, and much esteemed by the natives as "chow"), some pigeons about the size of bantam chickens, white parrots resembling small cockatoos, green parrots, and various water fowl of unknown names.

Capt. B—— and I ascended the river for a distance of about five miles, from which point we got a good view of Mt. Holcon which is said never to have been ascended by any white man. Far up the mountain side could be seen small clearings probably made by a wild tribe which has always refused to accept Christianity. They are reputed to be quite harmless and are very timid and we did not see any of them.

In this neighborhood the writer obtained a good idea of a tropical jungle, great areas being utterly impassable to anything less powerful than an 'elephant or a rhinoceros. There were occasional fields of grass twelve to fifteen feet high, the individual stems as thick as a broom handle, and so matted together as to be an effectual barrier to all progress. At first it was mistaken for a field of very dense sugar cane.

It was my misfortune to become separated from my guide, while shooting pigeons, and to lose my bearings completely. After a very strenuous time the river was at last found and the boat picked me up in an exhausted condition and bearing on my person such a complete collection of scratches and punctures that a month was scarcely enough time to complete repairs.

On the other side of the mountain are found numerous "tamarraw," an animal somewhat similar to the so-called "carabao" or water buffalo of these islands, but smaller and said to be found on no other island of this group and elsewhere only in the Dutch East Indies. They are reputed to be untamable, and are not much hunted by the natives who greatly fear them as they are about as amiable and dangerous as a grizzly bear.

The rest of this trip was without special incident but needless to say "Once was enough for me."

PHILADELPHIA ALUMNI CHAPTER BANQUET.

Victor Cochran, Zeta, '01.

At the close of the meeting of the Pennsylvania State Dental Association, June 28, 1906, the Philadelphia Alumni chapter held an informal banquet, inviting all Psi Omegas present to participate.

Boothby's was selected by the committee in charge, and promptly at 6:30, forty loyal members sat down to an intellectual as well as a material feast. Supreme Councilor, Brother Friesell, acted as toastmaster. His knowledge of men in general and Psi Omegas in particular especially fits him to perform this function and his style of introducing the speakers proved to be one of the features of the evening.

Dr. James Truman (Zeta) one of our oldest and most revered honorary members was first called upon, and in an enthusiastic manner expressed his interest in all that pertains to our fraternity and the welfare of those connected with it. The prolonged applause indicated that Doctor Truman's remarks had met with the approval and appreciation of all.

The next speaker of the evening was Dr. I. N. Broomell (Gamma) and like Dr. Truman he expressed a keen interest in our fraternity work and the advancement of its members. Dr. Broomell has been recently elected dean of the Dental Department of the Medico Chirurgical College and Sigma is to be congratulated upon having at the head of her school a man of his ability.

Dr. Joseph Head (Zeta) the next speaker, never loses an opportunity to inject into his audience a charge of that true Psi Omega spirit for which he is so well known and upon this occasion he was especially enthusiastic and interesting.

Brothers George W. Warren (Gamma), W. J. Roe (Gamma) and George Cupett (Sigma), each in his turn responded to the call of the toastmaster and in brief but forceful remarks added much to the intellectual feature of the evening.

Dr. Walter Neal (Gamma), is an accomplished story teller and elocutionist. His recitation of "Barbara Fritchie" in broken English was well rendered and delighted his audience.

Dr. P. E. Loder (Gamma) was present but was obliged to leave early in the evening.

Eta was well represented by Past Grand Master, Brother Wilbur who spoke of the sterling worth of her members and the earnest and effective work being done in the chapter.

Brother Holland (Zeta '06) spoke for the British in Psi Omega and in his inimitable style assured us of the loyalty of our brothers across the seas. Dr. Holland has since returned to Australia where we are reasonably sure a chapter will soon be organized.

After singing "Oh, You Must Be a Psi Omega Man" with vim and snap as it was never sung before, each went his way better satisfied with the world and with a determination, if possible, to be better Psi Omegas.

This banquet is the first of its kind held in this city and was a success far beyond our expectations. The committee, Bros. Nyce (Gamma), Standen (Zeta) and Chandler (Eta), is to be congratulated upon the successful result of its efforts.

Let us hope that all Psi Omegas will adopt this plan and where dental meetings of any kind are held, get together, have something to eat and a little talk, it need not be a banquet, but something to eat will be necessary.

THE N. D. A. MEETING.

E. H. Sting, S. C.

The meeting of the National Dental Association held in Atlanta, Ga., afforded the Supreme Councilors of Psi Omega an opportunity of meeting a large number of the members of our good chapters, Tau and Gamma Iota, besides attending the sessions. At this meeting was especially made apparent the fact that men of comparative youth are helping to shape the course of dental education in conjunction with men of more mature age. The writer was especially impressed with this fact upon his arrival at the Piedmont Hotel on a certain Monday morning at 1:30, to find a committee at work in the interest of the National Faculties Association. The members of this committee were two Psi Omegas and one "Barb," I think. These men were our venerable member of Alpha, Dr. M. W. Foster, Dean of the Baltimore College of Dental Surgery; Dr. Marshall, a man of less mature age, and our energetic, comparatively youthful Supreme Councilor, Friesell. Youth should have consideration for those who have given the greater portion of their lives and strength to the upbuilding of the profession; but I suppose the exigencies of the case demanded that time be secured as best it could for the transaction of business.

The Atlanta Dental Society made a successful effort to entertain the stranger dentists while in their midst; the most unique being the Georgia Barbecue held at the "Que Club."

Upon arrival at the club, the guests found everything in readiness, the pig and lamb roasted to a turn, the Brunswick stew properly seasoned and the "coffee" at the proper temperature.

Some six hundred mouths were to be fed, and the placing of the tempting edibles expeditiously at the disposal of such a crowd of hungry visitors was no easy task. The local dentists were pressed into service and waited upon the table, consequently Nyce, Friesell, and Sting had friends "at court" in the persons of Hill, Lorenz, and Holbeck, so that it was not long until very choice cuts of pig and lamb and a steaming dish of the famous Brunswick stew were being sampled. Everybody did justice to the occasion and it was a happy contented crowd which arose from the tables. Incidentally, it might be well to state that the ingredients of this stew must certainly be a State-secret for it is very jealously guarded. An effort was made to obtain the "formula" from our beloved Hill, but to no avail. However, a dish of stew, as served by the "Que Club," will go a long way in recompensing one for the arduousness of a journey to Atlanta.

After the repast speeches were in order; and here again, because of the demands of the audience, it was made evident that Psi Omega would be drawn upon to furnish the most pleasing morsel in this line. Every person who has heard him, and there are many who have had that pleasure, will concede that B. Holly Smith shines more brilliant than nearly all men in making an after-dinner talk. He sustained his reputation at Atlanta. The entertainment afforded at the "Que Club" was unique, new and gave the guests more real pleasure than could possibly any other form of entertainment.

Probably the most pleasing social event of the meeting was the banquet given at The Aragon Hotel in honor of Supreme Councilors Friesell, Nyce, and Sting, by the members of Tau and Gamma Iota chapters, Thursday evening, September 20th. After a reception in the parlors of the hotel, the party was conducted to a private dining room and proceeded forthwith to "lay waste" the menu.

Informal talks were then the order of the evening. Past Grand Master, De Los L. Hill of Tau, acted as toastmaster and in a neatly framed speech introduced the first orator of the evening. This proved to be Friesell, whom we all wanted to hear. In ending his talk he bestowed much praise upon one of the members present as follows:

"As a teacher of Operative Dentistry, it has been my aim to observe the operations of the best men in our profession in the making of gold fillings, and of late I have been taking special note of the methods of men who are making gold inlays; this was one of my special objects in coming to Atlanta as I knew that Psi Omega had within her ranks a man specially skilled in inlay work. It was a pleasure to have this young man demonstrate to me his methods of constructing inlays, step by step, and I want to say that I firmly believe that Psi Omega has in the person of Brother Lorenz an inlay worker without a superior in the United States."

Buford F. Boykin, Gamma Iota, '05' was next introduced and soon had the assemblage in an uproar. Boykin was able to "produce the goods" and the countenance of every person present was continuously wreathed in smiles during the time he had the floor.

Toastmaster Hill next introduced Mr. F. O. Foster of Atlanta, who entertained us with his Negro dialect stories. Mr.

Foster made apparent that "A little nonsense now and then is relished by the wisest men."

Talks of less length followed, then Toastmaster Hill in a few fitting remarks broke up the assemblage; good-byes were finally said and one of the most pleasant social functions was a subject for reminiscences.

The meeting of the National Dental Association was one of the most successful in the history of the organization. The method of having only one section on duty at a time proved popular and will probably be adopted at subsequent meetings. The papers were also very good, as were the clinics.

At the close of the meeting of the National Dental Association, the visiting practitioners departed feeling that they had been amply repaid for time and means spent in attending the meeting.

MATERIA MEDICA.

(The result of three years' careful (though enforced) study and research by the members of the Scientific Research Society of the Class of '06, College of Dental and Oral Surgery of New York.)

Latin Name:—Materia Medicosum.

Chemical Symbol:---$CR_2 I_7 Me_{23}$.

(Not official, and never will be.)

Synonyms—Craniosum Impenetrosum, Antimemorium and Dental Students' Delight.

Preparation—It is prepared by a complicated process, known to the ancients (Hippocrates having first prepared it), but unknown at the present day. This compound becomes old with age and has to be redistilled every ten years.

Description—It is a hard, amorphous subject, with a pungent odor, very tasteless and remains dry under all conditions. It is insoluble in the cerebro-spinal fluids. It burns readily (this has been proven by simple methods after state board exams.) but does not support combustion or life, except simple life in the twist house. Although it is omnipresent (during the term,) it is difficult to obtain and more difficult to keep when it is caught.

Dose—Four or five pages twice a week, taken before retiring and upon arising. There is no adjuvant nor corrective known.

Physiological Action:—

External:—

It cannot be absorbed by the unbroken skin. It is a caustic. It is a disinfectant, as it instantly destroys certain bacteria as the Bacillus hapiigoluckiis, Restococcus and Streptococcus dilatorius intercellularis.

Internal:—

Digestive Tract—It paralyzes peristaltic movements and diminishes the secretions. It is indigestible and is not acted upon by the gastric or any other juice.

Circulation—It is a heart depressant, causing that sinking feeling, the blood pressue, however, is raised.

Blood—It is a blood coagulant, liberating fibrin by reflex action. To think of it makes one's blood run cold.

Respiration—Causes the respiration to take the form of long drawn sighs and loud manifestations such as groans, accompanied by facial distortions.

Nervous System—When taken in moderate doses it is a limited stimulant, causing intermittent studious activity. In large doses it is a depressant. It is the best hypnotic we have. If taken frequently, causes loss of memory and abolition of reflex action.

Skin—A diaphoretic, causing a cold perspiration to appear when an effort is made to assimilate it.

Special Senses—Efforts to introduce it by the auditory apparatus are of no avail, as it is immediately excreted by the other ear. It is a mydriatic and an irritant to the optic nerves.

Toxicology:—

Acute Poisoning—Large doses have caused the most alarming symptoms, blues, lassitude, general malice, nausea, non compus mentus, and collapse followed by stoppage of the clock.

Treatment—Treat on general principles. Do not use a stomach pump. Give stimulants such as Wilson's or Hunter's mixtures, but never hypodermically, as it won't do any good that way.

Chronic Poisoning—Is altogether too common, due to the large and frequent doses given by professors of materia medica. It does not, however, act as an accumulative poison, as it does not require any effort to excrete it, but by repeated attacks upon the system it causes a general derangement.

Symptoms—Entire change in moral perceptions; the student will swear, lie and cheat during recitations, neglect his duties, and his temperature undergoes a complete change. (Note how these terrible symptoms resemble those of chronic opium poisoning.) Most of the symptoms of acute poisoning are also present. Most of the symptoms are subjective as the student tries to hide the objective symptoms from the examiner.

Treatment—Preventative treatment, but "that's up to the prof!" Unless the size of the lesson is cut down, all treatment is hopeless and in severe cases isolation in sanitariums may be necessary.

Therapeutics:—

Used generally for "cuts." As a hypnotic it has no equal, and its effect is more lasting and difficult to shake off. Acts as a tonic by a peculiar indirect action, causing a desire for more air, thus stimulating oxygenosis. Given to stimulate the action of the nerve cells of the cerebrum of studious students, but should not be given often nor in large doses, as it will destroy studious habits. In passing it might be well to state that solutions of seventy-five per cent. or over are necessary—in exams.

DENTISTRY—ITS EARLIER A   TORY.

Leon Barnett, Beta Epsilon, '05.

Dentistry is that branch of the healing art which has for its province the treatment of diseases and lesions of the human teeth and their replacement by substitutes when lost.

While civilized nations consider their teeth the most beautiful in their natural color and form, some nations mutilate their teeth by chipping, filing and altering their form, in some cases also staining them to conform to their peculiar ideas of beauty. Mutilation is practiced by certain wild tribes of Africa, New Guinea, Java, and the Tasmanian coast of Australia, and is prompted by fashion, superstition, or conformity with religious rites.

Filing of front teeth to points is practiced by Abyssinians to increase the savageness of their aspect and terrify their foes. With the Malays, filing the teeth is a religious act. In Indo-China and Japan, girls have their teeth stained black at the time of marriage. .

Early History.—Herodotis, the Greek historian, tells of the attention given to diseases of the teeth as well as of the eye and ear in Egypt. Belzoni and other writers claim to have found in Egyptian tombs artificial teeth made of ivory and wood, some of which were mounted upon gold plates.

Teeth in mummies are said to have been found filled with gold and a white cement but of this there is no positive evidence.

In 1884, Dr. Van Marter, of Florence, discovered in the museum of Corneto, Italy, skulls exhumed from Etruscan tombs in which pure gold wire was wound around natural teeth which indicated that in the spaces between where teeth were lacking, artificial or possibly human teeth had at some time been thus supported in place.

Later History.—During the eighteenth century dentistry became a subject of more critical inquiry and thorough investigation. Men of intelligence and education devoted themselves to it exclusively, and, as a result, its advancement in both literary and scientific directions during the nineteenth century has been most marked. This is evidenced by the fact that from 1800 to 1892 there were published in Europe and America some 200 volumes treating exclusively on the diseases of the teeth.

Until the latter part of the eighteenth century any advance in dentistry was confined to Europe, but since then the most rapid advancement has been made in the United States.

The first dentist practicing in the United States of whom there is any account, was one Le Maire who accompanied the French army in 1775-83, then came to this country. Soon after LeMaire's arrival, came an English dentist named Whitlock. The first native dentist is believed to be John Greenwood who began practice in New York about 1778.

I will quote one of the advertisements which appeared in some of the New York papers as early as 1784. The following appeared in "Rivingston's Gazette" of December, 24, 1783:

"Mr. Greenwood, Surgeon Dentist (lately arrived in this city), begs leave to acquaint the publick that he preserves the Teeth and Gums by removing an infectious Tartar, that destroys them and renders the natural purity of the breath offensive. He cures Scurvy in the gums; also fastens the teeth by causing the gums to grow up and adhere to them. He extracts and replaces the

Teeth, and makes them white. He substitutes Artificial Teeth in so neat a manner as not to be perceived from natural ones, without drawing the stumps or causing the least pain. They give a youthful air to the countenance, and render pronunciation more agreeable and distinct; in a word, both Natural and Artificial are of much real service—it is a folly to neglect them. And as he would ever have the work recomend him, he requires no pay from those that are not completely satisfied with his performances. He has Pills for the Tooth Ache, that seldom fail to give relief; likewise boxes of Tooth Powder and Brushes that will recomend themselves."

"N. B.—Mr. Greenwood will with pleasure attend those Ladies and Gentlemen who cannot conveniently wait on him at rooms in Mrs. Richardson's house, No. 24 at the Old Slip in New York."

Dr. Greenwood constructed entire dentures for Gen. Washington during 1790-95. They were carved from ivory and retained in the mouth by means of spiral springs. These dentures may now be seen in the Museum of the Baltimore College of Dental Surgery.

Then came Spencer from England, Gardette from France, Hudson from Ireland, and Koecker from London.

In 1820 there were about 100 practitioners, in 1892 the number was 18,000. The first dental school in the United States was chartered by the legislature of Maryland in 1839, with the title of Baltimore College of Dental Surgery. The Ohio Dental College at Cincinnati was chartered and established in 1845; the Pennsylvania College of Dental Surgery at Philadelphia was established in 1856, and the Philadelphia Dental College in 1865.

In 1892 the number of dental colleges in the United States was 38; the number of graduates from various dental colleges in the United States from 1880-92 inclusive was 6,329, while the number of graduates in 1892 alone amounted to 1,483.

The first diploma granted to a woman was in 1869. The first dental periodical in the United States was published at Baltimore in 1839; in 1892 there were seventeen.

The first dental society in the United States, the American Society of Dental Surgeons, was organized in 1840; in 1892 there were 130.

Rubber dam was first used by Dr. S. C. Barnum, of New York, in 1864; he was the inventor.

Active Chapters.

ALPHA—BALTIMORE COLLEGE OF DENTAL SURGERY.

E. J. Lawler, Editor.

Alpha sends greetings to all Psi Omegas, also reports all of her active members back for their respective duties.

The attendance at our college this year is very much larger than that of last year, especially in the freshman class, so that the juniors did not have such an easy time taking the freshies out for "orders" as did the juniors last year.

Alpha is not to have a house this year but she has leased the Beethoven hall, situated at 521 N. Howard street. We meet the second and last Wednesdays of each month, all visiting brothers will be welcome.

Our degree team will have a pleasant "job" shortly, as there are a number of good men who are to join our ranks.

On May 28, Alpha suffered a great loss in the person of an honored and distinguished honorary member, Thomas S. Latimer, M. D. Brother Latimer was the oldest member of the faculty of our college so that his death is all the more felt by the college and by the fraternity. He was a kindly man, a man above reproach and was beloved by all. He occupied the Chair of Physiology and Comparative Anatomy; when classed as a lecturer, he had few equals and no peers. Because of his great fluency of speech and wonderful vocabulary, it was easy for him to make his lectures perfectly understood by the students. His convictions were strong and his courage undoubted which were made evident long years ago by his record made in the interest of the Lost Cause.

Many of Alpha's '06 men have located and they feel greatly pleased by the encouragement extended to them by the older practitioners and by the public.

BETA—NEW YORK COLLEGE OF DENTISTRY.

George R. Christian, Editor.

To all Psi Omegas, the brothers of Beta send their best wishes as a symbol of greeting for the session now at hand.

In the vicinity of the college and the frat house things are again astir, for those who have laid dormant through the summer are again stretching their weary bones to drag themselves to the lectures and classes. However, Beta is not well represented in the circle of yawning, idle students. On the contrary we are being stimulated to extra exertion by knowing how our brothers are gaining distinction at the college and by viewing the appearance of the group of new men who are prospective members. Ten or twelve of these were entertained at the frat house last week and it will probably be stated in our next report that they are with us as members.

It is with regret that we had to part with Brothers John F. Areson, Bernard Du Bois and William A. Hopkins. The first two have transferred to the University of Pennsylvania and the third to the Philadelphia Dental College. We hope to hear favorably from them from time to time as the session wears away.

Wishing all a very happy, prosperous and successful season we anxiously await The Frater and news from our sister chapters.

DELTA—TUFTS DENTAL COLLEGE.

C. P. Haven, Editor.

Delta sends greetings to all sister chapters and to the Supreme Council.

The '06 members were wined, dined and bidden a fitting God speed; a banquet and reception having been held in their honor at the close of the year at which were also present President Hamilton, Secretary Briggs, and several members of our faculty. Sound and good was the advice given by these men to the members remaining as well as to those leaving to begin the practice of their profession.

The officers for the present year who will have charge of the welfare and guidance of Delta were named in Theta's editorial for last May. It is the general opinion that the interests of the chapter will be carefully and judiciously handled with such men at the helm and that success and advancement are assured. We have engaged and furnished a cosy little suite of rooms at 393 Massachusetts avenue and there all members of Psi Omega will be made welcome.

At our second meeting, Thursday, Oct. 18th, we "put through the mill," as one newly made Psi Omega has aptly termed our initiation, three worthy students, who, according to their past records, promise to be a credit to Psi Omega and to our profession. They are:

Harold E. Smith......................Athol, Mass.
Walter C. Brayshaw.........North Weymouth, Mass.
John H. Hollihan...............New Bedford, Mass.

We sincerely hope that all sister chapters have as bright an outlook for the coming year as has Delta.

EPSILON—WESTERN RESERVE UNIVERSITY.

C. C. Rogers, Editor.

Epsilon chapter is entering upon a year which bids fair to be a very prosperous one. We commenced this year with ten undergraduate members. We lost by graduation last June four members, Brothers Pontius, of Akron, O.; Bevard, of Elyria, O.; and Brothers Jones and Arosamena, of Cleveland.

We regret very much to announce the loss of Brother H. E. G. Wright, one of our most energetic members, who by a painful accident this past summer, lost several fingers, thus necessitating his abandoning his place in the ranks of our profession. At this writing the last word we have from Brother Wright is that he is entering into an engineering course. We desire to extend to Brother Wright our most sincere and heartfelt sympathy.

We have with us this year several new members in the faculty, viz.: Drs. Friesell, McLernon, Belford and Friedman, all

Psi Omegas. We give them a hearty welcome, and are looking forward to a very profitable year.

October 12th we gave a smoker at our room at the college which proved a very enjoyable and successful function. We have already pledged several new men, and have good prospects for others.

One of our Brothers, S. A. Allen, has this summer taken unto himself a wife. We wish to extend to Brother and Mrs. Allen our hearty congratulations.

We hear that our graduate members are all happily located and wish them all success.

ETA—PHILADELPHIA DENTAL COLLEGE.

Lewis B. Duffield, Editor.

It is with great pleasure that Eta sends forth greetings to the Supreme Council and to her sister chapters, sincerely hoping that a bright and prosperous year will be the future of every chapter of Psi Omega.

Last year was one of the most successful years Eta has ever had, but we look for greater things this year. We had the misfortune of losing our happy home at 725 North 18th street, but it appears that all things happen for the best, as we have more comfortable quarters at 1732 Spring Garden street, where we cordially invite members of all sister chapters to call at any of our meetings, which are held every Thursday evening.

We have several pledged men from last year, and quite a number from the freshman class of this year, whom we expect to initiate in the near future. We take pleasure in introducing the following officers for the coming year:

Grand Master.................Matthias H. Casey, '07.
Junior Master.................Maurice A. Buck, '08.
Secretary......................John A. Teeden, '07.
Treasurer.................... Joseph Borchardt, '07.
Senator.......................Richard Aicheles, '07.
Chief Inquisitor................George Whitely, '07.
Chief Interrogator..............Milliam Daniels, '08.

Historian....................Lewis B. Duffield, '08·
Inside Guardian..................Wm. Talcott, '08·
Outside Guardian.................Oscar Koenig, '08·
Editor.......................Lewis B. Duffield, '08·
Executive Committee—Stephen J. Casey, William Herlig, Maurice A. Buck.

THETA—UNIVERSITY OF BUFFALO.

H. E. Marshall, G. M., Editor.

Theta sends greetings to all Psi Omegas.

On account of so many brothers graduating, we are rather weak in numbers. Those of us who are left are entering heart and soul into the work of our frat.

We began the year by holding a smoker. There were quite a number of freshmen present, also some of our alumni members, so that our first social effort was voted a grand success. No new members have been initiated as yet, but we hope to introduce some soon.

At present we are located at 25 Best street, where all Psi Omegas are welcome to the shelter of our roof.

Theta is sorry to lose, for this year, Brother Harry F. Hoffman, who, on account of his eyesight becoming impaired, will have to discontinue his work. He was one of Theta's most ardent supporters and she hopes to have him with her another year. Also does Theta regret the loss of Brother W. C. Faust who has transferred to Kappa. We are sure Brother Faust will be an honor to Kappa chapter. Concerning those who graduated, Theta is proud of her record, having had three honor men in the c ass.

Congratulations were carried to Brother Backus, P. G. M., who was recently married.

Trusting our fraternal friends will experience a most successful year, Theta extends best wishes to each and every chapter.

IOTA—NORTHWESTERN UNIVERSITY.

C. S. Savage, Editor.

Here we are again, some of us, twenty-six of us, who were not ready to graduate with the rest of us, who have gone on before us. So we again wish to extend to every sister chapter and each individual member of Psi Omega our best wishes for a good, prosperous year.

School opened this year with a bright outlook for Iota, for she has, through the untiring efforts of our Grand Master, Brother Power and other energetic brothers, secured an elegant three-story furnished home at 389 Ontario street where each brother can go and enjoy home comforts with the frat men who remain at the new Iota home.

On Wednesday night, October 17th, we held open house for the purpose of getting our freshmen and junior friends together in order that all might become personally acquainted.

Piano and violin selections were rendered by Brother Wehrheims, his brother and a friend who are prominent musicians here in the city. The music was of the highest type and we applauded vigorously. Good smoking materials together with plenty of good coffee, sandwiches and "Powers' Powerful Punch" were served tastefully, thus tempting the appetites of all. By his reading Brother Kennedy aided greatly in making the occasion such a brilliant success

On Thursday night, October 18th, a regular meeting was held and several good men were proposed for membership and some others were found worthy of Psi Omega honors, whom we expect to receive October 27th.

Last May we lost by graduation ten of our strong men, and, while we are always glad to see our brothers graduate, we feel and notice the vacancy which their absence causes. Added to our numbers we have with us: Brothers T. P. Merchant, from Chi; E. A. Brown, from Chi, and T. E. Butler, from Beta Alpha. All good, energetic men. This year we expect to live a little closer together than in former years thus promoting the welfare of the chapter and the fraternity.

Iota extends a most hearty invitation to each member of Psi Omega to visit her in her new home should occasion permit.

MU CHAPTER, 1905-06.

KAPPA—CHICAGO COLLEGE OF DENTAL SURGERY.

E. L. Henderson, Editor.

Kappa lost thirteen members by graduation and has twenty-three undergraduate members with whom to start the year.

At our first meeting we welcomed Faust, of Buffalo, who transferred to us from Theta.

The Chicago College of Dental Surgery is enjoying a very prosperous year, there is a large freshman class and there are a large number of students from foreign lands enrolled.

Kappa extends greetings to all sister chapters.

NU—PITTSBURG DENTAL COLLEGE.

H. Boisseau, Editor.

The present scholastic year opens with Nu in a very prosperous and active condition. I am glad to be able to report to the fraternity in general that the dreams of Nu chapter in regard to a fraternity house are at last to be realized and we are at the present time just "moving in" and our home for the ensuing year will be 3334 Fifth avenue. At our first meeting this year it was resolved to "do something." Too much credit cannot be given to Duquesne chapter for the generous way in which she came to our rescue, for without her assistance it would have been almost impossible to have secured the house.

Nu has already initiated four candidates this year, all upper class men, and prospects are bright for good acquisitions from the freshman class.

Nu is glad to announce that Taylor, from Rho, is with us this year.

Nu men have been signally honored in the election of class officers and nearly every officer in both senior and junior classes is a member of our chapter.

Our Dean, Brother H. E. Friesell, has had added honors heaped upon him by his election to a chair in the Western Reserve Dental College.

Nu sends regards and best wishes to her sister chapters.

OMICRON—LOUISVILLE COLLEGE OF DENTAL SURGERY.

J. L. Selden, Editor.

As we have gathered together again for another year of work and study we first perhaps inquire about our recent graduates.

It is with great sorrow that we think of the early and sudden death of our brother, D. A. Lee, of Jackson, Ala. On his return from the State Board examination of his state, he was taken suddenly ill and died June 27th after less than three weeks' illness. Brother Lee was a very popular member of Omicron chapter; he possessed charming manners, was a good fellow, and a very good student. His death is mourned by teachers as well as by all his fellow students. A widowed mother and a sister to whom he was greatly devoted survive him.

Our Past Grand Master, A. A. Sherwood, passed the Connecticut State Board and has located at Groton, Conn., near New London, where he is doing well.

Brother Arthur Hudson surrendered his liberty to a charming young lady last July and is now happy and hard at work in New Albany, Miss.

E. A. Freer and Foster France are both located in Minneapolis, Minn. L. M. Doss is in Sulphur Springs, Okla. Dennis Beater is in Leitchfield, Ky., and his brother, T. T. Beater, is working the country around Big Clifty, Ky. R. C. Daniels is located in Owensburg, Ky. W. L. Barnett is now located in Mexico City, Mexico, care of St. Francis Hotel. The other brothers have not located permanently.

All of the undergraduates have returned with the exception of Brother C. C. Howard, who has gone to Los Angeles, Cal.

We are sixteen strong to begin active work this year. We anticipate a very busy year and a pleasant one.

The officers for this year are as follows:

Grand Master	E. N. Johnson.
Junior Master	F. S. Ewen.
Secretary	M. D. Gibbs.
Treasurer	R. S. Russ.
Chief Inquisitor	I. B. Simpson.
Editor	J. L. Selden.

Chief Interrogator....................B. C. McEwen.
Inside Guard............................D. C. Long.
Outside Guard........................M. T. Fordyce.
Senator.................................R. S. Mobbs.
Historian..............................R. L. Baker.

PI—BALTIMORE MEDICAL COLLEGE.

J. H. Kiniry, Editor.

At the opening meeting of Pi twelve answered to roll call. C. J. Coffy Newing transferred to a Dental College in Chicago and Wm. Lyons to the University of Maryland.

The boys all look well after their summer vacations and are still renewing old acquaintances.

We have a very large freshman class this year, about double what it was last year, also a number of new seniors and juniors.

Taking everything into consideration, we look forward to a large chapter for the coming year, as we already have eight pledged men who will be initiated soon.

Our officers for the present year are:

Grand Master.........................T. W. McGee.
Junior Master........................M. H. Haag.
Secretary.............................H. H. Ring.
Treasurer.............................F. P. Davis.
Inside Guard.........................T. N. Wood.
Outside Guard........................F. Lena.
Historian............................Wm. Lyons.
Editor...............................J. H. Kiniry.
Chief Inquisitor.....................A. Hooper.
Chief Interrogator...................A. D. Elkins.

The Pi boys are well pleased over the senior class election. All except one of the students honored, by their class mates, with a class office are members of our chapter. The brothers honored are: J. J. Power, President; M. W. Haag, Vice President; H. H. Donahue, who is a member but has not received the "trimmings," Secretary; F. P. Davis, Treasurer; H. H. Ring, Historian; F. Lena, Sergeant-at-Arms; Executive Committee—Thos. W.

McGee, J. D. Gregg, H. A. Hooper and E. M. Talbott. Mr. E. M. Talbott being the only man not a Psi Omegan.

Pi lost six members by graduation last spring. They were F. Braley, P. G. M., who is now in company with a dentist at Warterbury, Vt.; F. St. John, who is nicely located and enjoying a good practice at Spartanburg, S. C.; E. L. Major, who expects to open his office in Greenfield, Mass.; Jas. McKean, at Paterson, N. J.; W. J. Rackey at Walton, N. Y., and A. M. McLane at Mt. Vernon, N. Y.

Pi extends greeting to all sister chapters and wishes them a very prosperous and successful year.

BETA SIGMA—COLLEGE OF PHYSICIANS AND SURGEONS.

L. R. Packwood, Editor.

Our college was completely destroyed by dynamite and fire April 19th, but the new building is being rushed to completion, and by January 1st will be completed. At present we are attending lectures and expect to almost finish this part of the course by January 1st, after which time we will work in the Clinic.

Material will be plentiful and the future looks brighter than ever for the advancement of our college.

The quake scattered our members to the four winds but we are proud to say that most of them were loyal to the P. & S., and are with us once more. Brother Patterson entered the University of California, and Brother Baldwin is in New York City.

Our freshman class numbers about twenty and there is some good material in it. Our members who took the State Board made a good showing, considering the disadvantages under which they labored. Owing to the quake it was hard enough to get plenty to eat and a place to sleep, without studying for a State Board. Some were unable to take the examination, as they lost all of their instruments and did not have the necessary fee. It was thought for awhile that the college would be saved, so most of the boys did not make an effort to save their instruments, but later, when it could plainly be seen that the city was doomed, it was too late to enter the college, as it was surrounded by soldiers and later blown up by dynamite.

Although we now labor under hardships, we expect to see our college once again one of the best institutions in the United States.

Owing to the generosity of the railroads and the people at every station with their ham sandwiches, our escape was made from the city and we were landed at home more or less haggard, but not broken in spirit. Brother McGregor and your Editor met the members of Chi in Portland April 25th, and we wish to thank them for the treatment we received at their hands. P. G. M. Fivall and Brother Davis took special pains to entertain us and we hope that, at some future time, we may have the pleasure of showing them our college and city.

Our officers for the ensuing year are:

Grand Master	E. Downs.
Junior Master	J. H. McKay.
Secretary	C. A. Gromaire.
Treasurer	D. F. Mulvihill.
Senator	H. G. Ryan.
Chief Inquisitor	H. B. Smith.
Chief Interrogator	W. Robinson.
Inside Guardian	E. A. Kruse.
Outside Guardian	C. F. Riley.
Historian	J. E. McGregor.
Editor	L. R. Packwood.

RHO—OHIO COLLEGE OF DENTAL SURGERY.

Edw. McCurdy, Editor.

Rho begins the session's work with enthusiasm and fresh from a healthy vacation.

We are still located at the Hotel Emery and have a membership of twenty.

Rho lost three energetic brothers by graduation: Hook, Bannister and Mannon.

Rho transfers Bro. Chas. Taylor to Nu chapter in Pittsburg. Taylor is a loyal frat man and we regret his loss, but wish him success in his new college.

Pi of Baltimore, Md., transfers W. L. Bixby to Rho.

Rho desires to thank Brothers Burger, D. D. S., and Williams, D. D. S., for their talks at the last meeting.

We contemplate initiating the following pledged men October 26th:

H. M. Schweinsberger..................Hillsboro, O.
James Turner..........................Walton, Ky.
R. R. Kelsey.........................Covington, O.
M. M. Maupin.........................Cincinnati, O.
N. A. Cunningham.....................Defiance, O.
W. J. Rule...............................Clyde, O.
William McCochran..................Saginaw, Mich.

Rho extends hearty greetings to all sister chapters and wishes them a pleasant and successful year.

TAU—ATLANTA DENTAL COLLEGE.

W. A. Holbeck, G. M., Editor.

We are just getting under headway.

A large number of our members were delighted to have the opportunity of meeting the members of our Supreme Council, Brothers Nyce, Friesell and Sting, in September. On the 20th of September members of Gamma Iota and Tau joined in givnig a little dinner at the Aragon in their honor. The following menu was served:

Manhattan Cocktail
Broiled Pompano
Lemon Butter　　　　　　　Julienne Potatoes
Blue Ribbon Celery　　Queen Olives　　Mixed Pickles
Tenderloin of Beef with Mushrooms
Potato Croquettes
Sauterne

Broiled Spring Chicken on Toast
Asparagus   French Peas
Whole Tomato Salad
Neapolitan Ice Cream
Assorted Cakes
Bent's Wafer Crackers   Coffee
Rocquefort Cheese

Ample attention was given to the menu, then Toastmaster Hill called upon various persons for a "talk." In each instance the talk was forthcoming so that the occasion was replete with humor and sage advice. Besides the guests, the following active and alumni members were present:

Dr. R. H. Calhoun   Dr. DeLos L. Hill
Dr. W. H. Sherard   Dr. F. E. Webb
Dr. G. W. Bledsoe   Dr. Nat G. Oattis
Dr. G. A. Milner   Dr. A. H. Corley
Dr. Joe Eby   Dr. W. L. Northern
Dr. H. A. Lorenz   Dr. W. A. Holbeck
Dr. C. E. Buchanan   Dr. K. Armstrong
Dr. B. F. Boykin   Dr. J. C. Thomson
Dr. W. C. Hodnett   Dr. G. H. Stevenson
Dr. J. N. Weems   Dr. J. E. Walker
                Mr. F. O. Foster

Tau introduces the following new members: Roy Marshall Huntley, '07; Wm. Wallace Westmoreland, '08; Dougas McIntyre, Jr., '08; Spencer F. McJunkin, '07; Jas. R. Jackson, '07; Wade L. Taylor, '08, and Anderson Mayo Hedick, '08.

Our officers for this year are:

Grand Master...................W. A. Holbeck, Texas.
Junior Master..................H. G. Sheats, Georgia.
Secretary......................J. G. Spencer, Texas.
Treasurer......................D. S. Aycock, Georgia.
Chief Inquisitor...............H. L. Smith, Georgia.
Senator............A. S. Cromartie, South Carolina.
Chief Interrogator.............W. L. Cook, Florida.
Historian......................C. G. Butt, Georgia.
Inside Guard.........G. H. Stevenson, Pennsylvania.
Outside Guard..................H. D. Smith, Alabama.

UPSILON—UNIVERSITY OF SOUTHERN CALIFORNIA.

F. L. Osenburg, Editor.

We of Upsilon greet Psi Omegas again after the long vacation and take pleasure in extending our best wishes for a continuance of the prosperity of our sister chapters.

Seven brothers returned to college to perpetuate the life and good-fellowship of Upsilon chapter. We lost a large number of members by graduation, news of whom will be forthcoming in a future letter.

Brothers E. E. Osenburg, L. L. Day, J. C. Magill, Chas. Lanler, H. B. Harwood, F. J. Fitzgerald and F. L. Osenburg are again in college lending aid and comfort to the freshman, sympathy to the junior, and advice to the faculty. The joyous laugh of Brother Peck and the baritone of Baldwin will not re-echo through our halls this year—more is the pity. Brother Ross, formerly with the '04 class, has joined us once more, also Brothers C. W. Endicott, of Chi, and C. C. Howard, '07, of Omicron.

We are looking forward to a prosperous year.

The freshman class, the first to enter under the increased requirements, promises well, so that we have, at this writing, a number of fine fellows "in pickle" for the coming autumnal "high jinks."

Several of our later graduates have been honored with appointments on the faculty, among them being Hopkins, '06, and Goodman, '05, in Porcelain and Brother McCoy, '06, in Orthodontia.

PHI—UNIVERSITY OF MARYLAND.

A. M. Berryhill, Editor.

College opened October 1st, with all of our active members present except Spears and Blakeslee.

Brother Spears passed the West Virginia State Board last June and is practicing at Bluefield, W. Va.

Brother Blakeslee is at his home in New York City.

Phi lost eight worthy men by graduation.

There is a good attendance in each of the three classes at our school this year; the freshman class gives promise of developing good fraternity men, so Phi feels that the best men will eventually enlist in Psi Omega's ranks.

At the last meeting of last year we decided to discontinue the Inter-Chapter frat house. We have made no plans to supply the want this year, as yet.

Our officers for the present year are:

Grand Master............................R. O. Apple.
Junior Master...........................W. H. Perrin.
Secretary..............................A. P. Scarborough.
Treasurer..............................E. B. Howle.
Senator................................R. W. Williams.
Chief Interrogator......................S. E. Douglass.
Historian..............................L. J. Peyrau.
Inside Guard...........................S. Tuaki.
Outside Guard..........................P. C. Southaul.
Editor.................................A. M. Berryhill.

CHI—NORTH PACIFIC DENTAL COLLEGE.

John E. Swanberg, Editor.

Again the privilege has been granted us to assemble our chapter for another college year.

Chi starts the year with an active membership of sixteen and four honorary members. Six brothers were lost last year by graduation. Three of our members have transferred to other schools, namely: E. A. Brown and T. P. Merchant to Northwestern University in Chicago and Iota; C. W. Endicott to Los Angeles and Upsilon.

We are glad to welcome O. H. Whaley from Beta Zeta, St. Louis, Mo., as a member of Chi this year.

Our officers for the present year are:

Grand Master............................A. T. Jones.
Junior Master...........................L. G. McAloney.
Secretary..............................L. E. George.
Treasurer..............................D. Dahlman.
Inside Guard...........................C. Wintermute.

Outside Guard..........................W. A. Short.
Historian.................................W. Murdy.
Editor....................................E. Swanberg.
Chief Inquisitor........................A. Brighouse.
Chief Interrogator......................R. Eshelman.

We are exceedingly pleased to note the spirit manifested among the brothers this year which indicates a progressive year for Chi. Chi will soon be reinforced by the addition of several new members and a decided effort will be made to make this the banner year in the history of Chi.

During vacation, our worthy secretary, L. E. George, became a benedict and returned to college beaming and happy. Chi bespeaks for the happy couple a long, prosperous life.

Following are the names and addresses of the brothers who graduated last June:

Clyde Mount........................Wallowa, Ore.
F. R. Davis...........................Rainier, Ore.
E. M. Senn.............................Vale, Ore.
C. H. Fixott........Marquam Building, Portland, Ore.
J. D. Sheehan.....484 Burnside Street, Portland, Ore.
E. H. Miller.........................Portland, Ore.

Lastly, Chi sends greetings to the Supreme Council, sister chapters and all Psi Omegas.

PSI—OHIO MEDICAL UNIVERSITY.

S. E. Spangler, Editor.

By these notes and through the columns of The Frater, Psi sends greetings to all sister chapters and best wishes to all of their and her own alumni members for the present year.

With the graduating class of 1906 Psi lost the following brothers:

William Hand..........................Toledo, O.
Clarence Eshelman.....................Toledo, O.
Marvin Powell.........................Columbus, O.
T. Alfred Smith......................Monticello, Ky.
Alvin Cole............................Fostoria, O.
W. A. Whitacre........................Delaware, O.

P. A. Wineland........................Bloomdale, O.
Thomas Sonnanstine,.....................Marion, O.
Arthur Silas Pilkinton................Pewams, Mich.
Henry J. Friedman....................Cleveland, O.
Irwin A. Bottenhorn...................Columbus, O.

Altho our chapter lost eleven good men by graduation, the opening of another college year found seventeen active members here and ready to work for the interests of Psi Omega. Their efforts have not been in vain as the following, Wm. Carter, George Hawkins, George Moore, Harry Oliver, Dennis Welch, Arthur Knoderer, Edward Warner, William Warren, Paul Gabel, were initiated into the mysteries of Psi Omega on September 25th, and before this article appears in print there will have been added five more names to the roll of Psi chapter.

If no preventing Providence intervenes between now (October 23rd) and October 26th, we will have administered the solemn rites to the following pledged men: Joseph Williamson, Roy Bode, Amplius Galvin, Everett Stewart, Sperry Claypool.

Much credit is due E. J. Wylie and team for their untiring efforts in leaving no stone unturned during the September initiation to make it a success and we feel reasonably sure that Wylie and helpers will do likewise in the near approaching one.

After the initiation at Fraternity Hall on September 25th, the chapter enjoyed a spread given in honor of the newly initiated men. Every one present expressed satisfaction at having become a Psi Omega.

While at this point it might be well to "blow" a little about Psi chapter as perhaps the chance will not come to us soon again although we hope present conditions may never change unless to grow better.

We are now located at 50 Buttles avenue, in a chapter house with our own furnishings. We have an enrollment of thirty-one, or soon will have, as active members, together with three alumni men and two honorary members in this city.

H. M. Semans, Beta '95, A. M., D. D. S., is now Dean of the Dental Department while Brother Cottrell has the Chair of Prosthetic Dentistry in the University. Dr. Deyo has charge of the Freshman Prosthetic Laboratory and Dr. Bottenhorn is assistant to Dr. Cottrell and has charge of all extracting. Dr. Powell is located on Town street, this city, and is doing fine. These last three named are alumni members All the class officers in the senior and junior classes are Psi Omegas and the president of the freshman class is a member, while the other officers are pledged men and will soon be members of our chapter.

Brother Cann is captain of this year's foot ball team, Brother Taylor, student manager of same. Brother Shumway is secretary of the college Y. M. C. A., while the writer of this article has the honor of being vice president. Brother Warner (J. H.) is editor-in-chief of the Phagocyte—our college paper, and Brother Wylie is president of the O. M. U. Republican club. To use a slang phrase "we are surely in it" this year at least.

Dr. Eshelman, '06, was married recently to Miss Ethyl Mae Blue, of Colorado, and Dr. F. M. Lose, '05, was married a short time ago, but the writer is sorry to state that he is, up to this time, unable to learn the lady's name and address. Psi surely wishes both the above couples many happy years of wedded life.

Drs. Ray White, '05, E. B. Carpenter, '05, and W. A. Whitacre, '06, visited the chapter house recently.

Mr. Van Doren, of Aberdeen, Wash., visited Grand Master Sherwood several days of last month.

Brother Cann spent a Sunday recently at Jackson, O.

C. C. Patton had as guest a Mr. Hyde, from Cambridge, O., on September 23rd.

E. C. Greiner, book keeper for the National Biscuit Co., of Zanesville, O., visited with S. E. Spangler October 22nd and 23rd.

Fearing that we may weary some good reader of this journal with news of and about Psi we will stop for this time, wishing one and all a prosperous year.

BETA ALPHA—UNIVERSITY OF ILLINOIS.

T. E. Butler, Editor.

Beta Alpha sends greetings to all chapters, and to Psi Omegas everywhere.

We have the pleasure of introducing two new members— George W. Wheeler and A. J. Zimouth. Class night was a very enjoyable occasion, many of our boys being among the honored ones. J. V. Vita as class historian, and W. B. Tym gave selections which showed careful and earnest preparation, and S. L. Worthington, in an excellent speech, presented a beautiful oil painting, on behalf of the senior class, to our Dean, Dr. B. J. Cigrand. Our '06 boys all passed the State Board examinations.

Brother E. F. Klumb, our chief inquisitor, who was compelled to leave college before the final examinations on account of a nervous breakdown, is back with us again this year, ready for the forthcoming initiations. The boys are taking hold of the work with a will and are sanguine and optimistic. Notwithstanding this year of small freshmen classes, we look forward to a prosperous and successful year.

BETA GAMMA—GEORGE WASHINGTON UNIVERSITY.

W. H. Hildreth, Editor.

Another college year has begun, with it comes the perplexities of new studies, new professors, and new faces; from the owners of the latter we hope to find worthy successors to those who graduated last June. To be a worthy successor of either of the '06 men will be no mean task for any man. What the senior delegation lacked in numbers they made up in abilty, both brothers being graduated in the honor class. Brother Harrison, the retiring Secretary, received the Gold Prize for the best Operative Work and Brother Clinton, the retiring Grand Master and Editor, received honorable mention. Thus the only two Psi Omegas in the class carried off two out of the three honors.

Beta Gamma's Fourth Annual Smoker was held the week after commencement, at which there was a goodly gathering of the brothers, graduate and undergraduate, in spite of the inclement weather and a rival attraction in the form of the banquet of the joint convention of the District of Columbia and Maryland Dental Associations.

An abundant and well-assorted menu received the first and most serious consideration of the brothers, after which Grand Master Clinton called the assembly to order to listen to toasts more or less serious, as follows:

Good Fellowship...................Dr. J. Hall Lewis.
The Ethical Practitioner..........Dr. H. C. Thompson.
The Fraternity....................H. Shirley Bowles.
The Profession...................Dr. J. H. P. Benson.
Achievements.............................Dr. Cogan.
Prosthesis.......................Dr. Allen S. Wolfe.
The House of Mirth................Dr. A. B. Crane.
The Ladies........................Dr. Jack Madert.
Not Yet, But Soon...............Dr. Bob Schumacher.
The Goat........................Walter H. Hildreth.
"Hoot Mon"......................G. B. R. Macdonald.

The banquet broke up in the wee sma' hours after the installation of the following officers for the ensuing year:

Grand Master.....................Geo. R. Macdonald.
Junior Master....................John T. Vivian, '07.
Secretary..................Charles G. Shoemaker, '07.
Treasurer.......................George F. Peck, '08.
Chief Inquisitor ....Herbert S. Murdoch, '08.
Inside Guardian.................Henry C. Young, '08.
Historian...................J. Walter Bernhard, '08.
Editor.....................Walter H. Hildreth, '08.

Dr. Allan S. Wolfe, of this city, a member of the George Washington University Dental Faculty and an honorary member of our chapter, was married on July 21, 1906, to Miss Bessie L. Dalley. Dr. Wolfe is a loyal member of the chapter and is always ready to come around on "frat" nights and give us friendly counsel and lend his presence in all that furthers the interest of Psi Omega. The chapter heartily congratulates him.

Brother Charles G. Shoemaker, of the senior class, also committed matrimony this summer. The lucky lady was Miss Lucia M. Rittenhouse, of Scranton, Pa. "Shoe" sought to steal a march on the boys by getting married in the middle of the summer, but an energetic brother interviewed every Psi Omegan in town with the result that a solid silver chocolate set, suitably inscribed with the Psi Omega emblem, had a prominent place among the numerous wedding presents. Verbal congratulations have showered upon Brother Shoemaker since college opened.

Brother J. Walter Bernhard became the proud father of a daughter, Dorothy, in the midst of the final examinations, last June. He says he is glad it is a girl (fathers always are satisfied with the sex of their first child), but it is our private opinion that he would have preferred a little dentist.

College opened auspiciously this fall with several additions to the upper classes, but the freshman class fell off considerably in numbers. The falling off is, without doubt, due to the increase in the tuition from $110.00 to $150.00 per annum, and to the fact that the Board of Trustees has announced that beginning with Fall of 1908, the college will be a day institution exclusively.

On Saturday night, October 13th, we held our first smoker in the new commodious chapter rooms. Honorary members, graduate brothers, undergraduate brothers and guests participated; bountiful refreshments and smoking materials were served.

Brothers Thompson and Wolfe, of the George Washington University Faculty and Bowles of the Georgetown University Faculty, addressed the boys on the value of fraternities to the undergraduate and graduate, and other kindred subjects; Brothers Crane and Madert each gave us a characteristic talk. We believe that our guests were favorably impressed with our chapter, and that several desirable new members will soon be numbered with us.

BETA DELTA—UNIVERSITY OF CALIFORNIA.

Leighton C. Brownton, Editor.

Much has been said and written of the great conflagration of last April, but it will probably be of interest to all Psi Omegas to know that Beta Delta passed through it without loss, except to individual brothers, and that to-day she stands firmer and stronger than ever, ready to benefit by the new condition of things and to do her utmost in the furtherance of Psi Omega principles. Our old infirmary was burned and a number of our boys lost their entire outfits. The night before the fire we had a very enjoyable dance at our hall on O'Farrell street (which escaped the fire) and it was only a few hours later that the city was awakened by the terrible earthquake. Our college building on Parnassus avenue was only slightly damaged and has been refitted with laboratories, a splendid infirmary with gas, electricity, and every modern convenience, so, taking it all in all, we are going to have a better course this year than ever before.

With the opening of this semester Beta Delta found herself strongly intrenched. Brothers Patterson and Smith are with us from Beta Sigma, and Brother Sexton from Beta Zeta.

We have been working hard and have accomplished much for this early in the semester. The new quarters, which were secured, are commodious, convenient and altogether satisfactory to the boys. We have held one smoker and a dance and are now planning another for the near future. Grand Master Carter is doing splendid work toward outlining our fraternal and social plans for the semester, so we anticipate a very active season.

The freshman class this year is small so there is keen rivalry between the three frats in our college for new material—the result is that Beta Delta has three of the best men in the class, pledged.

The junior class held its election a short time back with the result that our boys were honored with the offices of President, Vice President, Secretary, Sergeant-at-Arms and Editor and Manager of "Chaff," our college annual.

I must not forget to mention our orchestra, alias "The German Band," which was organized recently and which includes L. E. Carter, piano; A. R. Southeimer, first cornet; A. L. Sexton, violin; H. S. Bibbero, trombone; F. Randal, flute, and J. C. McManus, second cornet. The band furnished music at our last dance and acquitted itself very creditably. We are particularly favored in having a number of good musicians with us.

We were pleased to have with us at our last dance Brothers W. A. Cree and F. J. Colligan, '06 men, now practicing in this city.

Our membership at the beginning of this year is twenty. We lost seven men by graduation.

Our officers for this year are as follows:

Grand Master	L. E. Carter.
Junior Master	Leonard Martin.
Secretary	Don W. Byrne.
Treasurer	F. W. Meyer.
Senator	Jas. C. McManus.
Chief Inquisitor	H. S. Bibbero.
Chief Interrogator	J. E. Gurley.
Editor	L. C. Brownton.
Inside Guardian	F. A. Leslie.
Outside Guardian	H. A. Eggert.

We trust that our sister chapters obtained a good start for the year, and we extend to them and to the editorial staff of The Frater fraternal greetings.

BETA EPSILON—NEW ORLEANS COLLEGE OF DENTISTRY.

Leon Barnett, Editor.

Beta Epsilon extends greetings to all sister chapters.

The outlook for a prosperous year seems rather good.

Our first meeting was held on October 17th, and all the preliminary work for the present year has been attended to, there being only five members left from last year, it was urgently requested of every member that he exert all energy in procuring new members, but not to overlook the fact that only men of undoubted worth will be admitted to our midst. Several men have been proposed for membership and it is expected that quite a number of candidates will be ready for initiation the latter part of November when a new physical degree will be introduced by Barnett and Riess who have been using their spare time during the past summer whipping the new "stunts" into working order. I can safely say this degree will prove an innovation in every particular.

We are to take up the matter of formulating plans towards furnishing a Frat House this Fall and will expect all brothers to co-operate with us in this matter.

At our last meeting, held Thursday, October 25th, we were greatly entertained with a reading of a paper entitled, "The Early and Later History of Dentistry," by Brother Leon Barnett.

Our program for the coming year calls for the reading of papers by the members on different subjects.

The boys regret the loss of Dr. W. O. Talbot from the Faculty of the New Orleans College of Dentistry, through resignation, as he was well liked by all and is a great supporter of dear old Psi Omega. Brother Talbot occupied the chair of Professor of Orthodontia and ranks high among the prominent Orthodontists of this country.

BETA ZETA—ST. LOUIS DENTAL COLLEGE.

S. A. Lusby, Editor.

Another autumn has presented itself, causing the sun to be inclined southward and the trees to give up their foliage of green in response to nature's call; reminding the student that the time for him to return to or enter college is here. Familiar faces of brothers and associates are here, which recall to our memories pleasures of bygone days and impress upon us how fast the time has flown. We are back, some of us, for the last time, ready to absorb all we possibly can of knowledge pertaining to the profession we have chosen for our life's work.

After a careful survey of our freshman class, which numbers about twenty-five members, we are convinced that it contains much good material for the building up of our chapter.

We are sorry to lose Brothers, Bertram who went to Denver; Sexton to California, and Schindler to Washington University, St. Louis, Mo. Beta Zeta wishes them success and a prosperous year.

We are very sorry and regret very much that Brothers, F. W. Wiseman, clinical instructor, and T. G. Hawley, demonstrator, during the past year will not be with us this year. These men will be greatly missed by all who knew them.

We are proud to announce that we have Dr. D. E. Morrow as superintendent of the infirmary and lecturer on Materia Medica this year. We also feel proud to announce that Doctor Morrow was taken into Psi Omega's ranks as an honorary member at our last meeting in October; he is a man of wide reputation, substantial character and pleasing personality.

We open this year with the outlook for a bright and prosperous future.

Beta Zeta extends to all sister chapters greetings and best wishes for a successful and enjoyable year.

BETA ETA—KEOKUK DENTAL COLLEGE.

Geo. R. Narrley, Editor.

At roll call several weeks ago seven of last year's members answered. Beta Eta having lost two by graduation, Coe, now located at Peoria, Ill., and Mitchell at Kansas City, Kans. Brother Mitchell has, as yet, been unable to practice, owing to serious trouble which he had with his eyes last spring. The sympathy of our entire chapter is extended to Brother Mitchell.

We already have two applications and very good prospects of securing good men from the present freshman class. As our work is starting under the most favorable circumstances, we are hoping for a year of prosperity and success.

BETA ETA CHAPTER, 1905-06,

Brothers J. T. Crouch and A. B. Thompson, Beta Eta '05, are now members of the Keokuk Dental College Faculty. We gladly welcome them as instructors and bespeak success for them.

We are anticipating a ride down the Mississippi River on Capt. Dodds' "Water Wagon;" we can carry about a thousand so there will be plenty of room for all.

GAMMA IOTA—SOUTHERN DENTAL COLLEGE.

J. E. Walker, Editor.

On Saturday, October 6th, Gamma Iota held her first meeting of the session, which was a very enthusiastic one. Every member seemed full of the fraternal spirit and began the session in a way that means business and profit to each one. We are proud to report at present twenty of the old members back, and full of determination. We have good prospects for additional members as we have an abundance of good material to work on. We are sorry to report the loss of two of our members who have gone to another school. R. H. Mills and H. C. Smothers have gone to Baltimore, and, while we are sorry to lose them, we commend them to our brothers in Baltimore.

We lost ten of our old men by graduation. C. C. Russell, of Mississippi, who was unable to be with us this fall, will return in January. Altogether we feel that we have a prosperous year before us and that much good will be accomplished.

On Thursday night, September 20th, during the meeting of the National Dental Association in Atlanta, it was the pleasure of Tau and Gamma Iota chapters to entertain the three members of our Supreme Council, Brothers H. E. Friesell, J. E. Nyce and E. H. Sting, at a banquet at the Hotel Aragon. About thirty active and alumni members were present and a delightful evening was spent. We were highly entertained by tales from each of these gentlemen who proved themselves worthy of the high honors bestowed upon them by their fraternity. We are proud to have had them with us and sorry that all our boys were not there to meet them.

Our officers for the year are:

Grand Master	W. P. Adams.
Junior Master	W. C. Humphries.
Secretary	U. G. Turner.
Treasurer	J. R. Watson.
Senator	E. C. Buchannon.
Chief Inquisitor	J. E. Young.
Chief Interrogator	V. R. Hawkins.
Historian	I. N. Kinnedy.
Inside Guardian	T. G. Hill.
Outside Guardian	F. McCrummen.

They have the support of our entire chapter.

GAMMA KAPPA—UNIVERSITY OF MICHIGAN.

Le Vant R. Drake, Editor.

Gamma Kappa sends greetings to all sister chapters and best wishes for a successful and prosperous year. All of last year's members are back excepting one who left us by graduation, Dr. C. V. Smith, of Shepherd, Mich. Our hopes and expectations for the coming year are running high. We are proud to say that we have a chapter house and are "at home" to all brothers at the Psi Omega House, 319 North Division. We have added five new names to our roll this year. We are meeting with great opposition from the other two fraternities, but the Psi Omega standard is becoming recognized and if the methods which our chapter has adopted are carried out we are bound to win. Our motto is "quality, not quantity." We take pleasure in introducing our new members:

L. T. Mount, '07	Ashtabula, O.
M. Clinton, '09	Pinckney, Mich.
D. W. Barr, '09	Cleveland, O.
H. E. Brady, '08	Kalamazoo, Mich.
B. H. Masselink, '08	Zeeland, Mich.

At our election last May, the following officers were elected:

Grand Master	W. W. Whipple.
Junior Master	H. T. Wallace.

Secretary..............................M. C. Ruess.
Treasurer........   ....G. T. Katner.
Chief Inquisitor......................R. Simmons.
Chief Interrogator....................J. W. Anson.
Inside Guardian..........................C. Keyes.
Outside Guardian......................G. H. Smith.
Historian................................R. Evans.
Editor..................................L. R. Drake.
Senator................................G. H. Smith.

GAMMA LAMBDA—COLLEGE OF DENTAL AND ORAL SURGERY OF NEW YORK.

Gotthard E. Seyfarth, Editor.

Gamma Lambda closed the college year 1905-6 with an informal but impressive little celebration at our chapter apartments on May 29th. This event will ever be a pleasant reminiscence of the closing of a remarkable college-session to all who had been fortunate enough to be present.

At the beginning of the last session there existed, at the College of Dental and Oral Surgery of New York, the Phi Theta Pi Dental Fraternity, which had been founded several years ago by certain enterprising undergraduates of our institution, but, at the close of the session, this fraternity had passed out of existence, having been taken under the sheltering wings of the great Psi Omega Dental Fraternity, and is now known as Gamma Lambda chapter.

When the Phi Theta Pi Fraternity was organized its founders cherished the highest and noblest ideals that man can possess and it was, even at that early time, their ardent wish that they might some day receive the grant of a charter from Psi Omega. These men graduated and became Alumni Members, but they always remained in close touch with their active brothers, giving advice and assisting them in every manner, that they might, likewise, support and encourage the fulfilment of their hopes. So a few years passed, the fraternity had grown materially, if not in numbers in quality; for the motto was and is ours to-day, "Not quantity, but quality." At last the day arrived when our wish was gratified; on the sixteenth of April Phi Theta Pi had become Gamma Lambda of Psi Omega.

At this last meeting in May, by special dispensation from the Supreme Council, we had the great pleasure to initiate, into active membership, the following graduate members of the "late" Phi Theta Pi, the first five being among her founders:

  Earl McCulloch....................Gloversville, N. Y.
  Albert W. Gates.....................New York, N. Y.
  Andrew H. Gunn....................New York, N. Y.
  Harold L. Baldwin.................East Orange, N. J.
  Sylvester B. Hursch...............New York, N. Y.
  J. Eugene Requa....................New York, N. Y.
  John F. Doherty....................New York, N. Y.
  Edwin C. Hall.......................Harrison, N. Y.
  William J. Tappen.................East Orange, N. J.
  Percy C. Spengeman................New York, N. Y.
  Albert E. Forshay....................Newark, N. J.

After the initiatory ceremonies refreshments were served and a good and jolly time followed. It was a worthy and appropriate ending of a year which had brought about such remarkable changes. May all future years of Gamma Lambda close as happy and prosperous, with the same encouraging outlook, as did this session, the first of the new chapter.

On October 5th we had the first meeting of this year, and, as all brothers have recuperated from the hard work of the last session, we expect to accomplish a great deal during the coming year.

The officers of Gamma Lambda for 1906-1907 are:

  Grand Master.....................Robert H. McLeod.
  Junior Master..................Daniel B. Thompson.
  Secretary.........................James D. Street.
  Treasurer.......................Frederick E. Pierce.
  Chief Inquisitor.................James A. Robertson.
  Chief Interrogator ....Edwin M. Graham.
  Senator..........................Corydon Palmer.
  Historian.......................Gotthard E. Seyfarth.
  Inside Guardian...................James B. McGrath.
  Outside Guardian..................George B. Ellor.

Gamma Lambda sends greetings to all sister chapters; may they all have a happy, prosperous and successful college year!

Editorial.

All communications for publication in The Frater should reach the Editor-in-chief on or before the 25th of the month preceding the date of the issue in which the article is to appear.

There was some confusion in mailing the May Frater because addresses of some active members were not received at all, or, if received, were incorrect. We still have a number of copies of this issue on hand and if any brother has not received his copy he can obtain it by advising the Editor-in-chief that it is desired.

MORE HONORS FOR PSI OMEGAS.

Psi Omegas are always glad to hear of honors gained by their fellow members. The beginning of this session finds a goodly number of Psi Omegas who have profited by their ability as instructors and their adherence to duty. Among those who have been honored by election to important posts is Dr. H. M. Semans, Beta,'97, who has been selected by the faculty of the Ohio Medical University as Dean of its Dental Department.

The rise of Brother Semans is typical of the rise of many men in other vocations of life. His literary education was obtained at Ohio Wesleyan University, from which institution he graduated, receiving the degree of Bachelor of Arts in 1890. He spent four years in post-graduate work and received the degree of Master of Arts from the same institution in 1894.

Entering the New York College of Dentistry, he was elected to membership and became a member of Beta chapter in 1895, graduating from the college in 1897.

Doctor Semans located in Columbus, O.; in 1898 he was appointed instructor in Dental Technics at the Ohio Medical

University; in 1900 he was elected to the Chair of Dental Anatomy and became Instructor in Operative Technics and Porcelain Inlay; in 1906 he was elected Professor of Operative Dentistry and Anatomy, also Dean of the Dental Department of the University. His rise from the lowest position on the teaching corps of the University to the most exalted position within the gift of the faculty was the result of his diligence and of his painstaking efforts in behalf of the students under his charge.

Brother Semans is the second member of Psi Omega, initiated into active membership, to attain such high honor.

In Baltimore, one of the founders of our fraternity, George E. Hardy, M. D., D. D. S., for a number of years Demonstrator of Mechanical Dentistry in the Baltimore College of Dental Surgery, the birth place of our organization, has been called to fill a more responsible position on the Faculty of that institution. Brother Hardy has toiled long and faithfully with the "green" students, by his tact and kindly bearing he at once gains the affection of those under his charge and thereby enthuses the men to greater effort in their work in his department. It is a pleasure to be able to chronicle in The Frater the selection of Doctor Hardy to fill the Chair of Physiology and Comparative Anatomy. We feel sure that the faculty has made a wise choice in his election and that the alumni to a man will heartily approve the act.

Professor Hardy, The Frater congratulates you.

Brother I. N. Broomell, one of Gamma's honorary members, has been called to the Deanship of the Medico-Chirurgical College in Philadelphia. His election is a popular one and much benefit to the college with him at its head will result.

Brother T. J. McLernon has been called to assume re-responsible duties at the Western Reserve University, Cleveland, O. To which city he removed his family and household goods in September.

Brother E. E. Belford, Beta Gamma, who has for the past two years been practicing in Toledo, O., has also been honored by the faculty of Western Reserve by being appointed to the Chair of Dental Prosthesis. Many brothers who attended the Triennial Convention at Saint Louis will remember Professor Belford as having taken very active part in the proceedings of that convention. All Psi Omegas, who know him, will wish him success in his role on the faculty of Western Reserve.

Harvey Van Doren Cottrell, Psi, has been further honored at O. M. U. by being elected Secretary of the Faculty; he has also been advanced to the Professorship of Prosthetic Dentistry.

Brother Crouch has been appointed Chief Demonstrator and Brother Thompson Assistant Demonstrator at the Keokuk Dental College. George Bienvenu, Beta Epsilon, '04, has been appointed Assistant Demonstrator in Prosthetic Dentistry in the New Orleans College of Dentistry.

DeLos L. Hill, one of the most active men in the organization and history of Tau, a delegate to the Third Triennial Convention, the prime factor in the organization of Gamma Iota and for the past few years a demonstrator in the Southern Dental College, has been elected to the Chair of Physiology by the faculty of that college. Brother Hill is an earnest, vigorous worker, an enthusiast in educational affairs, and well fitted for his work; consequently we feel that he will acquit himself in his new role with honor to his college, his fraternity and himself.

Because of this record of advancement made in one year by members of Psi Omega, we cannot help but feel that careful selection, in the first instance, by the chapter of her members to be the real reason why Psi Omega is so strongly represented on the various college faculties and demonstrating staffs. Other worthy members have been and now are occupying as important places in various colleges and these new names simply add to the grand total of Psi Omegas employed as dental educators.

SAN FRANCISCO RELIEF FUND.

The following contributions to the Relief Fund for Psi Omegas who suffered serious financial loss on account of the earthquake were received after The Frater went to press last May:

To total amount reported in May Frater	$366.00
J. L. Paul, Gallitzin, Pa.	1.00
Dr. Felix Keidel, Fredericksburg, Tex.	5.00
Beta Chapter, New York	10.00
Gamma Lambda Chapter, New York	10.00
Dr. Geo. B. Snow, Buffalo, N. Y.	25.00
Theta Chapter, Buffalo, N. Y.	15.00

Dr. O. M. Sorber, Manila, P. I......................... 10.00
Mu Chapter, Denver, Colo............................ 2.75
Nu Chapter, Pittsburg, Pa............................ 10.00

Total $454.75

We had hoped to have a complete report from the Relief Committee for this issue of The Frater, but the committee was not yet ready to report.

Brother Crane is of the opinion that The Frater was in error when it stated that he was the first to contribute to the Relief fund. The man who passes the hat around usually puts in his contribution first; possibly Brother Crane neglected to conform to custom, but we are inclined to think otherwise. The letter received from Brother Crane upon the subject is printed in full and whatever the verdict of our readers, it must be conceded that Brother Crane played a very prominent part in a worthy cause. The letter follows.

Washington, D. C., Sept. 4, 1906.
Dr. Edw. H. Sting,
    Editor, "The Frater,"

Dear Brother:—

Three days after the news of the San Francisco earthquake reached Washington, I was glancing over a "Frater" and happened to notice that we have two active chapters in the doomed city. It immediately occurred to me that some of our brothers there must be in pressing need of financial assistance. As I knew the brotherly love of the Psi Omegas in Washington so well from personal experience, I felt that they would consider it a privilege to contribute to any fund intended to relieve a brother in distress.

Sitting down at the 'phone with the call book open in front of me, I called up all those brothers having telephone connection and asked the following question: "If we find that any of our brothers in San Francisco are in need of assistance, and can locate a brother to handle the fund, how much will you contribute?" In each case the response was whole-hearted and generous, and in a few minutes I had over $35 guaranteed. I then sent a telegram, without charge, by courtesy of the local manager of the Western Union, to Brother C. H. Merritt, of Oakland, Cal., asking him if he would take charge of the contribution.

While awaiting his reply, $45 more was pledged at a meeting of Beta Gamma chapter and by other alumni members It gives me the greatest gratification to state that every member who was asked for a contribution gave gladly and freely according to his means.

It took me about ten days to receive a reply from Brother Merritt, but finally we received his telegram saying that our boys in "Frisco" were in urgent need of help and had lost everything.

With this telegram in hand it was an easy matter to collect the money that had been pledged and a New York draft for $80 was forwarded to Brother Merritt within two days after the receipt of the telegram, and on the same day that the first of the circular letters from the Supreme Council asking for contributions were received in Washington. Brother Merritt later acknowledged the receipt of the draft.

My object in writing this letter is that the men of Beta Gamma and Beta Theta chapters may receive the credit for the prompt generosity with which they recognized the needs of their brothers in San Francisco, and to correct the misstatement in the May "Frater" that I was the first brother to contribute.   Yours very cordially,
Arthur B. Crane, Zeta, '99.

ASSISTANT WANTED.

An all round man, thoroughly competent, at least two years' experience in an office. Good appearance and habits; registered in New York State. Address Private Practice, care of The Frater.

Personal and Alumni Notes.

J. C. Cloyd is practicing at Catlin, Ill.

C. R. Grissinger, Eta, '05, is located at Bedford, Pa.

M. R. Milne, Eta, '05, is located at Meyersdale, Pa.

V. W. Laughlin, Mu, '05, is located at Challis, Idaho.

T. A. Wilkins, Omicron, '05, is located at Gastonia, N. C.

W. J. Wriglesworth, Iota, '05, is located at Fernie, B. C.

A. H. Spicer, Zeta, '05, is with his father at Westerly, R. I.

L. W. Strong has removed to 209 State street, Suite 1112, Chicago, Ill.

"Mike" Griffin, Zeta, '05, is at 781 Manhattan avenue, Brooklyn, N. Y.

C. E. Hurdle, Beta Eta, '04, has removed from Augusta to La Harpe, Ill.

A. F. Dyer, Theta, '05, is located at 87 East First St., Corning, N. Y.

S. W. Reed, Gamma, '05, is located at Lake Side Inn, Lake Placid, N. Y.

Clarence S. McCord, Nu, '05, is located at 1334 Federal street, Allegheny, Pa.

Winthrop W. Thompson, Beta, '02, has removed to 383 Hancock street, Brooklyn, N. Y.

William J. Thorson, Iota, '04, is located at Seventy-fifth street and Ellis avenue, Chicago, Ill.

"Rusty" Bryer, Zeta, '04, is married and lives at 849 Lexington avenue, New York City.

J. C. Stillman, Zeta, '04, is assistant to Doctor Brown, of Lafayette avenue, Brooklyn, N. Y.

H. G. Bauman, Zeta, '05, is located at his home, 228 East Fifty-second street, New York City.

Harry N. Darrow, Zeta, '05, is with Dr. Trebaud, at 42 South Fourth avenue, Mount Vernon, N. Y.

C. M. Bowles, Altoona, Pa., has removed his office from the Trust Building to Sixth avenue and Fourth street.

G. M. Osterberg, Chi, '02, Seattle, Wash., has removed from the Pythian Building to 316-317 Eitel Building.

D. K. Campbell, Zeta, '05, has his office at 436 Gold street, Brooklyn, N. Y. His home is at 73 Hancock street.

J. W. Platt, Pi, '02, has removed from Gallup, N. M., to Roby, Texas, where he finds a climate and practice to his liking.

G. C. Mathison, Gamma, '95, has removed from the Canada Permanent Block to 325 1-2 Portage avenue, Winnipeg, Man.

J. H. LeBlanc, Beta Epsilon, '05, was a visitor in New Orleans during October. Le Blanc is practicing in Whitecastle, La.

J. C. Reichley, Phi, '04, moved into his new office on October 1st. Brother Reichley is located at 216 West Market street, York, Pa.

The readers of The Frater are indebted to C. B. Gifford, P. G. M., Phi, '06, for the set of Maryland State Board Questions contained in this issue.

H. Clay Hassell, Omicron, '98, Tuscaloosa, Ala., circulated among friends in Atlanta while attending the meeting of the National Dental Association.

Brother Martin Dewey has removed from 414 Hall to 307 Argyle Building, Kansas City, Mo. Brother Dewey is President of the Alumni Society of the Angle School of Orthodontia.

—•◇•—

B. A. Rees, P. G. M., Alpha, '04, Salem, W. Va., is entertaining a ten pound baby girl wich arrived in his home on October 19th. We are pleased to hear that the mother and child are both in good health.

—•◇•—

Brothers Riess, Sigma, '03, and Jensen, Rho, '03, of New Orleans, La., have removed their offices from the Medical to the Macheca Building. It is with pleasure that we note the recovery of Brother Riess from a recent illness.

—•◇•—

C. A. Worthington and his brother, S. L. Worthington, Beta Alpha, '06 men, have opened offices at Danville, Ill. They are "up against" fifteen advertising "joints" but will nevertheless be successful in establishing good practices.

—•◇•—

Brothers William Richardson and S. S. Grosjean, of New Orleans, "the inseparables," were in attendance at the meeting of the National Dental Association. Brother Richardson, please accept our apologies for calling you "Billy" Williams in the May Frater.

—•◇•—

J. R. Greening, Omicron, '05, is in Mexico. Some time ago he had the pleasure of calling upon M. F. Bauchert, Chihuahua, Mexico. He found Brother Bauchert to be a "fine" fellow who has made good money in his eight years of practice in Mexico.

—•◇•—

While in Denver, Colo., during the past summer, Leon Barnett, Beta Epsilon, 05, of New Orleans, La., was entertained by Wm. M. McKee, of Mu. Barnett has been re-assigned to the visiting staff of the Charity Hospital of New Orleans, as Visiting Dental Surgeon.

—•◇•—

T. E. Butler, Beta Alpha, '08, practiced dentistry in Australia before he came to the United States to enter the University of Illinois and thereby was entitled to take the Illinois State Board Examination. His work during his first year in school encouraged him to try the "Board" which he did and passed successfully. The future of this worthy brother appears bright indeed.

Marriages.

BAKER—HOLT.

E. W. Baker, Zeta, '04, and Miss Alice Holt were recently united in marriage. They reside at 119 West 121st street, New York City. Brother Holt has his office at his home.

PARK—REESE.

Earl Heath Park, Nu, '05, and Miss Daisy Reese were united in marriage on Thursday, October 4th, at the home of the bride, Hortons, Pa. Brother Park has a splendid practice at Marion, Pa., where the happy couple will make their home.

Necrology.

ROYAL HUTTON PIERCE, KAPPA.

It is with sorrow that we print the sad news of the death of our Past Supreme Councilor, Royal H. Pierce, of Duluth, Minn. Brother Pierce was about thirty-four years old; in his senior year at school he was Grand Master of Kappa chapter. Later, he served two terms as Supreme Councilor. Brother Pierce was married on April 24, 1906, to Miss Margaret Mellon, of Duluth, Minn.

The following in regard to Brother Pierce is taken from The Dental Summary:

"Dr. Pierce, of Duluth, Loses Life in Lake.—Dr. R. H. Pierce, while hunting in company with his wife, his brother and several friends, was drowned in Rice lake, near McGregor, Minn., October 13th, 1906. He went out in a small boat to shoot ducks, and in some unknown manner the craft was capsized. When he did not return to camp at night searchers were sent out in every direction, but it was not until to-day that the upturned boat and his hat were found.

"Dr. Pierce two years ago was chosen grand senior sagamore of the Improved Order of Red Men of the United States. His widow was a bride of only a few months. He was a prominent dentist of Duluth."

State Board Questions.

PENNSYLVANIA, JUNE, 1906.

Anatomy and Physiology.

1. How are bones classified according to their form? (b) Give an example of each. 2. Name the four divisions of the brain. (b) Give a general description of the surface of the brain. 3. Name five superficial muscles of the face. 4. State the origin and distribution of the seventh Cranial Nerve. 5. Describe the hip joint. 6. Define secretion. (b) Excretion. (c) Name three substances secreted. (d) Three substances excreted. 7. What is the pulse? (b) Describe the sounds of the heart. 8. What are the functions of the Pancreatic juice? 9. What are the functions of the medulla oblongata? 10. State the changes that occur in the blood while it passes through the circulatory system.

Special Dental Anatomy, Dental Histology, and Dental Physiology.

1. Describe the apical foramen. (b) The apical space. (c) State the contents of each. 2. What teeth should normally be present in the mouth of a child eleven years of age? 3. Define the following terms as applied to teeth: Triangular ridge, oblique ridge, transverse ridge. 4. Name the centers of ossification of the mandible. 5. How many layers has the tooth follicle? (b) What does each layer form or assist in forming? 6. Describe the odontoblastic cell as seen under the microscope. 7. Explain the origin of the epithelial cords of the permanent teeth. 8. How is the peridental membrane supplied with nerves? 9. What muscles are engaged in operating the mouth? 10. State the order and name the ages at which the deciduous teeth erupt.

Chemistry, Metallurgy, and Oral Surgery.

1. What physical and what chemical features distinguish metallic from non-metallic elements? 2. What is oxygen? (b) How may it be obtained? (c) State some of its leading affinities. 3. Form complete equations of the following:

$Ag NO_3 + HCl =$
$PbCl_2 + H_2SO_4 =$
$CaO + H_2O =$

4. State the chemical names of the following compounds: $KI, CaSO_4, HgCl_2, FeO, NH_4OH$.

5. Describe some metallurgic resemblances of gold and platinum. (b) What important differences are manifested in their dental employment? 6. What conditions insure perfect flow and spread of solder in blow pipe technic? (b) To what errors are cracked porcelains attributable? 7. Describe the dry process of refining gold. 8. State diagnosis, clinical features, and surgical treatment of epithelioma of the lip. 9. What injuries may result, and what functional disturbances may occur, through careless extraction of the superior third molar tooth? (b) What precautions should be observed? 10. State diagnosis and surgical treatment of fibro-ankylosis of the temporomandibular articulation.

Principles and Practice of Operative and Prosthetic Dentistry.

1. Describe the technic of making and inserting a porcelain inlay in a disto palatine cavity of an incisor. 2. What results are liable to follow the premature extraction of the deciduous teeth? (a) Incisors. (b) Cuspids. (c) Molars. 3. What is the distinguishing feature of pain caused by pulp irritation? (b) By what methods may it be diagnosed and located? 4. Distinguish between erosion, mechanical abrasion and caries. 5. How may metallic fillings be inserted in cavities sensitive to thermal changes, with comparative comfort and safety to the pulp? 6. Describe the construction and fusing of a banded porcelain bicuspid crown. 7. Describe the method of replacing a broken tooth in a continuous gum denture. 8. How may the model for the construction of an upper plate be modified, to improve the stability of the denture? 9. From what is purple of cassius made? (b) For what purposes is it used in dentistry? 10. Describe the construction of a full soldered gold base denture.

Dental Pathology and Bacteriology.

1. Distinguish between a benign and a malignant tumor. (b) Name one variety of each. 2. What syphilitic manifestations may occur in the mouth? 3. Give the etiology and pathology of mercurial stomatitis. 4. Differentiate between a fistula, an ulcer and an abscess. 5. Give the differential diag-

nosis of pulpitis and pericementitis.   6. Describe a method of staining bacteria.   (b) Why are bacteria stained?   7. Give the etiology and pathology of dental caries.   8. What is thrush?   (b)   What causes it?   (c)   Describe the symptoms.   9. Describe the process of making pure cultures from a mixed collection of bacteria.   10. What is septicemia?   (b) What causes it?   (c)   State the symptoms.

Anesthesia, Materia Medica and Therapeutics.

1. Differentiate local anesthetics and anodynes. (b) Give three examples of each. 2. Describe the physiologic action of ether administered as an anesthetic. 3. Describe the methods of administering cocain. (b) State the doses. (c) What are its antidotes? 4. How is alcohol obtained? (b) What kind is employed in medicine? (c) State its physiologic and therapeutic uses. 5. From what is aconite obtained? (b) Give its physiologic action. (c) Therapeutic uses, doses and antidotes. 6. Give the source of morphin. (b) Strychnin. (c) Atropin. State the dose and antidote of each. 7. How does a tonic differ from a stimulant? (b) From a restorative. Give an example of each. 8. Describe the physiologic action and therapeutic effect of heat. (b) Cold. 9. What is meant by chemical incompatibility of drugs? (b) By physiologic incompatibility. 10. Write a prescription containing Tr. aconite, Tr. opium, and water sufficient for eight doses. (b) Give directions for using. (c) State the amount of each drug in a dose.

MARYLAND, MAY, 1906.

Chemistry and Bacteriology.

1. What is meant by the term chemical energy? 2. What is meant by the term combustion? 3. What are oxides? Give two examples. 4. What is a saturated solution? 5. What are ptomaines? 6. Give Koch's rules in regard to the bacterial cause of disease. 7. Of what is water composed and how would you prove it? 8. What is the structure of bacteria? 99. Of what is a cell wall composed? 9. Of what do the contents of the cell consist?

Pathology and Therapeutics.

1. What is stomatitis? Give causes, symptoms and treatment for the simple variety. 2. Define cancrum oris. Give etiology, symptoms and treatment. 3. Define periodontitis. Give

symptoms, causes and treatment. 4. Describe alveolar abscess. Give its etiology, symptoms, treatment. 5. Describe alveolar pyorrhea; its etiology and treatment. 6. Give the derivation and medical properties of corrosive sublimate. State strength used in treating oral lesions. 7. What is dental caries? Its causes? 8. Describe the composition of nitrous oxide. In case of dangerous results following its use, what would you do? 9. Give the derivation and medical properties of aconite, and also its dental uses. 10. What is arsenious acid? Give dental uses and local antidote.

Anatomy.

1. Of what does the skeleton consist? 2. Name the bones of the face. Describe the superior maxillary bone. 3. Name the different parts of the muscular system. 4. Name and locate the salivary glands. 5. Name and describe the muscles which depress the lower jaw.

Physiology.

1. Describe the process of digestion. 2. Describe the changes produced in the air taken into the lungs by the process of respiration. 3. Name some kinds of cells found in man. What is epithelium? 4. What are the causes of the sounds produced by the heart? To what is arterial pressure due? How regulated? 5. Describe the corpuscles found in the blood. Describe their origin and function.

Operative Dentistry.

1. Give general rule for cavity preparation for gold filling; also cavity formation for porcelain. 2. What advantage has porcelain over gold as a filling material? Describe making a mesio-incisal porcelain filling for a central incisor. 3. How is gutta percha used as a filling material? 4. Describe the preparation of a root for a Logan crown. 5. What filling materials are used in deciduous teeth? When should the temporary molars be removed? 6. How would you prepare abutments for a bridge where the superior centrals and laterals are missing? 7. How would you prepare and fill with gold an approximal cavity in a central incisor where both labial and palatal surfaces are involved? 8. How prepare and fill a labial surface cavity that extends under the gum margin? 10. In what manner may a broken broach be removed from a root canal?

Oral Surgery.

1. Give some characteristics of sarcoma and epithelioma growths. 2. What are the usual causes of antrum diseases and give the most approved treatment? 3. Name the causes for im-

mobility of the jaws. 4. In what way might mechanical injuries produce exostosis? 5. Name the important symptoms of simple and compound fractures of the lower maxilla. 6. What is the difference between geminous and attached teeth? 7. Give the location of ranula, etiology, treatment. 8. What form of disease is established by the termination of periodontitis and suppuration? 9. Should an abscessed tooth be extracted at any stage? Give reason. 10. What is meant by an "intractable tooth pulp" and suggest a remedy.

Mechanical Dentistry.

1. Classify impression materials. 2. How may a shallow cup be easily and quickly modified in shape and adapted to a deep mouth without injury to the cup? 3. How can a lead counter die be obtained when the die is of an alloy that melts at a lower temperature than the counter die? 4. Of what are porcelain teeth composed? 5. Do thermometers vary in the registration of temperature? How may you test them? 6. Give the "dry process" of refining gold? 7. What is the pressure to the square inch in the boiler of a vulcanizer at 300 degrees F? 8. What is meant by atmospheric pressure in retaining a plate? 9. Describe the finishing of a vulcanite plate. 10. What is the fusing point of gold, silver, platinum, copper?

PHILLIPS' MILK OF MAGNESIA

"THE PERFECT ANTACID"
FOR LOCAL OR SYSTEMIC USE

| CARIES | SENSITIVENESS | STOMATITIS |
| EROSION | GINGIVITIS | PYORRHŒA |

Are successfully treated with it. As a mouth wash it neutralizes oral acidity.

PHILLIPS' PHOSPHO-MURIATE OF QUININE,
COMPOUND
TONIC, RECONSTRUCTIVE, AND ANTIPERIODIC

With marked beneficial action upon the nervous system. To be relied upon where a deficiency of the phosphates is evident.

The Chas. H. Phillips Chemical Co., New York and London.

Antiphlogistine

(INFLAMMATION'S ANTIDOTE.)

THE SPATULA

oftentimes will make unnecessary

THE SCALPEL

if it be used for the application of ANTIPHLOGISTINE hot and thick in the various inflammatory and congestive conditions.

ANTIPHLOGISTINE

Depletes Inflamed Areas,   Flushes the Capillaries,

Stimulates the Reflexes,   Restores the Circulation,

Bleeds but Saves the Blood.

The Denver Chemical Mfg. Co.,

Chicago, **NEW YORK,** London,
San Francisco, Sydney,
Denver. Montreal.

RATE

Official Organ
Psi Omega Fraterni

THE FRATER

Official Organ of The Psi Omega Fraternity.

PUBLISHED BY
THE SUPREME COUNCIL
In November, January, March and May,
AT TIFFIN, OHIO.

SUPREME COUNCIL

DR. EDW. H. STING,   91 E. Perry St., Tiffin, Ohio.

DR. J. E. NYCE,   1001 Witherspoon Bldg., Philadelphia, Pa.

DR. H. E. FRIESELL,   6000 Penn Ave., Pittsburg, Pa.

BUSINESS MANAGER.

DR. J. E. NYCE,   1001 Witherspoon Bldg., Philadelphia, Pa.

EDITOR-IN-CHIEF.

DR. EDW. H. STING,   Tiffin, Ohio.

SUBSCRIPTION.

One Dollar per year, payable in advance :: The Frater will be sent to all subscribers until ordered discontinued :: Send all communications to the Editor-in-Chief. :: Exchanges please send one copy to each of the Supreme Councilors.

Entered as second-class matter November 7, 1904, at the Post Office at Tiffin, Ohio.

FRATERNITY DIRECTORY.

Active Chapters.

ALPHA	Baltimore College of Dental Surgery.
BETA	New York College of Dentistry.
GAMMA	Pennsylvania Col. of Dental Surgery, Phila.
DELTA	Tufts Dental College, Boston, Mass.
EPSILON	Western Reserve University, Cleveland, O.
ZETA	University of Pennsylvania, Philadelphia.
ETA	Philadelphia Dental College.
THETA	University of Buffalo, Dental Department.
IOTA	Northwestern University, Chicago, Ill.
KAPPA	Chicago College of Dental Surgery.
LAMBDA	University of Minnesota, Minneapolis.
MU	University of Denver, Denver, Col.
NU	Pittsburg Dental College, Pittsburg, Pa.
XI	Milwaukee, Wis., Med. Col., Dental Dept.
MU DELTA	Harvard University, Dental Department.
OMICRON	Louisville College of Dental Surgery.
PI	Baltimore Medical College, Dental Dept.
BETA SIGMA	College of Physicians and Surgeons, Dental Department, San Francisco, Cal.
RHO	Ohio Col. of Dental Surgery, Cincinnati.
SIGMA	Medico-Chirurgical College, Philadelphia.
TAU	Atlanta Dental College, Atlanta, Ga.
UPSILON	University of Southern California, Dental Department, Los Angeles.
PHI	University of Maryland, Baltimore.
CHI	North Pacific Dental Col., Portland, Ore.
PSI	College of Dentistry, O. M. U., Columbus.
OMEGA	Indiana Dental College, Indianapolis, Ind.
BETA ALPHA	University of Illinois, Chicago.
BETA GAMMA	George Washington, Uni., Washington, D.C.
BETA DELTA	University of California, San Francisco.
BETA EPSILON	New Orleans College of Dentistry.
BETA ZETA	St. Louis Dental College, St. Louis, Mo.
BETA ETA	Keokuk Dental College, Keokuk, Iowa.
BETA THETA	Georgetown University, Washington, D. C.
GAMMA IOTA	Southern Dental College, Atlanta, Ga.
GAMMA KAPPA	University of Michigan, Ann Arbor.
GAMMA LAMBDA	Col. of Dental and Oral Surg. of New York.
GAMMA MU	University of Iowa, Iowa City.
GAMMA NU	Vanderbilt Uni., Nashville, Tenn.

Alumni Chapters.

New York Alumni Chapter....................New York City.
Duquesne Alumni Chapter....................Pittsburg, Pa.
Minnesota Alumni Chapter................Minneapolis, Minn.
Chicago Alumni Chapter.......................Chicago, Ill.
Boston Alumni Chapter...................... Boston, Mass.
Philadelphia Alumni Chapter.............Philadelphia, Pa.
New Orleans Alumni Chapter..............New Orleans, La.
Los Angeles Alumni Chapter.............Los Angeles, Cal.
Cleveland Alumni Chapter...................Cleveland, Ohio.
Sealth Alumni Chapter.......................Seattle, Wash.
Portsmouth Alumni Chapter..............Portsmouth, Ohio.

ALUMNI DIRECTORY.

Ada, O.—
C. W. Brecheisen, Psi, '02.
Aiken, S. C.—
G. A. Milner, Tau, '05.
Allegheny, Pa.—
F. H. Deterding, Nu, '05,
417 Third street.
Reynolds M. Sleppy, Nu, '04,
1915 Beaver avenue.
Altoona, Pa.—
Herbert R. Wehrle, Nu, '03,
Altoona Trust Bldg.
Arkadelphia, Ark.—
J. C. Settles, Omicron, '04.
Augusta, Ga.—
R. H. Calhoun, Tau, '04,
936 Broad street.
Baltimore, Md.—
Prof. W. Simon, Alpha,
1348 Block street.
Brooklyn, N. Y.—
Ellison Hillyer, Beta, '93,
472 Greene avenue.
Winthrop W. Thompson,
Beta, '02,
383 Hancock street.
Horace P. Gould, Beta, '95,
193 Joralemon street.
Warrington G. Lewis,
Beta, '01,
162 Clinton street.
Walter S. Watson, Beta, '02,
270 Halsey street.
Bowling Green, O.—
E. J. Frowine, Psi, '04.
Buffalo, N. Y.—
Wes. M. Backus, Theta, '04,
485 Grant street.
Chihuahua, Mexico.—
M. F. Bauchert, Beta, '96.
Chico, Cal.—
J. R. Young, Beta Delta, '03.
Box 515.
Columbus, O.—
H. M. Semans, Beta, '97,
289 East State street.
Cleveland, O.—
E. E. Belford,
Beta Gamma, '04,
E. 90 Place and Superior avenue.
Delhi, La.—
T. K. McLemore,
Gamma Iota, '06.
Edgefield, S. C.—
Augustus H. Corley, Tau, '04.

Florisant, Mo.—
G. S. Steinmesch,
Beta Zeta, '04.
Fort Gaines, Ga.—
R. H. Saunders, Tau, '05.
Fort Leavenworth, Kan.—
J. D. Millikin, Beta Sigma,
Dental Surgeon, U.S.A.
Fredericksburg, Tex.—
F. Keidel, Alpha, '04.
Gallitzin, Pa.—
J. L. Paul, Alpha, '01.
Gonzales, Tex.—
S. C. Patton, Tau, '03.
Hancock, Mich.—
Ralph W. DeMass,
Beta Gamma, '05,
Funkey Block.
Hull, Ill.—
L. H. Wolfe, Beta Eta, '05.
Iager, W. Va.—
G. E. Dennis, Phi, '05.
Ithaca, N. Y.—
A. M. MacGachen,
Theta, '03,
218 East State street.
Johnsonburg, Pa.—
H. C. Coleman, Nu, '03.
Johnstown, Pa.—
Owen Morgan, Alpha, '95.
Kaufman, Tex.—
Henry Hoffer, Alpha, '95.
Lafayette, Ind.—
A. R. Ross, Gamma, '03.
Lewistown, Pa.—
Curtis H. Marsh,
Gamma, '06.
14 E. Market street.
Liberty, N. Y.—
W. A. Buckley, Beta, '00.
Logansport, Ind.—
H. G. Stalnaker, Omega, '03.
Los Angeles, Cal.—
J. F. Curran, Kappa, '01,
1919 S. Grand avenue.
C. C. Jarvis, Upsilon, '04,
302 Severance Bldg.
Malone, N. Y.—
R. N. Porter, Gamma, '01.
Manila, P. I.—
O. M. Sorber, Nu, '97,
Dental Surgeon, U. S. A.
Mansfield, La.—
G. J. Griffiths, Tau, '03.

McKeesport, Pa.—
  W. D. Fawcett, Nu, '99, 508½ Fifth avenue.
Milwaukee, Wis.—
  E. J. Schlief, Xi, '97, 417 Wells Bldg.
  J. E. Callaway, Xi, '06, Suite 306, Stumpf and Langhoff Bldg.
Morganfield, Ky.—
  W. S. Green, Omicron,' 04.
New York City.—
  A. S. Walker, Beta. '97, 295 Central Park, West.
  E. W. Burckhardt, Beta,'04, Van Corlear Place, Kingsbridge.
  S. W. Van Saun, Beta, '00, Broadway and 74th St, The Ansonia.
New Kensington, Pa.—
  A. J. Rose, Rho, '03, Logan Trust Bldg.
New Orleans, La.—
  A. J. Cohn, Alpha, '99, 703 Morris Bldg.
  Leon Barnett, Beta Epsilon, '05, 703 Macheca Bldg.
  Rene Esnard, Beta Epsilon, '05, 612 Macheca Bldg.
Norristown, Pa.—
  D. H. Wetzel, Zeta, '02.
Oakland, Cal.—
  C. H. Merritt, Alpha, '98, 308-9 Union Savings Bank Bldg.
Oroville, Cal.—
  L. H. Marks, B. Sigma, '04.
Paso Robles, Cal.—
  W. G. Gates, Kappa, '05.
Paterson, N. J.—
  A. Dewitt Payne, Beta, '99, 160 Broadway.
Pikesville, Ky.—
  J. M. Williams, Rho, '05.
Pittsburg, Pa.—
  W. Emmory Ferree, Alpha, '00, 7138 Hamilton ave., East End.
  C. L. McChesney, Nu, '99, 98 Washington avenue.
  H. E. Friesell, Gamma, '95, 6000 Penn avenue.
Philadelphia, Pa.—
  A. F. Goddard, Gamma, '01, 15th and Chestnut Sts., 1302 Pennsylvania Bldg.
  A. P. Lee, Eta, '00, 3403 Chestnut street.
  J. E. Nyce, Gamma, '02, 1001 Witherspoon Bldg.
Port Clinton, O.—
  John G. Yingling, Alpha,'97.
Roby, Tex.—
  J. N. Platt, Pi, '02.
Rowland, N. C.—
  C. H. Lennan, Tau, '03.
San Francisco, Cal.—
  C. W. Knowles, M.D., D.D.S., Beta Sigma, '99, Rooms 101-7 Spring Valley W. Works Bldg.
  Thos. R. Morffew, Beta Sigma, Examiner Bldg.
Seattle, Wash.—
  Geo. T. Williams, Nu, '04, Snoqualmie Hotel.
  F. W. Hergert, Chi, '03, 651 Colman Block.
  C. P. Poston, Chi, 218 Lumber Exchange.
Springfield, Mass.—
  H. Everton Hosley, Gamma, '95, Phoenix Bldg.
St. Joseph, Ill.—
  H. E. Davis, Rho, '03.
St. Louis, Mo.—
  H. J. Braun, Beta Zeta, '04, 2850 St. Louis avenue.
  H. V. Pfaff, Iota, '99, 2217 St. Louis avenue.
Tiffin, O.—
  W. H. Holtz, Rho, '03.
  E. H. Sting, Alpha, '95.
  E. C. West, Psi, '02.
Topsham, Maine.—
  H. Q. Mariner, Sigma, '05.
Tuscaloosa, Ala.—
  H. Clay Hassell, Omicron, '98.
Upland, Ind.—
  J. A. Loughry, Psi, '04.
Union, S. C.—
  Jas. M. Wallace, Phi, '04.
Vinton, Iowa.—
  B. F. Schwartz, Iota, '04.
Washington, D. C.—
  Shirley W. Bowles, Eta,'98, 1315 New York avenue.
  C. L, Constantini, Beta Gamma, '03, 814 14th St., N. W.
Washington, Pa.—
  Howard R. Smith, Nu, '03, 17 West Chestnut street.
Waynesboro, Miss.—
  C. H. Gray, Tau, '04.
Winchester, Ky.—
  George S. Brooks, Rho, '02.
Westfield, N. J.—
  Theo. R. Harvey, Gamma, '94, 245 Broad street.
Williamson, W. Va.—
  Wm. S. Rosenheim, Pi, '05.
Wellsburg, W. Va.—
  K. C. Brashear, Psi, '02,

Swanburg,　　　　Osterburg,　　　　J. F. Alexander,　　　　Luithlen,
　　　Lee,　　　　　　　　　　　　　　　　　　　　　Palmer,
Williams,　　　　　Poston,　　　　　　Hergert,　　　　　W. Alexander.

THE FRATER.

Vol. 6.   January, 1907.   No. 2.

GAMMA NU—VANDERBILT UNIVERSITY.

E. Elwood Street. Editor.

Organized by H. E. Friesell, S. C., November 26, 1906.

The evening of November 26, 1906, started a new era in fraternity life at Vanderbilt University, Dental Department, at which time Alpha Kappa Delta, our local organization composed of staunch, tried and true men, was, with due ceremony, disbanded so that her members could organize and qualify as charter members of Gamma Nu chapter of the great Psi Omega Dental Fraternity.

Though Alpha Kappa Delta ceased to exist, the many pleasures enjoyed under her name will linger long in the hearts of each one of us; but the happiest moment to us was when we learned that, because of our Alpha Kappa Delta organization we would be enabled to become a part of Psi Omega.

Supreme Councilor, H. E. Friesell, administered the obligation to each of the following candidates who will be known as the charter members of Gamma Nu:

Edward L. Williams, '08	Monroe, N. C.
Walter E. Simms, '09	Modesto, Cal.
E. Elwood Street, '08	Clarksville, Texas.
A. Clifford Braly, '08	Nashville, Tenn.
Arthur J. Moreland, '07	Metropolis, Ill.
Albert M. Gregory, '07	Smyrna, Tenn.
Leslie W. Noel, '08	Nashville, Tenn.
Clifford McCain, '08	Bogata, Texas.
Chas. R. Layton, '08	Rockport, Ky.
Louie F. Wilson, '08	Mobile, Ala.
Wesley T. Merritt, '07	Jackson, Miss.
Arnette P. Williams, '07	Furman, Ala.
Hawthorn M. Fuller, '07	Centreville, Ala.
James N. Sledge, '09	Greensboro, Ala.
Joseph K. Williams, '07	Corinth, Miss.

Chas. D. Dillard, '07 .... Huntsville, Ala.
Hubert R. Penny, '08 .... Garner, N. C.
James B. Jones, '09 .... Murfreesboro, Tenn.
John A. Byrd, Jr., '09 .... Nashville, Tenn.
Theodore M. Wilson, '07 .... Jenifer, Ala.

Then the jeweled Psi Omega pins were distributed to each member.

The first business transacted by the new chapter was the election of officers, which resulted as follows:

H. M. Fuller .... G. M.
E. L. Williams .... J. M.
J. K. Williams .... Sec.
T. M. Wilson .... Treas.
A. C. Braly .... C. Inquisitor.
L. F. Wilson .... C. Inter.
A. J. Moreland .... Inside G.
W. T. Merritt .... Outside G.
J. N. Sledge .... Hist.
E. E. Street .... Editor.
L. W. Noel .... Sen.

Because of the fact that there are two other National Dental fraternities represented by chapters at Vanderbilt, we will never cease in our efforts to maintain Gamma Nu the proud leader of them all.

At present, our future seems decidedly bright because we start with a fine lot of fellows who are enthusiastic and congenial.

Since our organization, we have had quite a number of encouraging letters from sister chapters and from individual members of the fraternity and it is the desire of the members of Gamma Nu to assure all that we appreciate the interest taken in us and the hearty welcome which we have received.

REPORT OF THE SAN FRANCISCO RELIEF COMMITTEE.

E. P. James, Chairman.

Oakland, Cal., Dec. 10, '06·

Dear Brother Sting:

I am mailing under separate cover the relief committee report. I regret very much not having been able to send it some three weeks ago as promised but was delayed in getting the signatures of the other members of the committee. As it is Brother Merritt's signature is omitted on account of his absence from the state.

The distribution of the fund was considerably delayed on account of the difficulty of locating the brothers. The plan of cash distribution being adopted only after failure to make satisfactory arrangements for a discount with the dental depots. The 20 per cent offered not being considered sufficient.

In submitting this report I wish to extend the thanks of the committee to the Supreme Councilors and the brothers who so generously responded to the call for assistance, particularly to those brothers from the stricken district who, themselves suffering great loss, were still able to extend sympathy and even offer material aid to more unfortunate brothers.

Yours sincerely and fraternally,

EDWIN P. JAMES,
Chairman of Committee.

Oakland, October 31st, 1906.

To the Officers and Members of the Psi Omega Dental Fraternity:

The following is a full report of the relief committee on the disbursement of the funds contributed by the members of the fraternity for the relief of brothers having suffered loss by the disaster of April 18th to 22nd, 1906.

Receipts.

Check sent by brothers of Washington, D. C.,
to Brother C. H. Merritt .... $ 80.00
Check sent by Supreme Council to Brother
Edwin P. James $374.75 $454.75

Disbursements $454.75

REPORT OF DISBURSEMENTS.

Boynton, G. D., 1760 Eddy street, San Francisco.
Loss $200. No position. Insurance none.

Bryant, William A. Honorary. 2941 Washington street, San Francisco.
Red Cross Volunteer. Loss: Entire office outfit and copy for "Oral Surgery" in process of publication. Insurance none.

Backwood, T. B., Beta Sigma, '07. Umatilla, Umatilla Co., Or.
Not in need of assistance.

Brownton, T. C. 1220 Laguna street, San Francisco.
Not in need of assistance.

Berger, Leroy O. Porter Bldg., Room 38, San Jose.
Not in need of assistance.

Byrne, —. Beta Delta, '07. 299 Mission street, Santa Cruz, Cal.
Loss $175. Insurance none. No position.

Bibbero, H. Beta Delta, '07. 115 East Main street, Stocton, Cal.
Not in need of assistance.

Colligan, F. J. Beta Delta, '06. 1391 Vallejo street, San Francisco.
Loss $300. Insurance none. No position.

Cranz, L. T. Beta Sigma. 1742 Sutter street, San Francisco.
Loss $3,000. Insurance $600. (Re-established since.)

Conroy, J. H. Beta Sigma, '08. 10 Sharon street, San Francisco.
Loss $50. Insurance none. No position.

Cane, G. H. Beta Sigma. 1026 60th street, Oakland, Cal.
Not in need of assistance.

Cree, W. A. Beta Delta, '06. 1296A 9th avenue, San Francisco.
Loss $200. Insurance none. Re-established.

Carter, —. Beta Delta, '07. 792 McAllister street, San Francisco.
Loss $150. Insurance none. No position.

Downes, Ernest. Beta Sigma, '07. 535 B street, Santa Rosa, Cal.
Loss $1,500. Insurance none. No position.

Davis, H. P. Beta Sigma, '05. 1830 San Jose avenue, Alameda, Cal.
Loss $1,400. Insurance none. No position.

Dye, F. M. Beta Sigma, '06· 2328 Bowditch street, Berkeley, Cal.
  Loss $50. Insurance none. No position.
Evans, A. O. Beta Delta, '05· 792 McAllister street, San Francisco.
  Loss $1,000. Insurance $600. No position.
Eason, J. A. Beta Sigma. 1296 Turk street, San Francisco.
  Loss $1,500. Insurance $500. Serving in National Guard.
Eggert, —. Beta Delta, '08· Hotel Raphael, San Raphael, Cal.
  Not in need of assistance.
Ferguson, T. H. 2316 Eagle avenue, Alameda, Cal.
  Loss $1,000. Insurance none. No position.
Florey, Wm. D. 245 Chattanooga street, San Francisco.
  Loss $1,125. Insurance none. No position.
Fisher, Geo. N. Beta Delta, '06· Colony Center, Cal.
  Loss $150. Insurance none. No position.
Gallagher, C. V. Beta Sigma, '06· 3943 17th street, San Francisco.
  Loss $50. Insurance none. No position.
Griffin, J. J. Beta Delta, '06· Petaluma, Cal.
  Loss $75. Insurance none. Position in view.
Gromaire, C. R. Beta Sigma, '07· 2409 Sacramento street, San Francisco.
  Loss $25. Insurance none.
Guiley, —. Beta Delta, '08· Willets, Cal.
  Not in need of assistance.
Harvey, C. L. Beta Sigma, '05· 501 Ashbury street, San Francisco.
  Loss $1,000. Insurance none. No position.
Howard, E. T. M. D. Honorary. 1505 Devisadiro street, San Francisco.
  Not in need of assistance.
Hodghead, D. A. M. D. Honorary. 3435 Sacramento street, San Francisco.
  Loss $1,500. Insurance none. No position.
Hansen, C. T. 1006 McAllister street, San Francisco.
  Not in need of assistance.
Harper, —. Beta Sigma, '08· Porterville, Cal.
  Loss $65. Insurance none. Has position.
Knowlton, J. T. Honorary. Cal. General Hospital.
  Loss $2,000. Insurance $300. Position in view.
Kruse, E. A. Beta Sigma, '08· Sugar Pine Mills, Madera Co., Cal.

76 THE FRATER.

Loss $70. Insurance none. No position.

Knorp, F. F. M. D. Honorary. 3009 Sacramento street, San Francisco.
Loss $9,000. Insurance $3,000. Re-established.

Knowles, C. W. Beta Sigma. 2417 Washington street, San Francisco.
Loss $2,500. Insurance none. Re-established.

Levey, Wm. H. Beta Sigma, '02. 1630 Buchanan street, San Francisco.
Not in need of assistance.

Lane, W. R. Beta Sigma, '05. Fresno Flats, Madera county, Cal.
Loss $1,500. Insurance none.

Lassen, J. P. Beta Delta, '03. 1603½ Fillmore street, San Francisco.
Loss, complete office outfit.

Leslie, —. Beta Delta. Porterville, Tulare Co., Cal.
Not in need of assistance.

Moore, T. E. Beta Sigma, '01. 2033 Channing Way, Berkeley, Cal.
Loss $4,000. Insurance $600. Position in view.

McKay, J. H. Beta Sigma, '07. 32 Ray street, Victoria, B. C.
Loss $25. Insurance none. No position.

McGragor, J. E. Beta Sigma, '07. Nanaimo, B. C.
Loss $100. Insurance none. No position.

Mulvihill, D. F. Beta Sigma, '07. 855 Castro street, San Francisco.
Has position. Not in need of assistance.

Morris, E. H. Beta Sigma, '06. 1526 Geary street, San Francisco.
Loss $75. Insurance none. Practicing.

McCormic, J. J. Beta Sigma, '08. Redwood City, Cal.
Loss $25. Insurance none. Has position.

Martin, H. G. Beta Sigma, '06. 421 North Stanislaus street, Stocton, Cal.
Loss $175. Insurance none. No position.

Martin, —. Beta Delta, '07. Concord, Cal.
Loss $75. Insurance none. No position.

Nuckoll, H. M. Beta Sigma, '01. Turlock, Stanislaus Co., Cal.
Loss $4,000. Insurance $500. No position. (Re-established since).

O'Brien, J. Beta Delta, '03· Marysville, Cal.
No loss. Position in view.

Pescia, Attillio F. Beta Delta, '05· 1060½ 7th street, Oakland, Cal.
Loss $1,000. Insurance none. Contemplating re-establishing.

Patterson, R. F. 3943 17th street, San Francisco.
Loss $50. Insurance none. No position.

Pague, F. C. Honorary. Physicians' Building, Oakland, Cal.
Loss $3,000. Insurance none. Re-established.

Pieper, E. O. San Jose, Cal.
Not in need of assistance.

Rader, Geo. Beta Sigma, '02· Care of C. J. Rader, 3877 21st street, San Francisco.
Loss $2,500. Insurance none. Position in view. Living in park.

Robinson, W. H. Beta Sigma, '08· Vacaville, Tolano Co., Cal. Box 483.
Loss $150. Insurance none. No position.

Ryan, H. G. Beta Sigma, '07· 3943 17th street, San Francisco.
Loss $100. Insurance none. No position.

Rieley, —. Fresno, Cal.
Loss $1,180. Insurance $600. Position in view.

Ross, —. Beta Delta, '08·
Not in need of assistance.

Scannavino, Jno. Beta Delta, '05· 516 Pacific avenue, Alameda, Cal.
Loss $1,400. Insurance none.

Smith, R. S. Beta Sigma, '08· 519 Fillmore street, San Francisco.
Loss $40. Insurance none. No position.

Smith, H. B. Beta Sigma, '08·
Not in need of assistance. Has position.

Sarll, Frank E. Beta Sigma, '08· 2635 Sacramento street, San Francisco.
Loss $35. Insurance none. No position.

Sykes, A. E. Oakland Bank of Savings Building, Oakland, Cal.
Loss $2,500. Insurance $700. No position Re-established.

Southheimer, —. Beta Delta, '07· 97 Anzerais avenue, San Jose, Cal.
Loss $40. Insurance none. No position.

Therkof, G. H. Beta Sigma, '01· 74 Portola street, between Steiner and Pierce, San Francisco.
Loss $940. Insurance $250. Expects to re-establish.

Taylor, H. H. Beta Sigma, '06· 3943 17th street, San Francisco.
Loss $350. No insurance. No position.

Truitt, S. P. Beta Delta, '06· Lampoe, Cal.
Loss $350. Insurance none.

Van Wyck, Crittenden. Beta Sigma. 1944 Webster street, San Francisco.
Not in need of assistance.

Vicary, E. E. Beta Sigma, '06· 57 Montecito avenue, Oakland, Cal.
Loss $750. Insurance none. No position.

Vanderhurst, S. Beta Sigma, '06· Salinas City, Cal.
Loss $35. Insurance none. No position.

Watkins, W. H. Beta Sigma, '02· 615 Bay street, San Francisco.
Loss $500. No insurance. No position.

Wilson, C. W. Beta Sigma. 3943 17th street, San Francisco.
Loss $200. Insurance none. No position.

Whelan, W. A. Beta Sigma, '01· 632 Fillmore street, San Francisco.
Loss $1,500. Insurance none. Re-established.
Loss $750. Insurance none. No position.

Yount G. B. Beta Sigma, '04· 3733 Clay street, San Francisco.
Loss $160. Insurance none. Position in view.

Young, C. E. Beta Delta, '05· 1656 Bush street, San Francisco.
Loss $100. Insurance none. Established.

JOHN J. GRIFFIN,
JOSEPH LORAN PEASE,
CHAS. V. GALLAGHER,
EDWIN P. JAMES.

List of names of brothers whose mail was returned by the Post Office Department as unclaimed.

Name.   Last Known Address.

H. J. Chismore, 705 Sutter street, San Francisco.
W. O. Gray, 9 Mason street, San Francisco.
A. W. Morton, M. D., Hon., Parrott Bldg., San Francisco.
E. L. Jones, 498 Valencia street, San Francisco.
C. B. Root, 639 Ellis street, San Francisco.
S. L. Theller, 330 Pine street, San Francisco.

List of names of brothers from whom no reply was received, a number of them known to be O. K.

Name.   Last Known Address.

Winslow Anderson, M. D., Hon., 1025 Sutter street, San Francisco.
Thos. Morffew, Examiner Luilding, San Francisco.
Chas. E. Jones, M. D., Hon., 1118 Guerrero street, San Francisco.
H. D'Arcy Power, M. D., Hon., 305 Larkin street, San Francisco.
C. W. Mills, 1002 Union street, San Francisco.
A. W. Taylor, 1202 Union street, San Francisco.
F. W. Harris, M. D., Hon., 502 Valencia street, San Francisco.
Louis Jacobs, M. D., Hon., 1139 Geary street, San Francisco.
Francis Williams, M. D., Hon., 1392 Haight street, San Francisco.
J. S. Seymour, M. D., Hon., 24th and Castro streets, San Francisco.
Carrol O. Southard, M. D., Hon., Star King Building, San Francisco.
Russel H. Cool, 1312 Van Ness avenue, San Francisco.
H. S. McKellops, San Francisco.
E. E. Kelley, M. D., Hon., 751 Sutter street, San Francisco.
John Robertson, 2104 Market street, San Francisco.
J. W. Key, 1005 Filmore street, San Francisco.
V. P. Orella, 406 Sutter street, San Francisco.
G. N. Hein, 855 Market street, San Francisco.
R. L. Hursh, 1001 A. Guerrero street, San Francisco.

Norman Henderson, Alameda, Cal.
W. A. Twiggs, Danville, Cal.
C. H. Schultz, corner Jersey and Castro streets, San Francisco.
Shirley Ashby, 24th near Sanchez street, San Francisco.
W. S. Wright, Knox Building, San Jose, Cal.
C. S. Coe, Palo Alto, Cal.
H. T. Hinman, Third and F streets, San Jose, Cal.
H. S. Chandler, San Jose, Cal.
E. L. Dormberger, Nevada Building, San Jose, Cal.
Fred. T. Ashworth, 2497 Mission street, San Francisco.
Calvin D. Brown, 494 Valencia street, San Francisco.
—. Goodman, 522 East 11th street, Oakland, Cal.
P. D. MacSween, Modesto, Cal.
John B. Fox, 122 S. street, Santa Rosa, Cal.
— Myer, 1161 East 17th street, Oakland, Cal.
— McManus, Napa, Cal.
— Bliss, Santa Cruz, Cal.
— Gonzalas,, 851 Golden Gate avenue, San Francisco.

Following is a copy of circular issued. All payments have been made by check and canceled checks will be forwarded as they are returned by the bank.

EDWIN P. JAMES,
Chairman of Committee.

R. 301—1111 Washington Street, Oakland, Cal.

Oakland, Nov. 30, 1906.

Dear Brother:—

Kindly acknowledge receipt of the enclosed check for $, the amount voted to you out of the Psi Omega Relief Fund.

It was the desire of the committee to place the fund in the hands of the Dental Supply houses, that the brothers might have the benefit of a special discount. The Committee, however, was unable to make satisfactory arrangements to that end, and the plan of cash distribution was adopted.

Trusting that you are once more well on the road to prosperity, and wishing you a large measure of success in your future undertakings, we are,

Sincerely and Fraternally Yours,
EDWIN P. JAMES, Chairman,
1111 Washington street, Oakland.
C. HOWARD MERRITT,
J. LORAN PEASE,
J. J. GRIFFIN,
CHAS. V. GALLAGHER.

RECIPROCITY.

D. H. Wetzel.

Read at a Meeting of the Philadelphia Alumni Chapter Held at the Home of Brother Cochran.

To write and present a paper upon any subject whatever, before this learned body of professional men, is indeed a great undertaking. I fully realize how useless it would be for me to attempt to tell you anything about the practice of dentistry that you do not already know, so I have chosen the rather ambiguous, yet fully discussable, title, "Reciprocity," for my paper this evening.

I am sure you all know the meaning of the word. I will discuss it under two heads: 1. Reciprocity between Dentists. 2. Reciprocity between the Patient and the Dentist.

A good substitute for the word Reciprocity would be that old maxim "Do unto others as you would that others should do unto you."

Instead of jealousy, bickering, "knocking," and other evily conceived actions toward your fellow practitioner, how much more good could be accomplished by the adoption and practicing of just a little of the import of the Golden Rule.

Is it worth while for a Doctor of Dental Surgery to become an Ananias and to abuse his fellow practitioner for the sake of a few paltry dollars which he may, at the time, divert to his own pocket? Does not the loss of character more than pay for the small financial gain? Besides, will he not in time be rated by the public at his real value and will not his former malicious criticism react against himself? Do the older practitioners treat the recent graduate with proper consideration? It is quite true that in some instances they do, but in a great number of cases the young dentist is ignored by the older members in the profession; or efforts, concealed or open, are made to belittle the ability and general knowledge of the younger man where he deigns to enter into close competition with the great "I Am."

Cases are on record where a preceptor will stoop to intrigue in order to place his protege in an embarrassing position at some future time. For instance, one case, especially crafty, came to my attention where the preceptor advised his protege to pay but little attention to Dental Prosthesis, that he (the preceptor) would impart to him instructions in that branch of dentistry. Result, preceptor failed to keep his promise, the student because he neglected his mechanical work was at a disadvantage, which was a source of annoyance in more ways than one. The preceptor even going so far as to say to his patients "The young men in these days are not taught right; why there is Dr. Blank, just graduated, who cannot make a decent plate."

But Dr. Blank was quite well equipped to practice operative dentistry, extracted less teeth than his former preceptor, which fact soon came to the ears of the laity, and, finally, did learn to make a decent plate so that the old hypocritical preceptor finally surrendered and betook himself back to the old home, where he is now earning a bare living on the farm left him by his deceased parents.

Another case but different in nature—A young dentist sought advise from an older practitioner who had professed friendship for him and had offered his assistance at any time, consequently the younger man in time sought advice in reference to a charge for certain work; the old practitioner named a sum which was way above the prices which prevailed in the community. Result, patient thought the younger dentist's services too expensive and returned to her former dentist, who happened to be the old practitioner.

I cited the above instances to show that some older practitioners are afraid of their more youthful competitors and resort to unprofessional methods in an endeavor to handicap them in their work. How much more honorable would it have been for these men to have acted on the square with the young practitioners and really tried to assist them?

The old and the young should be honorable in their competition and, thereby, aid in making our profession an association of gentlemen of the highest type.

The other phase of the subject: Reciprocity between the Dentist and the Patient will not be dealt with at such great length, for I suspect that Lady Cochran will become anxious because of the lateness of the hour which the reading and discussion of this paper will occasion.

In many instances, the patient has somewhere absorbed the idea that dentist is but a synonym of High Finance, Standard Oil, or some equally obnoxious term. They come, dreading the operation and probable expense, without a full understanding of the time consumed in acquiring the necessary knowledge and manipulative ability to do the work skillfully and with thoroughness.

Thus when we have spent what seems to them a short or long time, according to the pain endured, in doing a certain operation and ask a reasonable fee for our services, we are immediately classed with brigands or some other such gentry.

Why is this? It is probably caused by the low prices of the inefficient, careless practitioner or by reading certain advertisements in newspapers wherein ridiculously low prices are named for certain work.

It is here that a litttle time spent in convincing the patient that full value has been returned for the money, by being honest in your explanation, that you will be rendering a real service in that you cause the patient to refrain from seeking the services of the ridiculously low priced man.

Of course the patient ought always have implicit confidence in the dentist; the patient probably does in your ability but, in some instances, rather laments the cost. Whatever you do, do not misrepresent facts to your patient, be fair and trust to Providence, or some other enlightening medium, to so direct the thoughts of your patient, that when the final day of judgment comes—the day of settlement—he will cheerfully say "Well done, thou good and faithful servant."

PRACTICAL POINTS.

G. A. Fletcher, P. G. M., Beta Gamma.

The observation of shortcomings in others often makes one sit up and take notice. Realizing how the student neglects, to his own disadvantage, the many small practical details which will save him time and patients, and knowing the value of commencing right, I offer the following points to young Psi Omegas, trusting they may be of value. Although all are not original I have not seen any of them in print.

A ten cent sugar bowl half full of a 10 per cent. solution of formalin and carbolic acid, colored with a few drops of tincture of budbear makes the pretty color of Glyco-Thymoline and an ideal disinfectant for instruments.

A finger bowl on bracket with one per cent solution of carbolic acid, a few drops of budbear and a little toilet water, makes an ideal hand sterilizer, sightly to patient and agreeable to the hands.

White Japanese napkins fastened by two rubber bands to the head rest, so that the top one can slide off, keep head rest clean and antiseptic.

Heavy white unglazed paper, cut in 500 lots to fit brackets, is far cheaper than napkins.

A one ounce amalgam bottle, with a small hole punched in cover, is a perfectly clean receptacle for floss silk.

A few strokes with an S. S. White bur stone, kept to a feather's edge with a piece of sandpaper, will give you three times the wear of your burs and they are always sharp. The time devoted to keeping them sharp is more than saved by never having a dull bur.

The ordinary fan motor is easily converted to run a lathe by having a machinist fit chuck to shaft and putting on a base board. Mine cost $7.00 complete and is as efficient as a $45.00 electric lathe.

A few drops of glycerine added to iodine and aconite will prevent an annoying iodine blister.

A tube of cold cream to apply to the chapped or cracked lips of patients will be appreciated by them.

An atomizer filled with a pleasant antiseptic mouth wash, to spray the mouth before examination, may save you from an infectious disease.

In using instruments always lay them with points toward you. It will save several hundred turns of the wrist during a busy day.

I submit these "points" with the best wishes to all Psi Omegas, to whom I gladly give and from whom I will as gladly accept information.

NOTICE TO PSI OMEGAS WHO CONTEMPLATE VISITING NEW ORLEANS DURING CARNIVAL.

Psi Omegas who may find themselves in our city, (New Orleans), during the Mardi Gras season would confer a favor on Beta Epsilon by registering at the office of Brother Leon Barnett, 703 Macheca Building, which is the chapter's down town headquarters.

It will be our greatest pleasure to show them around and make their stay quite enjoyable and one they will long remember.

Bring your wives and sweethearts with you. If convenient, notify Brother Barnett on which road you intend to arrive, so that a committee can meet you and assist in finding accommodations for you.

Please state as early as possible the number of persons in your party and date of your arrival.

The carnival season commences on February 8 and continues to the 13th.

Active Chapters.

ALPHA—BALTIMORE COLLEGE OF DENTAL SURGERY.

E. J. Lawler, Editor.

Alpha wishes all Psi Omegas a very happy and prosperous New Year. The holidays being over, the boys are again at work in earnest. During November and December Alpha initiated the following candidates, whom we take pleasure in introducing to the fraternity:

Louis August Theil, '07 .... Portage, Wis.
Max Lee Freeman, '08 .... Milton, Nova Scotia.
Samuel J. Holt, '09 .... Hanover, N. H.
Walter S. Braddock, '07 .... West Finley, Pa.
Horace N. Porter, '08 .... Cumberland, Md.
J. Edward H. Libby, '09 .... Portland, Me.
Souvereign P. Purvis, '07 .... Hamilton, N. C.
Henry Martin, '09 .... No. Grafton, Mass.
Albert Earl Hennen, '08 .... Fairmount, W. Va.
Thos. R. Kavanagh, '09 .... Kane, Pa.
Henry L. Fischer, '09 .... Waterbury, Conn.
Dennis M. Hoban, '09 .... Plains, Pa.
Alfred B. Thruston, '09 .... Sedalia, Mo.
John F. Barton, '09 .... East Hampton, Conn.

During January our number will be further increased by the initiation of several good men now pledged.

Brother A. E. Henan, of Nu, has transferred to Alpha.

During this term we had the pleasure of listening to several short talks delivered by alumni and honorary members.

BETA—NEW YORK COLLEGE OF DENTISTRY.

George R. Christian, Editor.

The brothers of Beta send good cheer and best wishes to all Psi Omegas hoping for their success and prosperity during the year of 1907.

Our chapter quizzes are very much appreciated, since, of late, we have been favored with the worthy attention and help of several alumni brothers.

During our last "massacre" the gentlemen mentioned below were favorably encountered and admitted to membership. The ill effects of the battle royal are now worn away and we respectfully bring forward for introduction to Psi Omegas the following good brothers:

Alfred M. O. Bartel, '09 .... New York City, N. Y.
Judson F. Bioren, '09 .... Newark, N. J.
John Louis Peters, '09 .... New York City, N. Y.
Harry James Roberts, '09 .... Jersey City, N. J.
Gustav H. Konecke, '09 .... Brooklyn, N. Y.
Arthur H. Boughton, '09 .... Newark, N. J.
Harrison V. Scudder, '09 .... Middletown, N. Y.
Henry G. Steinmeger, '08 .... Stapleton, S. I.

GAMMA—PENNSYLVANIA COLLEGE OF DENTAL SURGERY.

Gamma introduces to the fraternity the following members taken in during this school year:

Geo. C. Cohler, '07 .... Everett, Pa.
Adam L. Buddinger, '09 .... Mt. Carmel, Pa.

Warren G. Sherwood, '09 .... Rochester, N. Y.
Frank P. McGinnis, '09 .... Philadelphia, Pa
Arthur D. Smith, '09 .... Cordelia, Pa.
Ernest L. Smith, '09 .... Philadelphia, Pa.
Frank S. Dwyer, '08 .... Ansonia, Conn.
Timothy V. McGeehan, '09 .... Coal-Dale, Pa.
Stoddard Stevens, '09 .... Harpersfield, N. Y.
Jas. J. Durkin. '07 .... Providence, R. I.
Francis D. Dolan, '07 .... S amford, Conn.

DELTA—TUFTS DENTAL COLLEGE.

C. P. Haven, Editor.

Delta sends best wishes to the Supreme Council and to all sister chapters.

Delta is progressing this year as she never has before. We have drawn and are still drawing into the fold, the best timber of which Tufts Dental boasts. "Frat spirit" is steadily growing, and interest in everything Psi Omegan is boundless. We have received much encouragement from our instructors at the college, the large majority of whom are Psi Omegas, and, to our invitations to be present at our meetings, from time to time, they have gladly responded.

Since the last issue of The Frater Dr. Marshall and Dr. Kinsman of the college, and Dr. Parker representing the S. S. White Co., have given us some very good instructions in the different branches of our profession. Dr. Kinsman has also presented the chapter with a very beautiful picture which adds greatly to the "homelike" appearance of our rooms.

In the hall of the college we have had placed a tasty bulletin board for the publishing of such information as the committee deems advisable. Brother Freeman was the prime mover in this matter and to him we have extended a vote of thanks. Our new members taken in during November and December are as follows:

Harold E. Smith, '09 .... Athol, Mass.
Walter C. Brayshaw, '09 .... Weymouth, Mass.
John H. Hollihan, '09 .... New Bedford, Mass.
Walter E. Briggs, '09 .... Attleboro, Mass.
Harold E. Mangovan, '09 .... Bangor, Maine.
Charles J. McKenna, '09 .... New York City.
Carl W. Stegmaier, '09 .... Kingston, Mass.
John E. Keefe, '09 .... Fall River, Mass.
William E. Denier, '09 .... Somerville, Mass.

EPSILON—WESTERN RESERVE UNIVERSITY.

C. C. Rogers, Editor.

Epsilon sends greetings to all Psi Omegas, also the following report for the beginning of the mid-year term:

Since the beginning of the school year we have initiated into full membership the following:

W. G. Nightingale, '09 .... Cleveland, Ohio.
Myles E. Perry, '09 .... Elyria, Ohio.
Thomas J. Hill, '08 .... West Richfield, Ohio.
Daniel S. Teters, '09 .... Lakewood, Ohio.
Frank C. Campbell, '09 .... Cleveland, Ohio.
Chas. V. Kindig, '09 .... Rittman, Ohio.
Charles J. Kampfe, '09 .... Cleveland, Ohio.
Alfred C. Frost, '07 .... E. Liverpool, Ohio.

We regret very much to add that Brother Kindig has since abandoned the ranks of our profession.

All the new members have entered actively into the work which indicates a bright future for Epsilon chapter.

Early in December a banquet was held, at which were present Brothers McLernon and Belford of the faculty and Brothers Griffis and Rogers of the Cleveland Alumni chapter. Bountiful refreshments were served, after which we had smoking and a very sociable evening.

ZETA—UNIVERSITY OF PENNSYLVANIA.

Zeta introduces to the fraternity the following members taken in during this school year:

S. F. Williams, '07	Troy, Pa.
Albert D. Hequembourg, '09	Dunkirk, N. Y.
Chas. W. Swank, Jr., '09	East Mauch Chunk, Pa.
Robert E. G. Weysser, '09	Mauch Chunk, Pa.
Harry Le Roy Billings, '09	Springfield, Mass.
William J. Frost, '09	Springfield, Mass.
William J. Byrnes, '08	Pittsfield, Mass.
Wm. A. Lowndes, '07	Cottekill, N. Y.
J. Craig King, '09	Reynoldsville, Pa.
Isaac S. Lenderman, '08	Wilmington, Del.
Ellsworth T. Crilley, '08	Jersey City, N. J.
I. C. Gingras, '09	Turners Falls, Mass.
Harold C. McMahon, '08	Brewer, Maine.
William A. Brown, '09	Key West, Fla.
Harold E. Martin, '09	Philadelphia, Pa.

ETA—PHILADELPHIA DENTAL COLLEGE.

Lewis B. Duffield, Editor.

Eta sends the season's greetings to the Supreme Council and to all sister chapters.

Everything at Eta's headquarters is now in full swing. Many of the brothers are preparing to leave for their homes, there to partake of that bounteous Christmas dinner which dear mother has prepared for us; knowing that it will be all the more appreciated because of our three months' diet on boarding house hash.

Psi Omega has figured very prominently in the election of class officers for the ensuing year in the junior and senior classes, the result showing the following Psi Omegas elected:

Senior Class.

President	"Pop" Wm. R. Heilig.
Secretary	W. J. Heffeman.
Class Prophet	Stephen J. Casey.

Class Poet .... Geo. Wadlinger.
Class Artist .... C. O'Neil.

Junior Class.

President .... Jas. O'Connell.
Vice President .... L. B. Duffield.
Treasurer .... John Reddan.
Class Historian .... Ray F. Witz.

Secretaryship being filled by one of the fairer sex of our class.

Eta is pleased to announce the transference of two members from Zeta chapter into her house in the early part of the term, Brothers S. Snyder and L. V. Brendle, commonly known among us now as "Stanley and Lester."

Eta takes pleasure in announcing that some of her members are getting to be very sociable with the ladies of our college, resulting thus far in a surprise party which was given a few weeks ago by five of our brothers, namely: Jimmie, Maurice, Walter, Woodfin and Lewis, at which time a very pleasant evening was spent at the expense of Sarah and Lottie. The fore part of the evening was devoted to a Quiz on Bacteriology by Brother Jimmie, after which Brother Woodfin introduced a new game called "Rolling the Oranges," while the rest of the brothers told a few stories. After a late hour in the evening had been reached, we were invited into the dining room where was set before us a most delightful feast, during which time Brother Jimmie entertained us with a "History of his Life;" "How he Received That Smooth Surface on the Crown of His Head," and the "Conditions in the Far East."

Following Brother Jimmie's speech Walter and Sarah gave us a few new ideas on horse racing, and how to ride bare-back.

After which we bid our hostess' adieu, and departed to our respective homes, feeling delighted with the evening spent with the fair damsels.

Eta takes pleasure in introducing to the fraternity her new members to date:

Clifford E. Lewis, '08 .... Shelton, Conn.
Roy Franklin Witz, '08 .... Warren, Pa.
Angus V. Rose, '07 .... Syracuse, N. Y.
Walter P. Burns, '08 .... Louisville, Ky.
James W. O'Connell, '08 .... Westerly, R. I.

William W. Carson, '08 .... Kissimmee, Fla.
John A. Reddan, '08 .... Trenton, N. J.
Edw. J. Counihan, '09 .... Holyoke, Mass.
Thos. C. Joseph, '09 .... Wilkes Barre, Pa.
Hilmar F. Sommers, '09 .... Philadelphia, Pa.
Thos. L. Wilcox, '09 .... Philadelphia, Pa.
John W. Scherer, '09 .... Blooklyn, N. Y.

IOTA—NORTHWESTERN UNIVERSITY.

C. S. Savage, Editor.

To all members of Psi Omega Iota sends New Year greetings and best wishes for a successful year. Since the last writing the boys of Iota have been busy with school and fraternity interests.

On November 13, we spent a most delightful evening at a surpise party at the house, for the "house boys." It was ladies' night, and our lady friends joined us in the pleasures of the evening. Cards, music and dancing, ice cream and cake were the sources of our pleasures and that's no mistake.

During the football season, "Northwestern Dents" won all games between professional schools of the city and "Champions of Professional Schools" was accorded them in the athletic print. Of the team members three Psi Omegas played star games: Raymond Jones, full back; J. E. Forsythe, right half; H. Ross, right end.

Everything at school is moving on smoothly and if no bad luck is encountered there will be about 20 Iotas for graduation next May. At our last grand initiation we conferred honors upon the following gentlemen, and take great pleasure in presenting them as full fledged Psi Omegas:

Orlando V. D. Jones, '07 .... Chicago, Ill.
Walter Arthur Moore, '09 .... Walla Walla, Wash.
Robert William Reed, '09 .... Lincoln, Neb.
Roscoe L. Stout, '09 .... Chicago, Ill.
James H. Ross, '09 .... Chicago, Ill.
J. Ramon Jones, '07 .... Robinson, Ill.
Frank George Desmond, '09 .... Barabas, Wis.

Albert C. Rich, '07 .... Sterling, Ill.
L. Carl Allender, '07 .... Maryville, Mo.
Paul D. Fridd, '09 .... Valley City, N. D.
Geo. Thomas Reed, '09 .... Chicago, Ill.

KAPPA—CHICAGO COLLEGE OF DENTAL SURGERY.

E. L. Henderson, Editor.

Kappa is in a flourishing condition.

Our regular meeting programs are becoming very interesting. Our last one being both instructive and enjoyable. Dr. Roach gave us a talk on the indications, uses, and application of Mouldable Porcelain and Brother Meyers read a paper on Gold Inlays.

Dr. Thomas, of last year's class, is a frequent caller at our meetings, enlivening the boys with his ever ready stock of stories.

Kappa takes pleasure in presenting to the fraternity her new members for this school year:

Ira E. McCarty, '07 .... Enid, Oklahoma.
Joseph Harris Chute, '09 .... Minneapolis, Minn.
Albert E. McEvoy, '07 .... Dubuque, Iowa.

MU—UNIVERSITY OF DENVER.

Mu introduces to the fraternity the following member taken in during this school year:

Russell W. Vaughan, '07 .... Denver, Colo.

NU—PITTSBURG DENTAL COLLEGE.

H. Boisseau, Editor.

We are now comfortably located in our new home and many are the trials and tribulations of the sturdy Greeks who have associated themselves together here. Nu chapter had long been of the opinion that a fraternity house would do us good, and often in our meetings plans and schemes were discussed with that end in view, but nothing ever came of them until one day last October when we decided to do something. Committees were appointed —one to rent a house, the other to buy furniture. The house was rented and the furniture bought on time. The fellows moved into the house, hired a cook, and began to pay board. Committees were sent out to raise money. The Alumni were appealed to, with the result that enough money was forthcoming to pay for the furniture, most of which came from Duquesne Alumni Chapter. Such in brief is the history of how Nu happens to have a house.

We desire to say to the fraternity at large that the house is a success, in every sense of the word, and that all are pleased. It seems to have been just what was needed here at Nu chapter. All of our active members take a greater interest in the affairs of the fraternity and a much better attendance at our weekly meetings is one of the most noticeable, as well as one of the best features it has brought about. Considerably more work is required from the individual members, especially those living at the house, but this is disposed of with a will and in a way which is sure to bring success. Up to the present time the house has a little more than paid the running expenses, which is very satisfactory to those concerned. With a better location, that is, one closer to the college, where those members who take the noon meal at the college can be served, and cheaper rents, it seems that the house will become a source of revenue to the chapter.

Duquense Alumni Chapter meets with us once a month thus bringing the active and alumni members in closer touch.

We are pleased to announce that we had, during the holidays, the honor of a visit from one of the Supreme Council, Brother Nyce, who stopped over in Pittsburg on his way East from Chicago. Brother Nyce is one of the mainstays of our fraternity, and, as regards his personal disposition, is all his name implies.

Also Brother Hennen, last year of Nu, now of Alpha at Baltimore, paid us a visit during the holidays having taken his New Year Day dinner with us.

Just at the present time there is considerable doing among the Psi Omega boys here; Jan. 18, is the date set for our historic "Annual Trip to Millvale," the place where Pluto reigns and where our "barbarians" are transformed into Greeks. This year we have fifteen candidates who hope to undergo the ordeal successfully and after that date Nu will have the following new Psi Omegas on her chapter roll:

Thomas C. McClintock, '08 .... Dravosburg, Pa.
Fred Klawuhn, '08 .... Ridgeway, Pa.
Omer S. Ferren, '09 .... Dunbar, Pa.
Arthur G. Rinard, '08 .... Breezewood, Pa.
Ernest Ray Roberts, '09 .... Allegheny, Pa.
David R. Biddle, '08 .... McKeesport, Pa.
Louis B. Moore, '09 .... Wilkinsburg, Pa.
Roy D. Rumbaugh, '09 .... Crafton, Pa.
Homer C. Roe, '09 .... Allegheny, Pa.
Bruce J. Frazier, '09 .... Kittanning, Pa.
Frank H. Hoffman, '09 .... Jeannette, Pa.
Ed M. Craig, '09 .... Dunn Station, Pa.
Carl M. McNary, '09 .... Houston, Pa.
E. M. Donaldson, '09 .... Washington, Pa.
W. C. Horner, '09 .... Avalon, Pa.

XI—MILWAUKEE MEDICAL COLLEGE.

I. B. Thackray, Editor.

Xi chapter sends greeting to the Supreme Council and to her sister chapters.

We take pleasure in presenting the following officers for the coming year:

I. B. Thackray .... G. M.
W. M. Dettermann .... Jr. M.
R. H. Hanke .... Chief Int.
A. W. Sauter .... Senator.
B. W. Maercklem .... Sec'y.
J. Mortell .... Treas.

The boys are all with us again with the exception of the following lost by graduation:

James E. Callaway .... Milwaukee.
E. Musel .... Racine, Wis.
Walter T. Smith .... Sister Bay, Wis.
John Rule .... Iowa.

Our first smoker and banquet of the year was given on November 2, in our new club rooms on Grand avenue. About forty of the fellows attended and all reported a jolly good time. A feature of the program was a toast given by Dr. H. L. Banzhof, dean of the Milwaukee Dental College. He spoke on "The Relation of the Fraternity to the Man."

Xi takes pleasure in introducing to the fraternity her new members, our harvest up to December 20, '06:

O. C. Gamphere, '07 .... Milwaukee, Wis.
Richard D. Park, '09 .... Glenwood, Wis.
Paul A. Howell, '09 .... Lancaster, Wis.
Arno C. Gauerke, '08 .... Milwaukee, Wis.
Emil A. Nelson, '09 .... Milwaukee, Wis.
Carl M. Marcan, '08 .... Milwaukee, Wis.
Kaquo Omura, '09 .... Tokyo, Japan.
Adolph R. Lindow, '09 .... Elkhart Lake, Wis.
Walter J. Durkopp, '09 .... Middleton, Wis.

―•◇•―

OMICRON—LOUISVILLE COLLEGE OF DENTAL SURGERY.

Omicron introduces to the fraternity the following members taken in during this school year:

James E. Bailey, '08 .... Central City, Ky.
John H. Cadmus, '08 .... Orange, N. J.
Frank W. Monfort, '07 .... Bardstown, Ky.
John O. McCauley, '08 .... Morganfield, Ky.
Omer S. Meredith, '07 .... Big Clifton, Ky.
James D. Coleman, '08 .... Clinton, Miss.
George M. Rees, '08 .... Louisville, Ky.
Herbert L. Duncan, '08 .... Dixon, Ky.

PI—BALTIMORE MEDICAL COLLEGE.

Pi introduces to the fraternity the following members taken in during this school year:

James D. Gregg, '07 .... Liberty, N. C.
Joseph P. Stanley, '09 .... Laurence, Mass.
Harry A. V. Donahue, '07 .... Essex Junction, Vt.
James W. Davis, '08 .... Frewsburg, N. Y.
Charles E. Sherwood, '09 .... Southampton, Mass.
Harry A. Hotaling, '07 .... Sidney, N. Y.
William E. Jenkins, '07 .... Roxabel, N. C.
Lawrence P. McGovern, '09 .... Lynn, Mass.
Carroll H. Greene, '09 .... Stony Creek, Va.
Edward F. Gill, '09 .... Providence, R. I.
James E. Harden, '08 .... Providence, R. I.
John H. Williams, '09 .... Baltimore, Md.

BETA SIGMA—COLLEGE OF PHYSICIANS AND SURGEONS.

Beta Sigma introduces to the fraternity the following members taken in during this school year:

Alfred R. Vogelman, '08 .... Modeste, Cal.
F. August Koenig, '08 .... San Jose, Col.
Samuel H. Hall, '08 .... Stockton, Cal.
Gordon H. Jonasen, '08 .... San Francisco, Cal.
Wm. J. Nelsoon, '07 .... San Francisco, Cal.
Walter S. Thompson, '08 .... San Francisco, Cal.

RHO—OHIO COLLEGE OF DENTAL SURGERY.

Edw. McCurdy, Editor.

Rho has been progressing nicely this year, our total membership is now thirty-two. Burger and Williams are fequently seen at our meetings.

Rho takes pleasure in introducing the following men who were initiated during November and December:

James M. Turner, '08	Hamilton, Ky.
William F. Rule, '09	Clyde, Ohio.
Cornelius E. Pryor, '09	Graysville, Ohio.
Charles W. Noel, '09	Visalia, Cal.
Ralph R. Kelsey, '09	Covington, Ohio.
Napoleon A. Cunningham, '09	Defiance, Ohio.
Henry M. Schweinsberger, '08	Hillsboro, Ohio.
Malcolm M. Maupin, '08	Cincinnati, Ohio.
William McCaughrin, '08	Clachan, Ontario.
John N. Banks, '09	Salem, Va.
Samuel D. Marshall, '07	Florence, Ky.
James H. Shircliff, '09	Gormania, W. Va.

At our last meeting a very interesting lecture was delivered by H. H. Kratz, one of our most enthusiastic active members.

Taylor, of Nu, a former Rho lad, was a recent visitor.

We are in the midst of exams, preparatory to our holiday vacation.

SIGMA—MEDICO CHIRURGICAL COLLEGE.

H. M. Walters, Editor.

Our officers for the present year are:

Grand Master	Geo O. Barclay.
Junior Master	C. L. Crist.
Secretary	Geo. W. Wilkens.
Treasurer	J. B. Davenport.
Editor	H. M. Walters.
Historian	A. M. Gates.
Chief Inq.	Geo. Dillmore.
Chief Int.	Thos. J. Guilfoil.
Inside Guard	J. H. Schneider.
Outside Guard	Wm. Keyser.
Senator	Dr. Thos. J. Byrne.

The prospects for a frat house this year are very good. It is a necessity for fraternal advancement. With our list of active members we have reason to believe that in a very short time Sigma ought to be the happy possessor of a place where active fraternal spirit can be advanced.

We were very sorry to hear that Brother Wm. G. Dusto, '06, P. G. M., is sick at the home of his parents in Shenandoah, Pa., with spinal meningitis. Latest reports show that he is improving.

Brother J. B. Davenport, '07, who was in the Medico-Chirurgical Hospital, suffering from a slight attack of typhoid, is again attending to college duties.

Sigma wishes success to The Frater and all sister chapters.

We started this term with twelve active members, but with the fraternal spirit fully alive, we are having a good year.

We have initiated the following candidates up to Dec. 20, 1906:

Francis J. Cusack, '07 .... Philadelphia, Pa.
William E. Crolius, '08 .... Philadelphia, Pa.
Patrick J. Kane, '08 .... Scranton, Pa.
John P. Hacha, '08 .... Latrobe, Pa.
Ross J. Kelly, '09 .... Philadelphia, Pa.
Lucien B. Somers, '08 .... Philadelphia, Pa.
Earle W. Smith, '09 .... Philadelphia, Pa.
Clyde A. Smith, '09 .... Philadelphia, Pa.
Delmar H. Stocker, '09 .... Tunkhannock, Pa.
Douglas W. Webster, '07 .... Atlantic City, N. J.
Robert M. Haury, '09 .... Philadelphia, Pa.

After the initiation a fine luncheon was served. The evening was very pleasantly spent. Our new members are especially good ones and we are indeed proud of them.

TAU—ATLANTA DENTAL COLLEGE.

C. G. Butt, Editor.

On Tuesday evening, November 27, at 9 o'clock, the annual dance was given in Segadlio's Hall.

As the older members leave college, never to return, they are wont to look back with regret, knowing that they have danced their last dance as an active member of Tau; as new members enter, they look forward with special delight to this dance for they know, by hearsay at least, that a delightful time is in store for them.

But this dance was enjoyed even more than others, for, Gamma Iota, at the special invitation of Tau, was present on the above evening and thus, for the first time in the history of each, the two chapters intermingled, so that, as one fair lady present that evening remarked, "only by looking at my program could I discover that there were two chapters present." Each brother tried to outdo the other in favoring brothers of the other chapter. A mild punch was served during the evening. Truly, that was an evening to be long remembered by both chapters for such a strong bond of brotherly feeling was born as will never break.

The class honors this year were hotly contested, Psi Omega lost the honor of having the valedictorian by only four votes—as there is a class of fifty-nine, this shows that Psi Omegas stand high.

On the 13th of December, at College Park, G. M., Brother Holbeck, delivered an essay on "High Ideals" at a reception tendered the students of the Atlanta Dental College by the young ladies of Cox College, one of the foremost colleges of the South and, it is needless to say, his essay was one of the features of the evening.

Tau gladly presents new members taken in during November and December.

Douglas McIntire, Jr., '08 .... Marion, S. C.
Roy M. Huntley, '07 .... Wadesboro, N. C.
William W. Westmoreland, '08 ...... Columbus, Miss.
James R. Jackson, '07 .... Pontotoc, Miss.
Wade L. Taylor, '08 .... Greelyville, S. C.
Anderson M. Hedick, '08 .... Brooksville, Fla.
Spencer F. McJunkin, '07 .... Toccoa, Ga.
Karl A. Frieseke, Hon'y. .... Atlanta, Ga.
Lawrence E. Ethridge, '07 .... Montgomery, La.
J. Kennon Barrett, '07 .... Conyers, Ga.
George F. Miller, '08 .... Century, Fla.
David B. Patton, '07 .... Knoxville, Ala.
William E. Smith, '08 .... Edison, Ga.
Augustus B. Strozier, '08 .... Willis, Texas.

Lon Wimberly, '07 .... Terrell, Texas.
Forney M. Lawrence, '07 .... Cedar Bluff, Ala.
William T. Baird, '07 .... Eagle Lake, Texas.
Miller W. Laurence, '07 .... Ruston, La.
Calvin J. Grant, '08 .... McBee, S. C.
Killen M. Hodges, '09 .... Elm Grove, La.
Henry M. McLeod, '08 .... Jackson, Ala.

Tau is on a higher plane now than she has ever been since receiving her charter and her members are not only showing more enthusiasm than ever before, but are standing higher in their respective classes.

UPSILON—UNIVERSITY OF SOUTHERN CALIFORNIA.

Upsilon introduces to the fraternity the following members taken in during this school year:

Carimon J. Cresmer, '08 .... Riverside, Cal.
John G. Loughan, '09 .... Los Angeles, Cal.
Herbert H. Farnham, '08 .... Los Angeles, Cal.
William F. Whelan, '07 .... Santa Monica, Cal.
Alexander N. Lord, '08 .... Los Angeles, Cal.
Louis Felsonthal, '09 .... Los Angeles, Cal.
Thomas Lynn, '09 .... Los Angeles, Cal.
Fred P. Bolstad, '09 .... Bakersfield, Cal.
Herbert A. Ballagh, '09 .... Fresno, Cal.
Roy H. Chapin, '09 .... Escondido, Cal.
Charles E. Willoughby, '07 .... Los Angeles, Cal.
H. S. Duff, '07 .... Los Angeles, Cal.
John H. Stewart, '09 .... Santa Barbara, Cal.

PHI—UNIVERSITY OF MARYLAND.

Phi introduces to the fraternity the following members taken in during this school year:

John F. Anderson, '09 .... Statesville, N. C.
Richard G. Pyles, '08 .... Barnesville, Md.

Frank A. Lasley, '08 .... Gideon, N. C.
Raymond S. Neiman, '08 .... York, Pa.
John F. Kernodle, '07 .... Summit, N. C.
George B. Geyer, '09 .... Martinsburg, W. Va.
Travis S. Epes, '09 .... Dinwiddie, Va.
Edward J. Shortell, '09 .... Paterson, N. J.
Fred J. Marshall, '09 .... Norwich, Conn.
Elmo N. Laurence, '09 .... Raleigh, N. C.
Herbert W. Atchison, '08 .... Clarksburg, W. Va.
Edgar A. Harty, '08 .... Kingston, Jamaica.
Henry S. Gardner, '09 .... Martinsburg, W. Va.
James E. Funderburk, '08 .... Lancaster, S. C.
L. L. Belcher, '09 .... Welch, W. Va.

—•◇•—

CHI—NORTH PACIFIC DENTAL COLLEGE.

Chi introduces to the fraternity the following members taken in during this school year:

Arthur H. Williams, '08 .... Oregon City, Ore.
Walter I. Ferrier, '08 .... Tacoma, Wash.
Fred E. Casey, '08 .... Toppenish, Wash.
Lee G. Schell, '09 .... Hamilton, Ohio.
Marshall Y. Lucas, ... Armstrong, British Columbia.

—•◇•—

PSI—OHIO MEDICAL UNIVERSITY.

S. E. Spangler, Editor.

The holiday vacation, preceded by the mid-year examinations at O. M. U. has come and gone and all members of Psi are back and have buckled down to work once more. All came back fully recuperated from the effects of the examinations, revived in spirits by having spent a few days of rest among sweethearts and friends, and full of vim and vigor for the ensuing semester. Some of us hope to make this the last lap of the race at old O. M. U., and by May 7, 1907, hope to be eligible to enter the "sweepstake" race before the State Board in June. We

trust none may be barred from this chance to do his best for Psi Omega and O. M. U.

Many things have taken place since our last letter in which Psi was more or less interested. Sometime, about the third day of the third week in November, Psi held her third initiation of the year, taking in three good men. The newly initiated are Mr. Cowden, Mr. Clarke and Mr. Emmert, all of the freshman class. This increases our number of active members to thirty-five and before the school year closes we hope to make it even more as we have several good men, good prospects, in view. Our members initiated during November and December are:

Arthur T. Knoderer, '09 .... Columbus, Ohio.
William C. Warren, 08 .... Knoxville, Ohio.
George J. Hawkins, '08 .... New Franklin, Ohio.
Harry L. Oliver, '08 ... . Cambridge, Ohio.
William H. Carter, '08 .... Ravenna, Ohio.
Dennis G. Welch, '08 .... Ashley, Ohio.
George L. Moore, '09 .... Cambridge, Ohio.
Paul E. Gabel, '08 .... Dayton, Ohio.
Edward D. Warner, '07 .... Portsmouth, Ohio.
Joseph T. Williamson, '08 .... New Matamoras, Ohio.
Roy R. Bode, '09 .... Marietta, Ohio.
Sperry B. Claypool, 09 .... Ashley, Ohio.
Everett E. Stewart, '09 .... Beallsville, Ohio.
A. M. Galvin, '09 .... Wheeling, W. Va.
John G. Scheafer, '09 .... Columbus, Ohio.
Carl W. Emmert, '09 .... Portsmouth, Ohio.
Harry S. Cowden, '09 .... Quaker City, Ohio.
Earl G. Clark, '09 .... Fredonia, Pa.

On November 28 the chapter gave a dance at U. C. T. hall in honor of the alumni members who had come to town to witness the O. S. U. vs. O. M. U. foot ball game on the following day.

About thirty-five couples enjoyed the affair. Refreshments were served and all that were present went home knowing that Psi was not to be excelled in her social functions.

On the following day many alumni members, who did not arrive in time to attend the dance, came to the city to witness the great game.

Capt. Cann, Bro. Hawkins and Bro. Carter did good work throughout that game and aided materially in holding down the score.

During the week following Turkey Day week, the Ohio State Dental Society held its annual convention at the Great Southern Hotel in this city. Many of the boys who were here Turkey Day week remained over and many who were not here then came to attend the meet and paid the boys at the chapter house a visit.

Among those who paid us a visit since our last report were, Brothers C. J. Pressler, J. N. Brown, L. D. Pfouts, Radebough, A. Bobo, C. Brecheisen, Meek, White, Scatterday, Grant, Kirk, Carpenter, Whitacre, Smith, Sonnonstine, Pilkinton, Brooks, Brashear, Fackiner, Powell, and Deyo. All alumni members of Psi chapter. Supreme Councilor E. H. Sting, of Tiffin, O., and Ackeroyd, Zeta, of Dresden, O., were also with us.

On the evening of December 5, the boys gave a smoker at the chapter house in honor of our Supreme Councilor, E. H. Sting, and other members attending the convention. Speeches were made by Brothers Sting, Semans, Cottrell, and Pfouts. The rest of the evening was spent in conversation, singing of songs, and listening to the house orchestra. Every body smoked up in good style and voted the evening well spent. Come again Brother Sting, your remarks were enjoyed very much and we appreciated your visit with us.

Brothers Semans, Brashear, Cottrell, and Deyo attended the National Association of Dental Pedagogics held in Chicago December 26-27-28-29 and report a fine meeting, also a pleasant time.

Brother G. W. Grant, of Bucyrus, was recently married. Psi chapter extends congratulations to Dr. and Mrs. Grant and wishes them a long and happy wedded life.

Dr. Cottrell, Dr. Deyo, and P. G. M., John Warner together with two other gentlemen have organized a company known as the Capitol Dental Supply Co. and will soon be ready for business. Here's wishing them success.

BETA ALPHA—UNIVERSITY OF ILLINOIS.

G. W. Wheeler, Editor.

Beta Alpha is now located at 406 Ogden avenue, is prosperous and the boys are happy. We have taken into our ranks, since the opening of the school year up to January 1, '07, the following:

Laurence B. Murphy, '07 .... Chicago, Ill.
Ralph B. Driver, '07 .... Minneapolis, Minn.
Joseph A. Juzwick, '08 .... Laurium, Mich.
Mathias J. Seifert, M. D., Hon'y. .... Chicago, Ill.
Harry T. Spangler, '07 .... Plainfield, Ill.

One of our boys, L. H. Phifer, has recently taken unto himself a better half. Brother Phifer is one of our energetic young men. We congratulate him and wish for the couple many happy years.

While our chapter is not large, we are getting the good men from the different classes so that the standard, established in our chapter, is being maintained.

The Association of Dental Pedagogics, which recently met in our city at the Palmer House, extended congratulations to the University of Illinois for the fine exhibit and special mention was made of some of the work that was done by our boys.

We extend a cordial invitation to all members to visit us, when it is possible for them to do so.

—•◇•—

BETA GAMMA—GEORGE WASHINGTON UNIVERSITY.

W. H. Hildreth, Editor.

Beta Gamma sends heartiest New Year's greetings to all brothers, graduate and undergraduate, and wishes them success and prosperity for this and the years to come.

It is hard to realize that the college year is nearly half gone, yet time passes most rapidly when we have the most to do and the results accomplished bear witness to the success of our endeavors. There is an element in our University that is doing its utmost to throw obstacles in our path and prevent new men from joining our ranks. Nevertheless, with great satisfaction, I can say that Beta Gamma has overcome the opposition and by the dignified bearing of the brothers has given the college a better opinion of us than ever.

We gave our second smoker to the new men on November 17, on which occasion Brother J. H. P. Benson, of the faculty, gave us a very interesting and instructive talk on anomalous conditions accompanying the exfoliation of the temporary teeth;

treatment and results. These informal talks, or lectures, by brother members of the faculty and graduate brothers are a feature in our chapter and are delivered from time to time during the winter. Brother Arthur B. Crane, Zeta, '99, is booked to talk to us in the near future.

On December 8, we initiated the following men:

Wm. F. Lawrence, '07 .... Elmira, N. Y.
Herbert C. Hopkins, '09 .... Crawford, N. J.
Robert H. Clark, '09 .... Evansville, Ind.
Wm. R. Addison, '08 .... Superior, Wis.

Many graduate brothers assisted in the ceremonies, including several from the George Washington University and Georgetown University faculties. The usual banquet followed the initiation exercises. We believe that in the new brothers we have men who will make good Psi Omegas and who will be a credit to the fraternity.

It may be interesting to the readers of The Frater to know how the members of Beta Gamma are regarded by the student body, as evidenced by the class honors that have been thrust upon them at the recent class elections. Brothers W. L. Lawrence and C. G. Shoemaker are president and secretary, respectively, of the senior class. Of the four officers of the junior class, three are Psi Omegas, as follows: President, Brother J. W. Bernhard; Vice President, Brother H. C. Young, and Editor of the "Mall," Brother W. H. Hildreth

M. E. Harrison, Beta Gamma, '06, passed the District Board last July and has opened an attractive office in the fashionable section of this city. Brother Harrison's address is The Newberne, corner Twelfth street and Massachusetts avenue, N. W.

R. S. Clinton, another '06 man, is now plugging for the Board Exam and will take it early in January. Brother Clinton intends locating in Minneapolis in the near future and is trying the local examination just for practice and to see what board examinations are like.

BETA DELTA—UNIVERSITY OF CALIFORNIA.

Leighton C. Brownton, Editor.

The Frater was never more welcome or more thoroughly read than the November issue. Eight months and more had elapsed since most of us had seen one and we really felt out of touch with the rest of the frat. Now that we know how things have shaped themselves during the past months we feel more like our old selves of ante April 18.

As stated in our November editorial, Beta Delta as a chapter suffered but little from the effects of the fire, our chapter hall fortunately escaping—but there were a number of brothers who suffered serious financial loss. It is in behalf of these and in behalf of the remaining brothers that we wish to express our appreciation of the spontaneous and liberal spirit shown by the fraternity at large in raising the San Francisco Relief Fund. It came as a great boon to many brothers who were here during those trying weeks following the catastrophy and was the cause for much satisfaction among Psi Omegas in California in that it showed the true nature of the men who have helped and are helping keep our fraternity to the fore.

Three of our men were honored with election to office in the senior class: President, Leonard Martin; Vice President, Herbert S. Bibbero; Secretary, F. W. Meyer.

On the evening of November 16, we were entertained and instructed by a highly interesting clinic given by Dr. R. E. Farley whose topic that evening was "Seamless Crowns." The following week J. J. Griffin, P. G. M., related his experiences in actual practice, comparing what he learned in college with what he had learned since graduating.

Beta Delta takes pleasure in presenting the following new members to the fraternity:

Bert J. Hoffman, '07 .... Tulare, Cal.
James C. McManus, '08 .... Napa, Cal.
Gordon S. Rodda, '08 .... East Oakland, Cal.
Charles E. Harper, '08 .... Porterville, Cal.
Fred A. Ross, '08 .... Gilroy, Cal.

F. J. Colligan, '06, otherwise known as "Happy," alias "Hooligan," having acquired a remunerative practice, took the step which usually follows. We have been unable to get the name of the young lady, but wish them all happiness and success.

By the time this editorial appears in print, Brother F. A. Ross, of Gilroy, will have claimed the hand of Miss J. L. Holt, of San Benito. After the honeymoon they will reside in San Francisco until Brother Ross graduates. We extend congratulations to the young couple.

W. W. Leslie, '05, is located in the Chapman block, Porterville, and enjoys an ever increasing practice.

BETA EPSILON—NEW ORLEANS COLLEGE OF DENTISTRY.

Leon Barnett, Editor.

Beta Epsilon had one of her best initiations of the year on Thursday night, November 15, the following candidates running the gauntlet:

 Joseph D. Carter, '07 .... Abbeville, La.
 James F. Love, '07 .... Oakdale, La.
 Lawrence D. Landry, '08 .... Mark P. O., La.

The following clipping from the New Orleans Pickayune of November 16, will tell the tale of the initiation and banquet:

"The Psi Omega Dental Fraternity—and the name in itself suggests mystery to the uninitiated—held one of its revels last night, and after three victims had been offered up on the altar of mirth, the band rallied around a well-stocked board at the Old Hickory, and the night wasn't quite long enough for the things that were toward.

"J. D. Carter, Lawrence Landry and J. F. Love were the victims. They were put through all sorts of stunts in the Fraternity headquarters—were butted by the goat, bitten by the alligator, kicked by the mule and clouted by the giant, and all the while the hood-winks kept light from their eyes. Finally they were marched over rocky roads, booted along to make swift their gait, nudged and punched up a flight of steps, and when the hoods were removed they found themselves seated at a table with a whole host of 'garcons' rushing on smoking dishes, and the wine that cheers.

The old adage was verified, the wine lived up to its reputation and it was a cheerful crowd, full of jest and prone to guy the unfortunate who was not next to the 'proposition' which was hidden and which was referred to as the undercurrent suggested by the growth of tropical trees.

Grand Master G. T. Carman sat at the head of the board. primed to lay traps for the unwary, and near him were Junior Master E. L. Fortier, Secretary J. T. Reese, Dr. Leon Barnett, Editor for Beta Epsilon, who has held the exalted post for four years, and T. J. Green, the man who holds the money bags, and whose position is commonly termed treasurer.

"The recently initiated, with dinkey silk paper caps of the order of the jester's hood and bells on their heads, had seats of honor. Those present beside the officers, and the recently initiated were: Dr. A. G. Friedrichs, Dean of the New Orleans College of Dentistry; Dr. Oliver T. Reiss, Dr. H. A. Magruder, Dr. Paul de Verges, Dr. Lawrence D. Landry, Dr. S. S. Grosjean, Dr. A. Louis Ducasse, Dr. Emile H. Ramelli and Messrs. J. H. Rolling and J. D. Carter.

Favors were passed about, favors in keeping with the ceremonies—mysterious—favors that when opened proved to be fool's caps or arrangements of a similar caliber, and the general atmosphere was one of mirth and folly. As for the feast that was spread, it need only be said that Jacques Mayer did his best.

"Grand Master Carman, the first dictator of the festivities, selected J. T. Reese as toastmaster, and even if Mr. Reese does hail from the quiet precincts of the Carolinas, he proved himself 'all right' and discharged the duties of his office with a thoroughness that was convincing of ability."

Toastmaster Reese spoke, in part, as follows:

Brother Psi Omegas:

I count this a peculiar privilege and pleasure to bid you welcome this evening. Though totally unused to the pleasing ways of the orator, I at least have the gift of sincerity, so I bid you a hearty, loyal welcome.

We are a group of young men banded together by fraternal ties to assist, to emulate and encourage each other in a difficult task.

In the ascent of the steep hills of Dental science there are times when we feel over weary, over burdened and ready to fall from the ranks of climbers. Then it is that a comrade's hearty handgrasp, the sympathetic glow from the eye, and the warm words of cheer bring balm to the heart and courage to the spirit —so let us be ever loyal to each other.

The profession to which we are aspiring is a noble one— an important branch of the great healing art. Ours is to be the privilege to assuage pain and prevent distress. It is a profession whose boundaries are widening and instead of relieving, as of old, seeks to prevent pain and to instruct the uninitiated in the rules of hygiene. Let us of Beta Epsilon make ourselves worthy of our calling but, in order to accomplish this laudable end, abundant self sacrifice, study and discipline will be necessary.

Some of us will go out this year from our Alma Mater— perhaps never to meet again. I feel that I am but reaching the sentiments which live in every heart here when I wish for those who graduate, abundant success. I know that they will prove themselves worthy to be called Psi Omegas.

Brother Grosjean, the gentleman who made a hit with a feat of legerdemain in which a bunch of grapes and a banana figure, was the first speaker, and he devoted the time to going into details about the trick and endeavoring to enlighten the gathering.

Dr. Reiss, the well-known local practitioner, who organized the New Orleans branch of the fraternity, expended a fund of eloquence in impressing upon the members the course they should pursue in building up their society. The newly-elected candidates followed and Dr. Magruder came next, with an able address on the objects and purposes of the fraternity.

Barnett then told of his recent travels and made certain suggestions and then the toastmaster insisted that it was Dr. Friedrichs' turn. Dr. Friedrichs has a reputation as an after-dinner speaker, and the way he handed it out to the "brothers" that night was sufficient to serve for a while. Dr. Friedrichs was both comical and serious and after making the members roar with a string of excellent stories, he spoke upon the aim of the fraternity. He said that the brotherly feeling should be encouraged and that the fraternity, above everything else, should aim in the standard of excellence, the standard that would gain the recognition for the dental profession which it deserves.

Dr. De Verges gave the members a heart-to-heart talk. He had just come from the wedding of a very dear relative, and said that when it came his time to fall beneath Hymen's bond, everybody present would receive an invitation.

Dr. Landry spoke upon the development of the profession. Dr. Ramelli delivered an address upon the ethics of the profession, and Dr. Ducasse advanced some ideas for the broadening of the fraternity's work. Before the guests were through they even made Mr. Meyer, the host, talk, and the feast ended as it had begun, with a manifestation of genuine good-fellowship.

We are contemplating giving a smoker very soon and no doubt it will prove a success. The boys are preparing themselves to celebrate "College Night" and they anticipate a grand old time. College Night has become popular with the boys, and they all look forward to it each year.

Psi Omegas are in full force in regard to class officers this year. Psi Omegas hold the high offices in the senior class.

BETA ZETA—ST. LOUIS DENTAL COLLEGE.

S. A. Lusby, Editor.

The dawn of the new year is just tinging the Eastern horizon with its tint of gold. In bidding adieu to the associations and memories of the departing year, we hope we may have had experiences which we will profit by in the future.

In entering the new year we are confronted with a future which is pregnant with possibilities to those who are pure in heart and steadfast in purpose for the cause of fraternalism.

> What might be done if men were wise—
>   What glorious deeds, my suffering brother,
> Would they unite in love and right,
>   And cease their scorn of one another?
>
> What might be done? This might be done,
>   And more than this, my brother,
> More than the tongue e'er said or sung,
>   If men were wise and loved each other.

We are glad to announce the following additions to Psi Omega's ranks:

Lee R. Main, '07 .... Troy, Ill.
Paul Fitzgerald, '08 .... Micro, N. C.
George H. Slawson, '07 .... Salem, Mo.
Wendell T. Kitchell, '07 .... Newburg, Mo.

Brother Fitzgerald thought his riding the goat was quantum sufficit. Brother Main's modesty was a little shocked at the costume he had to wear the night he was given his second degree. We have the pledges of three or four more candidates who will probably be initiated at our next meeting.

BETA ETA—KEOKUK DENTAL COLLEGE.

Geo. R. Narrley, Editor.

Most all of the boys are on the way home now to spend the holidays and never since this school has been started has there been such a small number remaining here. All of the fraternity boys have made up their minds to have a good time this year. Several of our members will spend the vacation with Brother Coe, '06, of Peoria. A. B. Thompson, '05, our Asst. Dem. will return to Viola, Ill., and bring back a Christmas present in the shape of a bride. He certainly kept the matter a secret, for none of the fellows knew of it until he was ready to leave, but he surely will be given the glad hand when he returns.

Beta Eta is prospering. We have initiated the following candidates this year:

E. Lloyd McKenzie, '07 .... Payson, Ill.
Nicholas C. Hargis, '08 .... Lancaster, Mo.
J. Bernard Husley, '07 .... Keokuk, Iowa.

We have the application of another member of our faculty for honorary membership, several applications from juniors and some very good material to draw from in the freshman class.

Our initiation, several weeks ago, was an eye opener. Our Old Time Smoker was attended by eighteen active, would be, honorary and alumni members. It was certainly a "corker." We broke up in the wee small hours in the morning with the general opinion that Messrs. Sinotte, Arnold, and Hargis make a star smoker committee.

GAMMA IOTA—SOUTHERN DENTAL COLLEGE.

Gamma Iota introduces to the fraternity the following members taken in during this school year:

Percy I. Darden, '08 .... Goldsboro, N. C.
Enoch A. May, '09 .... Dobson, Miss.
Frank E. Hearn, '07 .... Sylva, N. C.
William G. Floyd, Jr., '08 .... Roanoke, Ala.
William J. Mitchell, '08 ...... Talladega Springs, Ala.
Dennis T. Turner, '08 .... Eatonton, Ga.
Stephen R. Hurtley, '08 .... McKenzie, Ala.
Alfred M. Jackson, '08 .... Inverness, Fla.
Robert L. Shirley, '08 .... Wingard, Ala.
Manning J. Flynn, '08 .... Rutledge, Ala.
Thomas S. Saxon, '08 .... Watkinsville, Ga.
Timon J. Burnham, '08 .... Magee, Miss.
James B. Webb, '08 .... Blackville, S. C.

GAMMA KAPPA—UNIVERSITY OF MICHIGAN.

Le Vant R. Drake, Editor.

Gamma Kappa wishes all sister chapters a Happy New Year. At the close of 1906 our prospects never looked brighter and we enter upon the new year with the determination to let every good man in our department know that there is a chapter of the Psi Omega fraternity here. Our endeavors to keep our standard high are being noticed by the men whom we desire to be interested in us. One of our professors said: "I can't help but admire the class of men in your fraternity." We feel gratified for those words because he is a member of one of the other fraternities. At our last meeting we took in one new member, and we take pleasure in introducing him to our brothers: William J. Seitz.

Our list of new members thus far this year is as follows:

Louis D. Mount, '07 .... Ashtabula, Ohio.
Martin R. Clinton, '09 .... Pinckney, Mich.
D. Winfield Barr, '09 .... Cleveland, Ohio.
Benjamin H. Masselink, '08 .... Zeeland, Mich.
Harper E. Brady, '08 .... Kalamazoo, Mich.

William J. Seitz '09 .... Henry, Ill.
Harry J. Fox, '08 .... Pigeon, Mich.

GAMMA LAMBDA—COLLEGE OF DENTAL AND ORAL SURGERY OF NEW YORK.

Gotthard E. Seyfarth, Editor.

Gamma Lambda, true to her promise, is doing splendid work right along, so we are proud to say that a great deal has been accomplished during the first three months of the college year. This may sound like self-flattery, but our officers are certainly doing their duty and I am sure that they will continue in their worthy endeavors. Although one of the "infant chapters" we have taken firm roots in the earth of fraternal progress and fear no difficulties, for no matter what may arise, we have the Supreme Council and the officers of Beta chapter to counsel us in times of trouble.

On the 16th of November we had the great pleasure to initiate into Honorary Membership Prof. William H. Haskin, M. D., formerly Professor of Oral Surgery at our college. While not a dentist himself, he has been so closely connected with and done so much for our profession, that we may justly say that he "belongs" to us as well as to the medical profession. He ranks high among his fellow practitioners and as an oral surgeon he has few, if any, superiors. Gamma Lambda is certainly very fortunate to have Prof. Haskin in her midst and Psi Omega may be proud in calling him one of her sons.

Three new men were put through the mill on the 7th of December and we are glad to say they live to tell the tale. These new brothers are:

Lewis H. Carr, '09 .... Newburgh, N. Y.
Matthew F. McPhillips, '09 .... Brooklyn, N. Y.
Raymond Sheerer, '08 .... Newburgh, N. Y.

Our meetings are well attended as there is always enough business on hand to make things interesting. The literary committee of our chapter is doing its utmost to make our meeting nights pleasant. Up to date we have had a number of articles read and discussed with promises of many more. As our graduate brothers are always well represented on these occasions, the undergraduates derive quite a little knowledge from the interchange of opinions by these older brothers, who speak from their own experiences. This and the fact that some of these talks are to be supplemented by practical demonstrations make them a valuable adjunct to our regular college course.

We believe in combining a little pleasure with our work once in awhile and have accordingly a few "spreads" and "smokers" to our credit. The informality which prevails on these occasions produces that "at home-like feeling" appreciated by those brothers who come from out of town, and it also again proves that we are all brothers of the large family of Psi Omega.

During the last month, we have been exchanging visits with Beta and we are on excellent terms with them. There is but one thing upon which we do not agree and that is in reference to our proficiency in a little game played by them, in which, as they say, they are more efficient than we could ever be. I think a championship tournament as soon after our mid-term examinations as may be satisfactory will be required to decide who really are the worst players.

At a recent meeting we had the pleasure of meeting Brother Blakeslee, of Phi, and we hope that all brothers who may in their wanderings stray to New York, will try to remember the existence of Gamma Lambda.

GAMMA MU—UNIVERSITY OF IOWA.

A. R. Hausen, Editor.

Gamma Mu sends greetings to all chapters.

We lost three brothers last year. Two by graduation, Schwims, now located at Peoria, and Daly, at Cambridge, Neb. Stockelah did not return to school. We will lose Hunsicker by graduation the first of February.

Gamma Mu takes pleasure in introducing the following new members:

H. D. Duncan, '07 .... Tipton, Iowa.
Herman A. Knott, '08 .... Tipton, Iowa.
Burr G. Saville, '07 .... Mount Ayr, Iowa.
William E. Moxley, '09 .... Ames, Iowa.

Kenneth McMartin, '07 .... Massena, Iowa.
John M. Tate, '08 .... State Center, Iowa.
Edwin O. Carter, '07 .... Nevada, Iowa.

Frazier and McGuire are pledged.

We have newly furnished chapter rooms a block from the dental building which are very handy to go to between classes.

Gamma Mu has given several small dances and one large one. We are now planning on a banquet to be given in the near future.

Brother Daly was married in September.

DR. T. J. McLERNON.

(Gamma.)

The resignation of Dr. McLernon of his position as Clinical Chief of our College Infirmary to accept a higher position in the Dental Department of the Western Reserve University at Cleveland, Ohio, will deprive the Stomatologist of his services in connection with the journal.

For about eight years, or practically during the entire life of the Stomatologist, Dr. McLernon has been its assistant editor, and his labors in connection therewith have contributed largely to the success of the publication. His ability as a stenographer enabled him to report the Saturday surgical clinics, and he gave much time to the correspondence and the gathering of the college and alumni news.

We are sorry to part with him, but at the same time we are pleased with his promotion, and believe he will make himself as valuable in his new field as he was in the old.

In the college infirmary he will be especially missed, for his services there were always appreciated by the students, who found him ever ready to extend a helping hand when needed.

Any instructor who wins the approbation of the Faculty and proves himself of real value to the students, as Dr. McLernon did, can feel assured that his efforts have met with success. No one need ask for greater satisfaction than this.—Stomatologist.

Alnmni Chapters.

PHILADELPHIA ALUMNI CHAPTER.

J. E. Nyce, S. C., Editor.

The Philadelphia Alumni Chapter held the first meeting for the fall on Wednesday evening, October 17, 1906, at the office of Brother Victor Cochran, 1628 North 17th street, with Grand Master, Brother H. D. Winsmore presiding.

A very interesting paper was read by Brother Daniel H. Wetzell on "Reciprocity," which was much enjoyed by all present. We will be glad to have "Pop" give us another hot shot in the near future. We had a large attendance for the first meeting, and the out-look for the winter is good. Several new names were added to our membership. Incidents of office practice were then discussed, after which Mrs. Cochran served hot coffee. Brother Cochran makes an ideal host, but his wife leads him. She thinks we need a ladies' auxiliary; so does Mrs. Mike.

Our next meeting was held December 19, 1906, at the office of Brother Wm. Marsh, 3754 Powelton avenue, with Grand Master, Brother H. D. Winsmore presiding.

Brother J. G. Lane read a paper on "Root Canal Filling," which was very interesting, bringing out a lively discussion by all present.

The following officers were elected for the coming year:

Grand Master	Victor Cochran.
Junior Master	J. G. Lane.
Secretary	R. E. Denney.
Treasurer	Wm. C. Marsh.
Editor	H. L. Chandler.
Ins. Guardian	D. A. Zurbrigg.

It was decided to hold the installation and a frat banquet on January 16, 1907, at Boothby's.

SEALTH ALUMNI CHAPTER.

J. F. Alexander, Chi, '03, Editor.

On December 12, 1904, Drs. Hergert, Palmer, Posten, Osterberg, Swanberg, Williams, Luithlen, and J. F. and W. G. Alexander met in Alexander & Alexander's office, there to discuss the advisability of organizing an Alumni Chapter in Seattle. All were heartily in favor of such a step and went right to work electing officers, selecting a name and appointing committees. Sealth, the Indian name for Seattle, was adopted as the name for the chapter. An application was made to the Supreme Council for a charter, which was duly granted, permitting us to launch our ship of fellowship to advance the cause of Psi Omega in this hustling Western city; to bring the brothers together and to renew the bonds of friendship formed in college days. Our chapter was a success from the first. We have fourteen active, enthusiastic members, all working in harmony for the common good of Sealth.

If any member of Psi Omega visits Seattle let him look us up, for he will be among friends. In 1909, the Alaskan-Yukon Exposition is to be held here. Work has already commenced on grounds and buildings. It will be something different from other expositions held on the coast. Greater and broader in its scope. The exposition will attract many visitors to our city. At this early date Sealth pledges to aid in making the visit of any brother to the exposition, one long to be remembered.

PORTSMOUTH ALUMNI CHAPTER.

P. W. Young, Editor.

The members of Portsmouth Alumni Chapter are getting along nicely, so is the chapter. We have had several very good meetings this fall which have been a source of profit to each one of us.

One of our members, Brother George H. Williamson, was united in marriage to Miss Emilie S. Dranillard, of Portsmouth, at the First Presbyterian church. Dr. Williamson is an alumnus of the Ohio College of Dental Surgery, '98, and is at present Grand Master of our Alumni Chapter. Brother Williamson and bride carry with them the best wishes of our chapter. Another of our members to give up celibacy is our esteemed Brother Frank A. Spencer, who quietly took himself to Edinburg, Ind., ostensibly upon a hunting expedition. There he was united in marriage to Miss A. L. Morrison, of this city, who was supposed to be visiting friends in Cincinnati. The sly couple kept their secret for some time, but eventually they were exposed and what the citizens of this commonwealth did to them was a plenty upon the fact of their marriage being verified. Spencer is now advising all young men contemplating matrimony to "do it openly," presumably being satisfied that secrecy in such matters is ill-advised. Brother Spencer is an alumnus of the O. M. U., '04, and Psi chapter. The friends and associates of the happy couple are united in expressing congratulations and best wishes for their future.

C. J. Pressler, Psi, '04, formerly with Dr. Jackson of this city, has purchased the practice of Dr. Hekel, of Waverly, O.

Reports are that Brother Pressler is doing nicely at his new home.

Editorial.

ALUMNI CHAPTER REPRESENTATION.

The alumni chapters are not as well represented in The Frater as they should be. With the exception of the Philadelphia, Sealth and Portsmouth chapters, little has been heard from them for some time. Good old Duquesne seems to have entirely forgotten The Frater—possibly caused by the absorbing task of raising that $50,000 for her new fraternity house. The New York chapter, one of our quondom contributors, is resting on her laurels. That good bunch down in New Orleans seems to have not recovered from the effects of election of officers, two years ago. Why not get the boys together, Brother Woodward? The Cleveland chapter ought to be called before the "faculty." The Los Angeles, Minnesota, Boston and Chicago chapters are also on the list of those from whom we would like to hear.

Why not start the New Year by injecting New Life into your chapters, Alumni members of Alumni chapters?

GENERAL FRATERNITY DIRECTORY.

Pursuant to the many demands for a complete General Directory, we wish to state that the directory is now being assembled and that it will be ready for mailing by the end of May, unless unforseen circumstances prevent.

It is hoped that ready assistance will be rendered, in getting out the work, by those who are in a position to be of service. If each new member will notify the Editor-in-Chief of any corrections necessary in his name and address, his kindness will be appreciated.

Corrections of names and addresses given in previous issues of The Frater will also be appreciated.

RELIEF COMMITTEE REPORT.

This issue of The Frater contains a comprehensive report from the Relief Committee which disbursed the funds to those who suffered loss in the San Francisco disaster. In behalf of the fraternity, The Frater takes this opportunity for thanking Brothers Griffin, Pease, Gallagher, James and Merritt for the time they gave and for the very thorough manner in which they discharged the duty intrusted to them. The report shows that the committee was discreet and impartial in disbursing the funds. It was deemed advisable to not print the amount of money voted to various brothers. A large number of brothers, who are mentioned in the report, were not in need of assistance, but news concerning them is included in the report for the information of their friends.

The report is on file in the office of our Grand Recorder, Supreme Councilor Friesell, where information not given in The Frater can be obtained by those who desire it.

CRYSTAL ANNIVERSARY OF PSI OMEGA.

In commemoration of the Fifteenth Anniversary of the birth of Psi Omega, plans are pretty well under way to celebrate, in unison, this event all over the country.

With fifteen years elapsed since our birth, one has but to look at the roll of our chapters to be assured that our organization is not only national in character but also that it is established upon a solid foundation. Reference to chapter editorials will readily reveal that, each year, a generous number of the graduates of the various colleges are Psi Omegas.

These in time enter into the practice of their profession in various sections of the country until, at this our Fifteenth Anniversary, there is scarcely a city or town of any importance which does not boast one or more members of our fraternity.

Thus has our horizon broadened from one lone chapter in 1892, with a handful of members, to 38 chapters in 1907 and a total membership of nearly 4,000.

These years of development have not been wasted; Psi Omega has continuously devoted her efforts to the establishment of strong, true, college fraternal life and has solved problems which required patience, prudence and courage, so that to-day she stands pre-eminent among Dental fraternities.

It is but meet that, consistent with our wonderful development and prestige, we should in some national manner celebrate this our Crystal Anniversary.

The plan, as promulgated to properly observe this event, is for each chapter to give a banquet, whether it be elaborate or modest, on the night of February 15, and at the hour of 8 o'clock Pacific, 9 o'clock Mountain, 10 o'clock Central and 11 o'clock Eastern time a standing toast be drunk, in unison, by Psi Omegas in all sections of the country.

A fitting souvenir of the occasion is suggested, some inexpensive remembrance which will become more dear to the recipient, not because of its intrinsic value but because of the associations and memories which its possession will recall. For, of all the friends we make, those of college days prove most sincere, especially among those lads of our own frat where selfishness and greed do not hold sway.

What nobler, grander sight can be conceived than this great number of Psi Omegas, so widely separated geographically, yet so closely united in spirit, simultaneously drinking a toast to their dear fraternity?

Personal and Alumni Notes.

C. D. Wright, Rho, '05' is practicing at Hillsboro, O.

Frank P. Duffy, Alpha, '06' is located at Riverpoint, R. I.

M. Throckmorton, Gamma, '05' is now located at Beaver, Pa.

W. H. Sherrard, Tau, '05' is now located at Williamston, S. C.

E. B. Strange, Beta Zeta, '05' is now located at Hillsboro, Ill.

G. D. Peters, Chi, '03' is married and is practicing in Portland, Ore.

F. J. Ebert, Zeta, '04' is now located at his home, Vancouver, Wash.

W. W. Shartel, Chi, '00' has removed from Lake City to Cedarville, Cal.

E. B. Hudson, Tau, '05' has removed from Watkinsville to Tallapoosa, Ga.

P. F. Lamm, Iota, '04' is located at 307 Hoffman building, Sedalia, Mo.

V. W. Laughlin, Mu, '05' has removed from Challis, Idaho, to Rockville, Mo.

G. C. Mitchell, Epsilon, '06' is practicing with Dr. Higgins, at Bellevue, O.

J. Condren, Eta, '05' is practicing at 1641 Fairmount avenue, Philadelphia, Pa.

E. J. Eveleigh, Theta, '04, is located at 427 North Salina street, Syracuse, N. Y.

B. E. C. Slawson, Beta Zeta, '06, is located at 3627 Broadway, St. Louis, Mo.

Hubert C. Bailie, Upsilon, '06, is now located at 508 Grosse building, Los Angeles, Cal.

G. A. Fletcher, Beta Gamma, '05, is now located at 7 Central avenue, Albany, N. Y.

A. W. Gaumer, Beta Eta, '04, is now located at Bloomfield, Ia., in partnership with Dr. Allender.

O. E. Day, P. G. M., Gamma, '05, is now practicing in Philadelphia, Pa., 1935 Christian street.

Emory C. Thompson, Alpha, Warren, Pa., became the happy father of a baby girl on Sept. 20, 1906.

Harold B. Adams, Zeta, '06, is associated with Dr. C. S. Hurlbut, at 332 Main street, Springfield, Mass.

L. M. Doss and Joe Eden, Omicron, '06 lads, have formed a partnership and are located at Sulphur Springs, Okla.

J. E. Nyce, Supreme Councilor, spent the holidays in Chicago, Ill., attending the meeting of Dental Pedagogics.

G. P. Bannister, Rho, '06, has removed from Dry Ridge, Ky., to Lexington. His office is in the City Bank building.

F. H. Deterding, Nu, '05, has removed his office from room 4, Sterritt building, to 417 Third street, Allegheny, Pa.

Theo. Jensen, Rho, '03, has discontinued the practice of dentistry on account of ill health. Brother Jensen has embarked in business in New Orleans.

J. E. Strasser, Nu, '00, has removed from Leechburg, Pa., to Los Angeles, Cal., hoping that the change of climate will be beneficial to the health of his wife.

The readers of The Frater are indebted to Stanley Reynolds, Gamma, '06, for the New York; to Ralph S. Clinton, Beta Gamma, '06, for the District of Columbia; and to C. B. Gifford, P. G. M., Phi, '06, for the Virginia questions printed in this issue.

C. B. Gifford, P. G. M., Phi, '06, is located at 231 Main street, Norfolk, Va., and will be glad to see all Psi Omegas visiting Norfolk next year, attending the Jamestown exposition. Brother Gifford will gladly render such aid to Psi Omegas as is in his power during the exposition.

The following, concerning H. E. Davis, Rho, '03, is taken from the Champaign (Ill.) Gazette:

"One of the most interesting meetings held by the Champaign-Danville District Dental Society, since its organization some two years ago, was the one held with Dr. H. E. Davis, at St. Joseph, on November 14. There was a good attendance and the papers and clinics on the program were unusually good. It was the annual meeting and the election of officers was held. Dr. Davis gave a banquet at his home at 6 o'clock which brought the members together for a social hour. This was voted one of the profitable features of the meeting. The next meeting will be held in Urbana, February 12."

Marriages.

SOULIER-AREGNO.

On Dec. 14, 1906, Eugene E. Soulier, Beta Epsilon, '05, and Miss Jeanne M. Aregno, of New Orleans, were united in marriage. Dr. Soulier is practicing in St. Martinsville, La., but came down to New Orleans to claim his bride. The Frater extends congratulations.

STRASSER-FARBER.

Henry Strasser, Phi, '06, soon after graduating announced his marriage to Miss Mamie Farber. Brother Strasser is associated with Dr. Schloendour, 521 North Charles street, Baltimore, Md., and was "Medal Man" in his class. His future is as bright, if not brighter, than that of any member of the class of '06. The newly wedded couple will reside at 924 Harlem avenue, Baltimore, Md.

COLVIN-IGLEHART.

Daniel C. Colvin, Phi, '06, and Miss Lucy Iglehart were united in marriage on Monday, June 11, 1906; P. G. M. Gifford, Phi, '06, acting as best man. Brother Colvin is now located at Hyndman, Pa., and says that he is doing well.

YOUNG-MARTIN.

Mr. Oscar F. Martin
announces the marriage of his daughter
Olive
to
Dr. Joseph Rankin Young
on Wednesday, November twenty-eighth
nineteen hundred and six
Chico, California

Dr. Young is a member of Beta Delta, '03, and a staunch supporter of The Frater. The Frater wishes for the happy couple many years of health and prosperity.

WOLFE-MILLER.

L. H. Wolfe, Beta Eta, '05, Hull, Ill., and Miss Lena Miller, of Quincy, Ill., were united in marriage at the home of the bride on December 20, 1906. Brother Wolfe represented his chapter at the Fourth Triennial convention of the fraternity which was held in St. Louis, Mo.

Necrology.

M. H. HEALY, ETA, '04.

It is with regret that we publish the sad news of the death of M. H. Healy, which occurred March 30, 1906. Brother Healy, upon graduation, commenced to practice his profession at Westerly, R. I. When the prospects seemed specially bright, his health failed, thereupon he went to El Paso, Texas, hoping to be benefited by the change, remaining there from October, 1905, to February, 1906. Not feeling benefited, he returned home, where on the 30th of March his death occurred.

ETHAN ALLEN FOSTER, PHI, '05.

It is with much sorrow that we print the sad news of the death of Brother Ethan Allen Foster, of Union, South Carolina. Brother Foster was Chief Interrogator of Phi in his senior year. Brother Foster was an exceptionally congenial young man, well liked by all those who had the pleasure of knowing him. Since graduating he practiced in his home town, Union, S. C., and was reported to be doing well.

State Board Questions.

VIRGINIA, 1906.

Operative Dentistry.

1. Relate the conservative treatment of the dental pulp. (a) Describe extirpation of the dental pulp, and detail the subsequent treatment required. 2. What treatment is indicated when the third molar is impacted? 3. What conditions of a mouth would indicate the necessary extraction of any remaining teeth? 4. Give the properties of non-cohesive gold. (a) Of cohesive gold. (b) Cite cases in which each is indicated, in order to obtain best results. 5. Give points that need to be guarded in locating and preparing a cavity for a porcelain inlay. (a) Describe the method of securing a proper matrix. 6. Define the conditions under which you would extract a temporary molar before the fifth year. (a) Under what conditions is the early extraction of the sixth year molar indicated? 7. What general rules have you adopted for the operating room, and in dealing with patients?

Chemistry.

1. State the difference between an element and a compound. 2. State the difference between a chemical compound and a mechanical mixture. 3. How are Salts obtained? (a) Give example. 4. Give process for obtaining oxygen. (a) Describe its physical and chemical properties. 5. How does chlorine occur in nature? (a) Give its atomic weight, physical and chemical properties, and how obtained. 6. Give symbol and atomic weight of zinc. (a) What compounds of zinc are commonly used in dentistry, and how are these compounds obtained? 7. What compound of arsenic is largely used in dentistry? (a) Give its physical properties and how obtained. 8. What is methyl alcohol? (a) How is it obtained? (b) Give characteristic difference between methyl and ethyl alcohol.

Materia Medica.

1. Give the derivation of the following drugs: Caffeine, chloroform, cocaine, and chloride of ethyl. 2. Give the physiological action of carbolic acid, digitalis, strychnine and nitrite of amyl. 3. Give the preparation and doses of mercury, opium and chalk. 4. Give the dental uses of borax, zinc chloride, iodine, alcohol and sulphuric acid. 5. Give the composition of Seidlitz powder and Dover's powder. 6. Give the antidotes for poisoning by aconite, iodine, arsenic and chloral.

Oral Surgery.

1. Classify fractures of the maxillary bones. (a) Describe the treatment for a simple fracture of the body of the lower jaw bone. 2. Classify dislocations of the lower jaw. (a) Give etiology, symptoms and treatment for its bilateral dislocation. 3. Define stomatitis. (a) Give symptoms and treatment for simple stomatitis. 4. Give etiology, symptoms and treatment for an alveolar abscess. 5. Give etiology, symptoms and treatment for tri-facial neuralgia. 6. What is ranula? (a) Give etiology, symptoms and treatment for ranula. 7. Give symptoms, treatment and prognosis of epulis.

Histology.

1. What are the vital functions of a cell? 2. Describe the colorless corpuscle. 3. How does enamel and dentine calcify? 4. Describe involuntary muscles and state where they are found. 5. Describe the medulated or white nerve fibres. 6. Describe enamel. 7. Describe the external coat of an artery.

Physiology.

1. Name five proteids found in the blood. 2. Name the enzyme and give the action of each. 3. Give the uses of sodium chloride in the system. 4. In what forms are fats, carbohydrates and proteids absorbed and circulated? 5. What would be the result of an exclusive diet of proteids and fats? 6. What causes blood to clot? 7. Name the causes of venous circulation. 8. Name the muscles used in quiet inspiration. 9. Give function of vagus and sympathetic nerves. 10. Of what does a reflex arc consist?

Pathology and Therapeutics.

1. Describe that form of the atrophy of the teeth known as Hutchinson's teeth and give the treatment for the condition.

(a) What teeth are usually attacked by this disease and of what disease are Hutchinson's teeth a diagnostic sign? 2. Mention some of the exciting and predisposing causes of caries of the teeth. (a) Describe briefly the production of lactic acid in the mouth and its action in producing caries of the teeth. 3. Describe exostosis of the cementum and give the etiology of the disease. (a) Name some of the reflex troubles caused by exostosis of the cementum. 4. What effect does the accumulation of salivary calculus have upon the teeth and soft tissues of the mouth? 5. What is pyorrhoea alveolaris? (a) Give the morbid anatomy of this disease and the therapeutic indications for its relief.

Anatomy.

1. Give the bone articulations and the muscle attachments of the inferior maxillary bone. 2. How many openings are there into the pharynx, and what are they? 3. Bound the sub-maxillary triangle and name the most important structures it contains. 4. Describe the maxillary sinus. 5. Name the branches of the third or spheno-maxillary portion of the internal maxillary artery. 6. Describe the anterior dental nerve. 7. Describe the masseter muscle.

Prosthetic Dentistry.

1. What materials are used as a base for artificial teeth? (a) Mention the advantages of each. 2. Describe the manner of taking an impression for cleft palate. 3. Give the component parts of artificial teeth. 4. Describe the best way of supplying a central incisor, when a plate is contra-indicated. 5. Name all the impression materials. (a) State the composition of each. 6. How soon after extraction would you insert a temporary plate? (a) How soon would you insert a permanent one? (b) Give all the points governing each case. 7. What is vulcanite? 8. Describe a Whiteside crown. (a) Give its advantages. 9. How would you correct a badly contracted arch? 10. Mention all the appliances and material necessary in making a shell crown.

Metallurgy.

1. Define an alloy. 2. Give the uses of platinum. 3. Name, in the order of their importance, five (5) noble metals. 4. What is a cupel? (a) When is its use indicated? 5. Why is aluminum not suitable for artificial dentures? 6. Give the composition of Mellott's metal and mouldine. (a) Give

their uses. 7. What is known as "pickling" a bridge? 8. What combination of metals is best adapted for clasps, and why? 9. State the composition of German silver. (a) Give its uses. 10. What is borax? (a) Why is it used in soldering?

DISTRICT OF COLUMBIA.

July, 1906.

Prosthetic Dentistry.

1. How may an impression be taken of a particularly sensitive mouth? 2. What is weighted rubber and for what used in dentistry? 3. Can silver be vulcanized next to rubber? 4. What is your method of taking a partial upper impression. 5. For what is aluminum used in dentistry? How is it annealed, and what is its fusing point? 6. How construct a crown for a bicuspid tooth, with porcelain facing, and tooth having a vital pulp? 7. What is an obturator? 8. Describe an appliance for expanding or enlarging the arch. 9. What combination of metals makes a good clasp for continuous gum partial plate? Give formula. 10. Describe method of obtaining an accurate bite for full upper and lower set.

Chemistry.

1. Name three acids commonly used in dentistry, and give specific use and formula of each. 2. Explain reaction of H_2O_2 on putrescent pulps. 3. Indicate by equation the reaction of zinc on HCl. (a) Write formula of ammonium nitrate. (b) Potassium nitrate. 4. Write names and give symbols of ten metals used in dentistry? 5. Distinguish chemically between oxychloride of zinc and oxyphosphate of zinc; state the conditions indicating the use of each in dentistry.

Oral Surgery.

1. Mention the materials used for sutures and describe the twisted or hair-lip suture. 2. Give etiology and treatment of syncope. 3. Is necrosis found more frequently in the upper or inferior maxillary? Why? 4. Define neurasthenia and give its symptoms and treatment. 5. How would you treat persistent bleeding after lancing the gums of a child?

Anatomy.

1. Describe osseous tissue and give its chemical composition. 2. Give a description of the inferior maxillary bone. 3. Mention the bones that enter into formation of the orbital cavity. 4. Describe the palate bone. 5. Mention the muscles of mastication and give their origin and insertion. 6. Describe the maxillary sinus. 7. Give a brief description of the facial nerve. 8. Mention the arteries from which the superior maxillary bone derives its blood supply. 9. Describe the superior vena cava. 10. Describe the salivary glands. Where do these glands empty?

Materia Medica.

1. What is meant by the active principle of a drug? Give an example. 2. Define antiseptic; disinfectant; germicide, and deodorant. 3. Describe astringents. Mention two. 4. Mention two heart stimulants and two heart sedatives. State dose of each. 5. In operations about the mouth what are the advantages of local over general anaesthetics? 6. Define escharotics; mention two and give their dental uses. 7. Give the mouth signs of mercurial stomatitis. 8. Distinguish between a narcotic and a hypnotic. 9. How should the injuries resulting from the local action of arsenious acid be treated? 10. From what is formaldehyde derived?

Operative Dentistry.

1. Name the kinds of filling materials and state their relative merits. 2. Describe your method of cavity preparation for filling with gold; porcelain, and amalgam. 3. What advantage has porcelain over gold or other fillings, if any? 4. How would you diagnose an abscess in its early stages, and how distinguish from a congested pulp? 5. How would you treat an abscess with a fistulous opening; and how a blind abscess? 6. How would you recognize pyorrhoea alveolaris, and how would you treat it? 7. How would you recognize gingivitis and what are its causes and treatment? 8. How would you recognize a case of antrum complication and how treat? 9. What treatment would you give in hemorrhage from extraction of a tooth? 10. What system would you consider most desirable in the treatment of a case of irregularity similar to model shown?

Physiology.

1. What is physiology as applied to dentistry? 2. What is the nature of saliva; analysis, and object? 3. Of what is the

mucous membrane composed? 4. How is the mucous membrane affected by smoking and alcoholic beverages? 5. What effect would these conditions have on artificial dentures? 6. What effect has saliva upon the teeth? 8. How would you control an acid reaction? 9. What is tartar; describe the different kinds, and their detrimental action? 10. What are adenoids? How do they affect the teeth?

Histology.

1. Does the enamel of teeth become harder after complete eruption? Explain. 2. Locate and describe Meckel's cartilage. 3. How does tooth enamel obtain blood supply at different stages of development? 4. Give functions and process of growth of cementum. 5. What is the tactile organ of a tooth? 6. What is amelification? 7. Give origin of dentine's nerve supply. 8. Give origin of pericementum's nerve supply. 9. What kind of tissue is dentine? 10. What are odontoblasts, and what kind of tissue?

Pathology and Bacteriology.

1. Define inflammation. 2. What are the first and last stages of unarrested inflammation? 3. Define and give a few of the causes of traumatic pericementitis. 4. What is the usual cause of septic pericementitis? 5. What pathological condition makes tooth containing putrescent pulp sensitive to pressure? 6. Give difference between parasitic and saprophytic fungi. 7. Which forms bacteria forming ptomaines? 8. Define propogation by fission. 9. Is heat or moisture more important to bacteria? 10. Define pyogenic bacteria.

NEW YORK, JUNE, 1906.

Fifteen questions are given on each subject. The candidate may answer any ten of them.

Anatomy.

1. What are the end bulbs of Krause? 2. Describe the minute structures of an artery? 3. Give a general description of the nervous system. 4. Describe the coccyx. 5. Describe the outer surface of the occipital bone. 6. Describe the palate bone. 7. Mention the points of interest on the inner surface of the su-

perior maxillary bone. 8. Describe the capsular ligament. 9. Give the origin, insertion and nerve supply of the levator labii superioris muscle. 10. Describe the sterno-mastoid muscle. 11. Describe the right coronary muscle. 12. Describe the internal maxillary artery. 13. What is the circle of Willis? 14. Describe the internal pterygoid nerve. 15. Describe the lingual nerve.

Chemistry and Metallurgy.

1. Name, giving formula in each case, three acids used in dentistry. Mention the specific use of each. 2. Differentiate chemical symbol and chemical formula. Give three examples of each. 3. Mention the principal changes in air during respiration. 4. Indicate the source of three of the following compounds: Lactic acid, acetic acid, oxolic acid, malic acid, tartaric acid, tannic acid. 5. Complete the following equations, writing the name of each compound:

$$No\ Cl + Ag\ No_3 =$$
$$2\ NoOH + Co_2 =$$

6. Describe a process of purifying sulfuric ether. Give the uses of sulfuric ether. 7. Define allotropism and give two examples. 8. Give the name and symbol of each of the halogens. 9. Describe a process by which most of the metals may be reduced from their oxides. 10. Write a formula for an 18 carat gold solder. 11. Write the chemical names of each of the following:

$$As_2 O_3,\ Su\ Cl_2,\ Zu\ Co_3,\ Fe\ Sc_4,\ KHCo_3$$

12. Name two reagents used in precipitating gold from its solutions. 13. Describe a process of etching on glass or porcelain. 14. What elements enter into the composition of all alkaloids. 15. Describe the chemical action when (1) iron rusts, (2) wood burns, (3) silver is tarnished by coal gas.

Oral Surgery and Pathology.

1. Give the etiology, diagnosis and treatment of phosphorous necrosis. 2. Give the etiology and the treatment of fracture of the inferior maxilla. 3. Name the varieties of dislocation. 4. Define inflammation. Give the symptoms of inflammation. 5. Give the etiology of ranula. Describe the treatment of ranula. 6. Describe the methods of administering nitrous oxide, mentioning the necessary precautions to be taken. 8. Describe the formation

of pus. 9. Give the treatment of acute synovitis. 10. Give the etiology and the treatment of epithelioma of the lip. 11. Describe the surgical proceedings for the extraction of an impacted wisdom tooth. 12. Describe a method of removing a foreign body from the pharynx without surgical operation. 13. Describe the formation of cicatricial tissue. 14. Give the etiology and the treatment of dropsy of the antrum. 15. State why an alveolar abscess may cause suppurative inflammation of the maxillary sinus.

Operative Dentistry.

1. Diagnose exostosis and specify the operations and the treatment necessary for its relief. 2. What causes thermal shock in teeth recently filled? Give preventive treatment. 3. Give the etiology of caries. Describe the varieties of caries and mention the operations necessary for the preservation of the teeth. 4. Diagnose congested pulp and give treatment. Describe the operation required. 5. Diagnose pulp stone and describe the operation and the treatment necessary. 6. Describe a method of keeping burs in a sterile condition and sharpened, ready for use. 7. Mention the form of tin that is most durable for fillings in teeth and give the technic of its use. 8. Describe the plugger points used for introducing and condensing a combination filling of noncohesive and cohesive gold. 9. Explain the surgical and mechanical uses of electricity in dentistry. 10. Differentiate dental abrasion and dental erosion. Give the treatment of abrasion. 11. State the conditions under which combination fillings of amalgam and gold are used. Mention the advantages of such fillings. 12. How may the cusps of broken teeth be restored by the use of gold and phosphate cement in combination? Describe the operation. 13. Describe the different deposits found on tthe teeth. Mention the characteristics of each and give treatment. 14. Describe the manner of preparing gold and platinum for filling cavities in teeth. 15. Give the treatment of pathologic conditions of the gums preparatory to filling teeth.

Prosthetic Dentistry.

1. What preliminary measures are necessary in order to obtain a correct impression of the mouth? 2. What conditions would indicate the selection of long bite thin anterior teeth for an upper denture? 3. Should the upper teeth or the lower teeth of an entire denture be the longer? Why? 4. Which teeth should bear the greatest pressure during the process of mastication? 5. How may porosity be avoided in vulcanizing thick pieces of rub-

ber? 6. Describe the method of attaching the teeth to a platinum plate in continuous gum work before the porcelain is applied. 7. Mention some of the uses in dentistry of fusible alloys. 8. How should a root be prepared for a collar crown? 9. How should a gold cap be adapted in relation to the neck of the tooth and the gum line? 10. Mention three distinct causes of deformities of the hard palate. 11. What is an obturator? 12. With which set of teeth should the prevention of malformation begin? Explain. 13. Mention some of the conditions to be considered in the treatment of irregularity of the teeth. 14. Describe the process of making and adjusting a splint for a lower jaw fracture between the second bicuspid and the first molar. 15. Describe an appliance for securely retaining in place the lower natural incisors after they have been loosened by violence.

Therapeutics and Materia Medica.

1. Mention the advantages and the dangers of the hypodermic administration of medicine. 2. Define the term resolution as used in reference to diseased tissue. 3. Describe nitrate of silver. State the dental uses of nitrate of silver. 4. Describe atropine. State when the use of atropine is indicated and mention its hypodermic dose. 5. Name the antidote for (1) iodine, (2) arsenious acid, (3) carbolic acid. 6. Define astringent, stimulant, anodyne. 7. State why children can bear sedatives better than they bear stimulants in the complications of first dentition. 8. Describe the methods of administering cocaine to produce anesthesia. 9. What effect on blood pressure has (1) ether, (2) chloroform? 10. Mention the contra-indications to ether anesthesia. 11. Define incompatibility of drugs. Give examples. 12. Mention the drugs used in the treatment of syphilitic lesions of the oral cavity. State how they are used. 13. State how the injuries resulting from the local action of arsenious acid should be treated. 14. Name the four parts of a prescription. 15. Write a prescription for pyorrhea alveolaris.

Physiology and Hygiene.

1. Mention the forces that keep the blood in circulation. 2. Name the tissues of the human body. 3. What are (1) villi, (2) valvulae conniventes? 4. Describe the peridental membrane. State the function of the peridental membrane. 5. Give the approximate number of chemical elements found in animal tissues. Name the five most important. 6. Which of the cranial nerves are nerves of special sense? 7. What causes blood to coagulate? Does the blood ever coagulate in the living body? Ex-

plain. 8. Give the physiology of (1) stomach digestion, (2) intestional digestion. 9. State the origin and function of the dental pulp. 10. Differentiate mucous membrane, serous membrane and synovial membrane. State the function of each. 11. Name the varieties of epithelium. State the functions of epithelium. 12. Explain why it is necessary to drink water. 13. What influences the color of the blood in circulation? 14. Name some of the diseases that may be caused by drinking impure water. 15. Mention some of the local and constitutional effects of using tobacco.

Histology.

1. Describe the cells composing the skin. 2. Describe the osteogenetic layer of the periosteum. 3. Describe the amoeboid movements of the white blood corpuscles. 4. What tissues are derived from the mesoderm? 5. Give the microscopic appearance of yellow elastic tissue. 6. Describe the nerve supply of the salivary glands. 7. Describe a nerve fiber. 8. Describe the structure of cancellous bone. 9. Give the microscopic appearance of the lymph node. 10. Name the varieties of cells that cover the mucous membrane. 11. Describe osteoblasts. 12. How do the portal vein and the hepatic artery terminate in the liver? 13. Describe the cells of areolar tissue. 14. Describe odontoblasts. 15. Give a description of the submaxillary gland.

PHILLIPS' MILK OF MAGNESIA

"THE PERFECT ANTACID"

FOR LOCAL OR SYSTEMIC USE

| CARIES | SENSITIVENESS | STOMATITIS |
| EROSION | GINGIVITIS | PYORRHŒA |

Are successfully treated with it. As a mouth wash it neutralizes oral acidity.

PHILLIPS' PHOSPHO-MURIATE OF QUININE,

COMPOUND

TONIC, RECONSTRUCTIVE, AND ANTIPERIODIC

With marked beneficial action upon the nervous system. To be relied upon where a deficiency of the phosphates is evident.

THE
ATE

THE FRATER

Official Organ of The Psi Omega Fraternity.

PUBLISHED BY
THE SUPREME COUNCIL
In November, January, March and May,
AT TIFFIN, OHIO.

SUPREME COUNCIL

Dr. EDW. H. STING,   91 E. Perry St., Tiffin, Ohio.
Dr. J. E. NYCE,   1001 Witherspoon Bldg., Philadelphia, Pa.
Dr. H. E. FRIESELL,   6000 Penn Ave., Pittsburg, Pa.

BUSINESS MANAGER.

Dr. J. E. NYCE,   1001 Witherspoon Bldg., Philadelphia, Pa.

EDITOR-IN-CHIEF.

Dr. EDW. H. STING,   Tiffin, Ohio.

SUBSCRIPTION.

One Dollar per year, payable in advance :: The Frater will be sent to all subscribers until ordered discontinued :: Send all communications to the Editor-in-Chief. :: Exchanges please send one copy to each of the Supreme Councilors.

Entered as second-class matter November 7, 1904, at the Post Office at Tiffin, Ohio.

FRATERNITY DIRECTORY.

Active Chapters.

ALPHA	Baltimore College of Dental Surgery.
BETA	New York College of Dentistry.
GAMMA	Pennsylvania Col. of Dental Surgery, Phila.
DELTA	Tufts Dental College, Boston, Mass.
EPSILON	Western Reserve University, Cleveland, O.
ZETA	University of Pennsylvania, Philadelphia.
ETA	Philadelphia Dental College.
THETA	University of Buffalo, Dental Department.
IOTA	Northwestern University, Chicago, Ill.
KAPPA	Chicago College of Dental Surgery.
LAMBDA	University of Minnesota, Minneapolis.
MU	University of Denver, Denver, Col.
NU	Pittsburg Dental College, Pittsburg, Pa.
XI	Milwaukee, Wis., Med. Col., Dental Dept.
MU DELTA	Harvard University, Dental Department.
OMICRON	Louisville College of Dental Surgery.
PI	Baltimore·Medical College, Dental Dept.
BETA SIGMA	College of Physicians and Surgeons, Dental Department, San Francisco, Cal.
RHO	Ohio Col. of Dental Surgery, Cincinnati.
SIGMA	Medico-Chirurgical College, Philadelphia.
TAU	Atlanta Dental College, Atlanta, Ga.
UPSILON	University of Southern California, Dental Department, Los Angeles.
PHI	University of Maryland, Baltimore.
CHI	North Pacific Dental Col., Portland, Ore.
PSI	College of Dentistry, O. M. U., Columbus.
OMEGA	Indiana Dental College, Indianapolis, Ind.
BETA ALPHA	University of Illinois, Chicago.
BETA GAMMA	George Washington, Uni., Washington, D.C.
BETA DELTA	University of California, San Francisco.
BETA EPSILON	New Orleans College of Dentistry.
BETA ZETA	St. Louis Dental College, St. Louis, Mo.
BETA ETA	Keokuk Dental College, Keokuk, Iowa.
BETA THETA	Georgetown University, Washington, D. C.
GAMMA IOTA	Southern Dental College, Atlanta, Ga.
GAMMA KAPPA	University of Michigan, Ann Arbor.
GAMMA LAMBDA	Col. of Dental and Oral Surg. of New York.
GAMMA MU	University of Iowa, Iowa City.
GAMMA NU	Vanderbilt Uni., Nashville, Tenn.

Alumni Chapters.

New York Alumni Chapter	New York City.
Duquesne Alumni Chapter	Pittsburg, Pa.
Minnesota Alumni Chapter	Minneapolis, Minn.
Chicago Alumni Chapter	Chicago, Ill.
Boston Alumni Chapter	Boston, Mass.
Philadelphia Alumni Chapter	Philadelphia, Pa.
New Orleans Alumni Chapter	New Orleans, La.
Los Angeles Alumni Chapter	Los Angeles, Cal.
Cleveland Alumni Chapter	Cleveland, Ohio.
Sealth Alumni Chapter	Seattle, Wash.
Portsmouth Alumni Chapter	Portsmouth, Ohio.

ALUMNI DIRECTORY.

Ada, O.—
C. W. Brecheisen, Psi, '02.
Aiken, S. C.—
G. A. Milner, Tau, '05.
Allegheny, Pa.—
F. H. Deterding, Nu, '05,
417 Third street.
Reynolds M. Sleppy, Nu, '04,
1915 Beaver avenue.
Altoona, Pa.—
Herbert R. Wehrle, Nu, '03,
Altoona Trust Bldg.
Arkadelphia, Ark.—
J. C. Settles, Omicron, '04.
Augusta, Ga.—
R. H. Calhoun, Tau, '04,
936 Broad street.
Brooklyn, N. Y.—
Ellison Hillyer, Beta, '93,
472 Greene avenue.
Winthrop W. Thompson,
Beta, '02,
383 Hancock street.
Horace P. Gould, Beta, '95,
193 Joralemon street.
Warrington G. Lewis,
Beta, '01,
162 Clinton street.
Walter S. Watson, Beta, '02,
270 Halsey street.
Bowling Green, O.—
E. J. Frowine, Psi, '04.
Buffalo, N. Y.—
Wes. M. Backus, Theta, '04,
485 Grant street.
Chihuahua, Mexico.—
M. F. Bauchert, Beta, '96.
Chico, Cal.—
J. R. Young, Beta Delta, '03.
Box 515.
Columbus, O.—
H. M. Semans, Beta, '97,
289 East State street.
Cleveland, O.—
E. E. Belford,
Beta Gamma, '04,
E. 90 Place and Superior avenue.
Delhi, La.—
T. K. McLemore,
Gamma Iota, '06.
Edgefield, S. C.—
Augustus H. Corley, Tau, '04.
Florisant, Mo.—
G. S. Steinmesch,
Beta Zeta, '04.

Fort Gaines, Ga.—
R. H. Saunders, Tau, '05.
Fort Leavenworth, Kan.—
J. D. Millikin, Beta Sigma,
Dental Surgeon, U.S.A.
Fredericksburg, Tex.—
F. Keidel, Alpha, '04.
Gallitzin, Pa.—
J. L. Paul, Alpha, '01.
Gonzales, Tex.—
S. C. Patton, Tau, '03.
Hancock, Mich.—
Ralph W. DeMass,
Beta Gamma, '05,
Funkey Block.
Hull, Ill.—
L. H. Wolfe, Beta Eta, '05.
Iager, W. Va.—
G. E. Dennis, Phi, '05.
Ithaca, N. Y.—
A. M. MacGachen,
Theta, '03,
218 East State street.
Johnsonburg, Pa.—
H. C. Coleman, Nu, '03.
Johnstown, Pa.—
Owen Morgan, Alpha, '95.
Kaufman, Tex.—
Henry Hoffer, Alpha, '95.
Lafayette, Ind.—
A. R. Ross, Gamma, '03.
Lewistown, Pa.—
Curtis H. Marsh,
Gamma, '06.
14- E. Market street.
Liberty, N. Y.—
W. A. Buckley, Beta, '00.
Logansport, Ind.—
H. G. Stalnaker, Omega, '03.
Los Angeles, Cal.—
J. F. Curran, Kappa, '01,
Suite 615,
Auditorium Bldg.
C. C. Jarvis, Upsilon, '04,
302 Severance Bldg.
S. W. Clapp, Upsilon, '06,
24 Muskegon Bldg.
Malone, N. Y.—
R. N. Porter, Gamma, '01.
Manila, P. I.—
O. M. Sorber, Nu, '97,
Dental Surgeon, U. S. A.
Mansfield, La.—
G. J. Griffiths, Tau, '03.

McKeesport, Pa.—
  W. D. Fawcett, Nu, '99,
    508½ Fifth avenue.
Milwaukee, Wis.—
  E. J. Schlief, Xi, '97,
    417 Wells Bldg.
  J. E. Callaway, Xi, '06,
    Suite 306, Stumpf and Langhoff Bldg.
Morganfield, Ky.—
  W. S. Green, Omicron,' 04.
New York City.—
  A. S. Walker, Beta. '97,
    295 Central Park, West.
  E. W. Burckhardt, Beta,'04,
    Van Corlear Place, Kingsbridge.
  S. W. Van Saun, Beta, '00,
    Broadway and 74th St. The Ansonia.
New Kensington, Pa.—
  A. J. Rose, Rho, '03,
    Logan Trust Bldg.
New Orleans, La.—
  A. J. Cohn, Alpha, '99,
    703 Morris Bldg.
  Leon Barnett, Beta Epsilon, '05,
    703 Macheca Bldg.
  Rene Esnard, Beta Epsilon, '05,
    612 Macheca Bldg.
Norristown, Pa.—
  D. H. Wetzel, Zeta, '02.
Oakland, Cal.—
  C. H. Merritt, Alpha, '98,
    308-9 Union Savings Bank Bldg.
Oroville, Cal.—
  L. H. Marks, B. Sigma, '04.
Paso Robles, Cal.—
  W. G. Gates, Kappa, '05.
Paterson, N. J.—
  A. Dewitt Payne, Beta, '99,
    160 Broadway.
Pikesville, Ky.—
  J. M. Williams, Rho, '05.
Pittsburg, Pa.—
  W. Emmory Ferree, Alpha, '00, 7138 Hamilton ave., East End.
  C. L. McChesney, Nu, '99,
    98 Washington avenue.
  H. E. Friesell, Gamma, '95,
    6000 Penn avenue.
Philadelphia, Pa.—
  A. F. Goddard, Gamma, '01,
    15th and Chestnut Sts., 1302 Pennsylvania Bldg.
  A. P. Lee, Zeta, '00,
    3403 Chestnut street.
  J. E. Nyce, Gamma, '02,
    1001 Witherspoon Bldg.
Port Clinton, O.—
  John G. Yingling, Alpha,'97.

Roby, Tex.—
  J. N. Platt, Pi, '02.
Rowland, N. C.—
  C. H. Lennan, Tau, '03.
San Francisco, Cal.—
  C. W. Knowles, M.D., D.D.S., Beta Sigma, '99,
    2417 Washington St.
  Thos. R. Morffew, Beta Sigma, Examiner Bldg.
Seattle, Wash.—
  Geo. T. Williams, Nu, '04,
    Snoqualmie Hotel.
  F. W. Hergert, Chi, '03,
    651 Colman Block.
  C. P. Poston, Chi,
    218 Lumber Exchange.
Springfield, Mass.—
  H. Everton Hosley, Gamma, '95,
    Phoenix Bldg.
St. Joseph, Ill.—
  H. E. Davis, Rho, '03.
St. Louis, Mo.—
  H. J. Braun, Beta Zeta, '04,
    2850 St. Louis avenue.
  H. V. Pfaff, Iota, '99,
    2217 St. Louis avenue.
Tiffin, O.—
  W. H. Holtz, Rho, '03.
  E. H. Sting, Alpha, '95.
  E. C. West, Psi, '02.
Topsham, Maine.—
  H. Q. Mariner, Sigma, '05.
Tuscaloosa, Ala.—
  H. Clay Hassell, Omicron, '98.
Upland, Ind.—
  J. A. Loughry, Psi, '04.
Union, S. C.—
  Jas. M. Wallace, Phi, '04.
Vinton, Iowa.—
  B. F. Schwartz, Iota, '04.
Washington, D. C.—
  Shirley W. Bowles, Eta,'98,
    1315 New York avenue.
  C. L. Constantini, Beta Gamma, '03,
    814 14th St., N. W.
Washington, Pa.—
  Howard R. Smith, Nu, '03,
    17 West Chestnut street.
Waynesboro, Miss.—
  C. H. Gray, Tau, '04.
Winchester, Ky.—
  George S. Brooks, Rho, '02.
Westfield, N. J.—
  Theo. R. Harvey, Gamma, '94, 245 Broad street.
Williamson, W. Va.—
  Wm. S. Rosenheim, Pi, '05.
Wellsburg, W. Va.—
  K. C. Brashear, Psi, '02,

EPSILON 1906-1907.

THE FRATER.

Vol. 6.　　　　March, 1907.　　　　No. 3.

EVOLUTION.

James E. E. Morrison, Rho, '05

Evolution, as the world understands it, embraces everything and everybody; the atom and the mass; the individual and the aggregate. It includes the past, it is the present, and reaches into the future. The general mythological idea of evolution was that everything sprang from chaos. The earth was the first to issue, then sprang up plant life; later man came to dwell on this fair earth, and, as time elapsed, the highest type of humanity was created, namely, the Dentist.

Similar crude conditions among various peoples naturally produce similar crude products. Later, similarly advanced conditions produce similarly advanced philosophic ideas, or an orderly form of evolution. Thus we find, out of the crude, prehistoric tooth carpenter, the cultured, scientific, evolutionized dentist. As differentiations in the physical realm of nature have led from the simple to the complex, so successive changes have led from the simple form of dentistry, viz: the removal of the teeth and their replacement by artificial means, up to a specialized profession, ranking among the first and best. A profession teaching the prevention and preservation rather than the extermination.

The growth, development, progress and evolution of the dental profession depends largely on the growth, development, progress and evolution of those persons who make it their life study. The history of most nations has been one of progression. There has been a constant struggle to surmount base conditions, to ameliorate physical hardships, to clear mental obstructions, to conquer ignorance, to learn, to think and to do. Thus, on individuals, who are not too weak or indifferent to be overcome by the great marching forces of time, depend the degree of progress of our profession. Contributing to the aggregate, as drops contribute to the ocean, as fleeting April showers help to swell Spring freshets, as single rain storms help to form floods whose inundations sweep away entire cities, our small contributions improve or dethrone the high standard already reached by Dental Surgery

Progress, nothing but progress, is the cry of every up-to-date dentist. Specialization is at hand and that member of the profession, who formerly found time to practice dentistry in its entirety, now devotes himself to the enthronement of porcelain; to the etiology of pyorrhea; to the pathological effect of saliva; to orthodontia technology; to prosthesis; to oral surgery. All point to a larger conception of life on the part of the dentist, whereby he may contribute his share to a more elevated tone and vitalizing force in dentistry, and thereby shape its life and destiny co-equal or above that of other liberal professions.

It is argued in these strenuous times that the requisite of success is concentration of thought and energy in one direction, yet the man of force and influence achieves distinction as much by his broader culture as by his skill in technology. It is the privilege of the dentist, the ambitious dentist who strives to lofty ideals, to go outside of his text books and find a most helpful adjunct to his daily work by familiarizing himself with the arts—that phase of art as we see it illustrated upon the canvas, in sculpture, in architecture and music. A knowledge in blending of proper colors would prove of immense value to those who would excel in porcelain work and certain features of dental prosthesis. As for architecture, many of its cardinal principles confront us daily. In music, the orthodontist improves or destroys a voice according to his degree of proficiency.

How often in the past have we found dentists of great mechanical skill and ability, who had no influence and commanded little respect in the community because of lack of education. It is the strong, cultured, evolutionized dentist of to-day who has influenced the world for good, and has raised the standing of our profession in the eyes of the world.

It is the educated dentist, the man of the greater mental training, who has raised the artisan or mechanically skilled workman to the lofty pinnacle now occupied by the Doctor of Dental Surgery.

The bells are proclaiming the birth of a new era, they are full of new tones, clearer and more joyful than ever before. The past has added greatly to the degree of progress. Wonders have been wrought, and to what extent these wonders, and the wonders to come will be developed, depend largely on the evolutionized dentist.

"The heights of great men reached and kept,
 Were not attained by sudden flight,
But they, while their companions slept,
 Were toiling upward in the night."

PERSONAL EXPERIENCES IN KINGSTON.

Leicester D. Samuel, Phi, '06·

A week or two before the terrible earthquake the weather had been exceptionally cool for that part of the world, and then became normal again and was absolutely ideal. Apart from a depressing heat, which I must admit I took no notice of, there was really nothing to indicate that this awful calamity was at hand.

On the morning of January 14, I had before me the prospects of a successful future, having my appointment book full for the balance of the week and a neat sum due for services rendered; but natural forces intervened, and, by Monday afternoon three of my patients were dead. Others were ruined financially, since their places of business were destroyed and the chances of receiving insurance money were very slim, as many companies refused point blank to pay insurance, some were willing to pay one-third of the losses, while the rest sent down an inspector to determine the extent of the losses.

On that memorable Monday afternoon at two o'clock my patient arrived, accompanied by her aunt who came to have her mouth examined; I found quite a large amount of work necessary and made an appointment for the following Monday. The aunt then left.

I made a gold filling for the niece, had placed the mallet and points aside and was making preparations to polish, when that well known shake commenced in the usual gentle manner. The young lady looked up at me and exclaimed, "Oh, an earthquake!" "Yes!" I said, "I wish it would stop now." It was getting worse and I wanted to get her out of the chair so that we might get out of the building, but the quake was at its highest, and, try as hard as I might, I could not take my foot from the floor to alter the position of the chair. The poor girl had covered her face with her hands and was evidently paralyzed with fright and could not move.

The noise was like the roar of artillery, the flooring underneath my feet felt as though it was lifting and shifting; I do not believe I could have walked out of the place without falling. I did not try to do that, however. I saw my cabinet fall over, the wall on my left cracked from corner to corner, the wall in front appeared as though it was being jerked in opposite directions, the window in front of me sprung loose, rocked, and fell into the garden below, then the wall came crashing down and it seemed to me that the earthquake then ceased. With the falling of the walls, complete darkness enveloped us and it was almost impossible to grope my way around. I extricated my patient, who seemed quite dazed and inclined to give way, but I was able to persuade her that the quake had ceased and that danger was over. While conducting my patient out of the office, I was met by my brother who had just run up, hatless and out of breath, to know how I had suffered. He then told me that my father was unhurt and together they were going home. Their destinations being in the same direction as that of my patient, she accompanied them. Then remembering the three ladies on the second floor, from whom I rented my rooms, I rushed to their assistance. No steps were to be seen. It was like climbing a pile of bricks. The upstairs was a chaos of fallen furniture, clothes from the presses, etc. One lady was pinned down by a heavy press but with much effort I managed to release her. I saved what I could for them in the shape of money and valuables, and advised them to get out of the house as soon as they could and to keep out of it.

My father and brother having left for home and knowing that they would report me safe, I ran into the street bound for my aunt's house to see how they had fared there. I was more than surprised to see the streets as I found them on the way. The atmosphere was like a dense fog from the dust; people were running frantically up the street, shouting, crying, praying, and several bus loads of injured people passed me; people, half covered with bricks, were lying in the streets, begging for assistance. I could not stop to help them until I had ascertained whether my own people were in a similar position and in need of the little help which I could render. On my way across the park, I noticed that the steeple of the Parish church had tilted and that the four clocks had stopped at the hour of the earthquake; on the opposite side of the park, fire was raging and moving in the direction of the hospital. I turned up Orange street to where my aunt resided. The house was in a similar condition as that of my office. I entered over fallen walls, but found no occupants; I began to fear that they had been killed and covered by the bricks; but, on going to the lawn, I found them all huddled together in the far corner. Three of her boys, my aunt informed me, had not yet arrived. They were in the city; I could give her no information regarding them; I then left her to go home and ascertain the condition of affairs there.

I cannot describe the condition of the streets, each one seemed to be worse than the other. About half way home, I saw one of my sisters in a bus. She was in an awful state of fright and, seeing me, jumped out while the bus was yet moving, to ascertain if I had seen father. He is alive, I assured her, and I was greatly relieved to learn from her that others at home were alive, though slightly injured. I then had time to look at her; she was half dressed and without shoes; the bus had left us and I was too fatigued from my long journey to carry her. I was just about to remove my shoes and give them to her, when I saw a phaeton, belonging to Mr. Mangus, out next door neighbor, drive up with only the coachman in it.

He took us home where we found only one missing, my father's brother. I volunteered to go back and look for him. I shall never forget that afternoon and the South Camp Road. The ladies, in the condition in which they had been forced out of their beautiful homes, crying pitifully to me to look for their husbands, fathers or brothers. My best friends, maddened by their grief and anxiety, frantically pacing the street. I ran as fast as my tired legs would allow and on the way learned that my uncle lay covered with bricks, in front of his store, and that he could get no one to assist him. The fire was now raging and the noise had increased rather than abated. My run had become a hobble. On arriving at the store, I saw a body lying prostrate with a hat drawn over the face. I lifted it hurriedly and saw the face of a friend, and not my uncle. I was informed that my uncle had been sent to a hospital. Then I was accosted by a young lady, my patient's sister, who implored me to help her find her husband. I learned from her that her aunt, Mrs. John D. Eisser, with whom earlier in the afternoon I had made the appointment, had been killed by a falling wall at her home. We were just about to go in search of her husband when we were informed by a friend that he had seen him alive. I then went to the hospital, and, when not a hundred yards away from the gate, I met another uncle and my brother coming out; they told me that uncle had just died. This was a sad blow, as he was a second father to us and our grief can better be imagined than described. I soon, however, realized the fact that there was work to be done, so we set to work and rendered such assistance as we could.

My remaining uncle and myself then secured a van, which was fortunately at our neighbor's place, it being one of the delivery vans belonging to his firm, and that night we brought the body of my uncle and placed it in the coach house. As may be imagined no one slept that night. At about midnight, I heard a great uproar in the street and saw people with bundles running and limping, as fast as they could up the street, shouting "move up, get to the mountains, the wave is coming." I managed to gather that a great tidal wave was expected and all were advised to move up as far as possible; I confided this bit of intelligence to my uncle, and, in the state of mind that we were in, it was agreed that it would be better if the wave cleared us all off together, so we remained, sitting, waiting, sorrowing; our homes ruined, our future darkened. It was an awful night. On an average of every two hours we felt an earthquake and each one added to the terror and horror of the disaster. A constant wail was heard from the race course, where thousands had assembled, and where, up to the present, thousands still remain, homeless and grief stricken.

Day eventually dawned. Camp Road now assumed a different aspect. Instead of anxious, hopeful inquiries, my poor grief stricken friends' faces told the tale that I had already guessed.

Thanks to the beautiful weather that followed, we were able to live in the open without any covering, every one being too scared to enter a house. As time passed, however, we gathered sufficient courage to occupy the stables and coach house, which, being made of wood, survived the shocks. Then came the news that two American battle ships had arrived with food and tents, and it seemed to me, very soon after came the report that the governor had refused their kind assistance. The feeling of the people in Kingston toward Sir Alexander Swettenham was one of hatred and disgust for his action, and he was made to know it through every possible means.

Fortunately for us the stock of several grocery stores was saved, this afforded us food until help arrived.

When I left, two weeks after the earthquake, the conditions were very little improved and I am afraid it will be a long time before anyone will risk putting up a building of any size. For my part I hope never to return. I hope to make Baltimore my home and maybe some day I will have an office of my own again; at present I must try and secure a position whereby I can obtain the necessities for making a fresh start.

Whatever I may be, or whatever I may do, I will ever carry in memory the scenes caused by this terrible earthquake which caused so much damage, woe, and loss of life in the space of half a minute.

"TOAST FOR CRYSTAL ANNIVERSARY."

Composed by Stone, Smedley, and Dillon, of Zeta.

Just fifteen years ago this hour to-night
   Was born a brotherhood of love and right,
To which the name Psi Omega was given;
   A name deep in our hearts with love engraven.

Thy works we cannot view but with just pride,
   And marvel at thy progress with such giant stride;
Thy spirit fosters in each loyal heart
   Ideals, which, with labor, success impart.

To-night throughout the land each voice is raised
   Extolling thy virtues, resounding thy praise,
Pledging with truth, to be ever faithful,
   And for the honor, to be ever grateful.

May never fall the standard thou hast sought;
   May thousands more partake the bounty brought;
May success with thee form a golden link,
   That such may ever be, dear brothers, drink.

TO PSI OMEGA.

Anonymous B. Young.

"We've met together, boys, tonight,
  To celebrate with mirth,
The Fifteenth Anniversary
  Of Psi Omega's birth.
Aye, glad we are this feast to share
  With brothers old and new;
And to our loved fraternity
  May each heart e'er prove true.

Then to the winds for these few hours
  We'll cares and troubles fling;
From East to West, from North to South,
  Hear the loud echoes ring.
Hold high our glorious standard, boys,
  That future years may know
The meaning of our chosen name—
  'P——— O———.'

All honor to our founders, who
  In eighteen ninety-two,
Gave to the undergraduate
  His 'fourteen ninety-two.'
All honor to our Councilors three,
  Who, loyal, brave and true,
Have piloted our ships of state,
  Alpha to Gamma Nu.

Years flit away, and silver gray
  Shall soon our brows adorn,
But the memory of this glad night
  Shall ne'er from us be torn.
So let us all our goblets raise,
  All filled from Nature's brew,
While boundless joys for P. O. boys
  Shall be our toast for you."

Active Chapters.

BETA—NEW YORK COLLEGE OF DENTISTRY.

George R. Christian, Editor.

With the echo of merry sounds still in our ears, we submit this little editorial as an emblem of salutation to all brothers of Psi Omega.

On the evening of February 15, in one of the spacious banquet halls of the Hotel Manhattan, the New York Alumni Chapter, Gamma Lambda, and Beta held their Annual Banquet. It was even a more elaborate affair than the dinner of the past year.

The worthy Dr. William Jarvie was the guest of honor. He with Dr. A. L. Northrop, Dr. W. W. Walker, Dr. S. G. Perry, Dr. J. Bond Littig, Dr. A. R. Starr, Dr. C. A. Meeker, Dr. W. H. Haskin, and Dr. Ellison Hillyer occupied chairs at the main table which was the center of attraction during the evening. From this region issued the following toasts:

"Fraternity" .... Dr. A. L. Northrop.
"With and Without Psi Omega" ...... Dr. Wm. Jarvie.
"Wisdom and Wit" .... Dr. W. W. Walker.

These were interspersed with the musical selections of an able orchestra and a vocal piece "Mona," sung by Brother Konecke which was encored by another piece. Both were rendered perfectly. Brother Griesmer also favored us, by changing the classic to "rag-time." Even the piano seemed pleased.

The menu which was excellently served was as follows:

Huitres
Creme de Tomatoes
Celerie   Olives   Radis
Bass Saute a la Meuniere
Concombres   Pomme de Terre Hollandaise
Fillet Mignon a la Cheron

Choux de Bruxelles
Sorbet au Kirsch
Pullet Grille sur Toast
Salade de Lettue
Biscuit Tortoni
Gateaux Assortis

Fromage   Mocco
Cigars   Cigarettes

The souvenirs were champagne glasses with the fraternity emblem engraved upon them. The cigar bands and cigarettes were also stamped with the Psi Omega shield, in colors. The event was so well planned that not a hitch occurred, which was most pleasing; we heartily thank the committee which consisted of Brothers Griesmer, Jurka, and Peters of Beta; Curtis, Pierce, and Street of Gamma Lambda, and Bryer, Edwards, and Hillyer of N. Y. Alumni. Dr. E. Hillyer is to be especially congratulated upon the success of the affair and we especially thank him for the devotion of his time, efforts, and ability to making the event such a success.

There was evidently some fascination in the basement of the hotel, for, during the short intervals of relaxation, some of the boys managed with more or less difficulty to descend the many marble stairs in search, it seemed, of the fountain of youth.

A toast was drunk to Brother Gutelius, of Beta, who is now on his way to China to practice. He was graduated last year and sacrificed a most promising opportunity here to ply his profession in the land of rice and laundrymen. We wish him all success and shall often recall the able services rendered by him to Psi Omega in the office of Grand Master of Beta.

Beta sends best wishes to the Supreme Council and to all Psi Omegas.

GAMMA—PENNSYLVANIA COLLEGE OF DENTAL SURGERY.

J. J. Durkin, Editor.

Gamma sends best wishes to the Supreme Council, and to all sister chapters.

Conditions at Gamma are most flourishing and better than ever.

Psi Omega came out on top, as usual, in the senior class election, electing her men at will. The following brothers were honored by their classmates: Geo. F. Bonnick, president; W. P. Luffbary, vice president; J. J. Durkin, secretary, and F. D. Dolan, poet. The executive committee: J. H. Dougherty, chairman; J. F. Foltz, and Geo. P. McCall. Record committee: A. B. Carey, chairman; J. J. Connally, and A. M. Berger. Class day committee: Franklin Ellis, Frank S. Dwyer, and M. C. Farrell.

Gamma wishes to announce that Psi Omega's Crystal Anniversary was fittingly celebrated in our fraternity house, 818 Spruce street, on the 15th of February. A very bountiful feast was placed before Gamma's members. At the strike of eleven our old friend and teacher, Dr. Kreithman, acting as toastmaster, ordered a standing toast to Psi Omega which was responded to with a will. Toasts were responded to by our Grand Master, G. F. Bonnick, and by recently initiated members. It was with regret that we observed the approach of an early morning hour, which forced the merry-makers to cease.

At our regular weekly meeting of the 19th of February, we had the great pleasure of having with us Brother Nyce, of the Supreme Council.

DELTA—TUFTS DENTAL COLLEGE.

C. P. Haven, Editor.

The Crystal Anniversary of Psi Omega was celebrated by Delta with a banquet at the Hotel Clarendon, at which every member was called upon to "make a noise like an orator" and oratorical indeed were the noises made. Chief Inquisitor Percy N. Nordgren delivered the address of the evening and spoke in part as follows:

"At this our Crystal Anniversary celebration, let us carefully consider what our fraternity is and what it stands for. We all know that Psi Omega is the largest and best dental frat in the world, that her growth has been phenomenal; starting with one lone chapter in the Baltimore College of Dental Surgery in 1892, we now have in 1907 fifty active and alumni chapters. Because of what has been accomplished for her members and for the profession in those fifteen years, are we not justified in feeling proud to-night that we have the honor of being Psi Omegas?

"So, from to-night on, fellows, let us work for our individual interests but also let us continue our efforts for the welfare of dear old Psi Omega. Let our greatest aims be to cultivate the social qualities of our members and to render assistance to a brother whenever it is possible for us to do so.

"To-night we unite in hailing the spotless white and the friendly blue and pledge in our brotherhood to each other to be true, so that when the toil, the joys of our college days are gone we will ever hold in fond memory the pleasures and associations of Delta. Let us raise our glasses and drink to the welfare and prosperity of our dear old frat—To Psi Omega."

Delta introduces to the fraternity three new members, namely:

Armond Dyon, ... N. Attleboro, Mass.
Frank Stalker .... Holyoke, Mass.
Mark Lishler .... Boston, Mass.

The following resolutions were adopted by the chapter, Delta having recently lost one of her faithful members:

Whereas, Divine Providence has seen fit to remove from our midst our beloved brother and fellow-member, Arthur Stanley Lowe, be it hereby

Resolved, That we, his brothers in Psi Omega, have lost a worthy member and a faithful friend.

Resolved, That with all subservience to the will of our Creator, we none the less mourn the great loss of our friend and brother and extend to his family our heartfelt sympathy and condolence.

Resolved, That a copy of these resolutions be sent to the family of our deceased brother, that they be recorded in the minutes of this chapter, and be published in The Frater.

Henry F. Brackett, Jr., G. M.
R. E. Channing, Sec.

EPSILON—WESTERN RESERVE UNIVERSITY.

C. C. Rogers, Editor.

Epsilon sends greetings to all Psi Omegas and congratulations on the Fifteenth Anniversary of our organization. We celebrated the event in a manner befitting the occasion. At ten o'clock we gathered in the dining room of the Baldwin hotel, there being present thirty-three active and alumni members.

The affair was opened by Toastmaster Frost. Toasts were responded to by Brothers Brown, Belford, McLernon, Rogers, Pettibone, Friedman, Mitchell, Pheneger, Reid, and Smith.

Excellent and bountiful refreshments were served, which with the delightful and pointed remarks of the above mentioned brothers, put us in good spirits both mentally and physically.

We take pleasure in announcing the marriage of Brother E. E. Belford, our Professor of Prosthetic Dentistry. Epsilon extends to his bride and himself her heartiest congratulations and best wishes for a long and happy wedded life.

ZETA—UNIVERSITY OF PENNSYLVANIA.

S. F. Williams, Editor.

On February 15, Zeta held a memorial supper in the chapter house in honor of the Crystal Anniversary of the fraternity. We had a very enjoyable evening listening to the many remarks of different brothers. At exactly eleven, p. m., the chapter rose in unison and drank to the toast selected for the evening. A great deal of credit is due Brothers Stowe, Dillon and Smedley for the beautiful, fitting toast, which they composed for the occasion. The chapter decided to have the toast engraved on a panel, so that it could be kept and handed down from year to year in memory of the Fifteenth Anniversary.

Zeta takes pleasure in announcing that Brothers Filbert and Downdes were elected editor-in-chief, and assistant business manager, respectively, of the 1907 Dental Record. As we have only ten senior members in a class of ninety-eight, and as the other two fraternities combined against us in election, this goes to show the popularity and grade of Psi Omega men.

We are enjoying a very prosperous year and sincerely hope that all sister chapters are having the best of success. We extend to all Psi Omegas our most heartfelt greetings.

ETA—PHILADELPHIA DENTAL COLLEGE.

Lewis B. Duffield, Editor.

The beginning of 1907 has indeed marked an epoch in our chapter, for never have we been so progressive as at the present time.

We take great delight in announcing the dedication of our new assembly room on Friday evening, February 15, '07, at which time the Fifteenth Anniversary of our fraternity was also celebrated. The evening was spent in a most enjoyable manner. Grand Master Casey gave us a brief history of Eta from her infancy to the present time, after which the brothers were entertained with instrumental and vocal selections, and, at a late hour a luncheon was served, of which all the members partook actively.

One of our biggest events of the season took place on Thursday evening, February 21, at the Continental Hotel, the occasion being our Annual Banquet. This banquet was the most successful which we have ever had. All present were full of life and vim, especially toward the finish.

The banquet was opened with an address by Toastmaster Casey, after which we were addressed by the following alumni brothers:

Dr. Dudley Guilford .... "The Profession."
Dr. C. F. Wilbur .... "The Alumni."
Dr. S. W. Williams .... "Past Recollections."
Dr. Thos. C. Stellwagen .... "Our Instructors."

The following menu was served:

Canape au Salpicon	Cocktail
Oysters, Migonette	Sauterne
Mock Turtle	
Celery	Olives farcie
Pattie of Sweetbreads	
Fillet de Boeuf, aux Champignons	
Browned Suet Potatoes	Brussels Sprouts
Psi Omega Punch	Cigarettes
Roast Turkey	Cranberry Sauce
Mashed Potatoes	Asparagus on Toast
Waldorf Salad	Claret
New England Plum Pudding	Roquefort Cheese
Cafe Noir	Cigars

Eta takes pleasure in introducing the following brothers who were initiated into the bonds of brotherly love at the last initiation: T. L. Wilcox, '09; E. Cunningham, '09; B. Shearer, '09; T. C. Joseph, '09, and H. F. Sommers, '09.

THETA—UNIVERSITY OF BUFFALO.

H. E. Marshall, G. M., Editor.

Theta celebrated the Crystal Anniversary of Psi Omega with a banquet at the Mansion House. Theta was joined by the alumni members on this occasion and a most enjoyable evening was passed. Brother Backus, P. G. M., acted as toastmaster. Every member responded with a toast, but the cream of the bunch was Brother Jellie's "When I Was Run Over by the Salvation Army Wagon." We marvel at his being alive to tell the tale.

At promptly eleven o'clock all arose and drank a toast to the future progress of Psi Omega.

Among the various topics discussed on this occasion was the formation of an Alumni Chapter. The project was heartily endorsed by all alumni members present, and we are looking forward to the foundation of the new chapter with pleasure.

On the whole this was one of the most enjoyable evenings Theta's members have had, bringing together as it did the active and alumni members.

IOTA—NORTHWESTERN UNIVERSITY.

C. S. Savage, Editor.

Iota is, as ever, actively engaged in the forward movement for the interest and welfare of the chapter and the fraternity. For the past two months the boys have been very busy, some of them dissecting, while others have been plugging gold and placing water-tight amalgam fillings for the "points."

We have spent some good times at the house during the past month, and the subject of maintaining the frat house is one which is discussed with much favor.

On February 15, the boys were very happy to celebrate the Fifteenth Anniversary of this splendid fraternity of ours, and, I am pleased to report, Iotas got right in line and were able to drink a toast to Psi Omega at sharp ten o'clock on Friday evening at a banquet in honor of the occasion. The entertainment committee selected the Saratoga Hotel, where a choice banquet hall was placed at our disposal. We counted twenty-two strong and were sorry that the rest of the boys could not be with us. Brother Bill Kennedy was chosen toastmaster and, at a few minutes to ten, with a few well chosen remarks, proposed the toast "Godspeed Psi Omega and all Psi Omegas." All hands gave thanks to the committee, composed of Brothers Wehrheim, Heap and Linne for the manner in which they had arranged for the occasion. The spread was a good one and everyone was in the best of humor. "Mark" Myles was the "Village cut up" and is thinking of doing a vaudeville stunt in the near future. Paul Fridd acted as assistant and was there with "bills." Tom Shuttleworth told a few good stories which were applauded.

Roy Pfouts proposed a pretty toast. "Babe Rich" and Allender told us how it felt to be at a P. O. banquet. Grand Master Power proposed a toast to the ladies. Linne told a story which reminded "Mark" of a coon story he once heard, so we had a round of stories. Roy Heap, Johnnie Wehrheim and Al. Linne told us of the troubles of an entertainment committeeman. Junior Master Beck made a good talk in which he expressed the regret of the juniors and freshmen in losing so many good seniors at graduation time. "Tom" Thompson and Guy Stirling told a few good yarns. Desmond was introduced as the ladies' man and told a story. "Dorsey" Brown, "Jake" Wipp and "Tom" Merchant made appropriate talks. "Bobbie" Reed, Walter Moore and Roscoe Stout all were there with a talk and stories.

Glee club members sang appropriate songs and Brother Stout led in yells. At midnight a toast was proposed to our foreign brothers; after which all sang "Auld Lang Syne" and voted the occasion the most enjoyable of the year.

Iota takes great pride and pleasure in presenting to the fraternity two new brothers: Arthur Nelson Wilen and Charles Allen McLean.

KAPPA—CHICAGO COLLEGE OF DENTAL SURGERY.

E. L. Henderson, Editor.

Kappa extends her best wishes to all sister chapters.

The evening of February 15 found us sitting down to a sumptuous banquet at the Hotel Bismark to celebrate the Crystal Anniversary of our dear frat. Promptly at 10 p. m. Grand Master Hooker proposed a standing toast to Psi Omega which was drunk with a will; a moment later the boys broke loose in cheers for Psi Omega and Kappa chapter.

MU—UNIVERSITY OF DENVER.

I. R. Bertram, Editor.

Some of our sister chapters are, perhaps, beginning to think that Mu chapter has fallen by the wayside, but, after our sorrows have in a way been laid aside, we are again working for the good of Psi Omega. On account of the sickness and death of our Editor, Brother McKee, we did not have an editorial in the January Frater. We are indeed sorry to state that two of our members of the senior class, Brothers McKee and Montgomery, each of whom not only stood high as a fraternity man but as students, have passed out of our ranks.

Gone from our ranks are they,
  Gone from this world of strife,
Our brothers not dead, but away,
  Living a happier life.

And while we miss them here,
  We are hoping to meet them up there,
Called by our parents, so dear,
  Where joy shall take place of despair

Mu held a banquet at the Savoy Hotel, February 15, celebrating the Fifteenth Anniversary of Psi Omega. It was an evening that will long be remembered in times to come. Before the banquet we had the pleasure of taking into our ranks Dr. Edward F. Dean, Professor of Anatomy in the Dental and Medical Department of Denver University. Dr. Dean is a man of high standing with his fellow practitioners and we are sure that he will make a true, full-blooded Psi Omega. We also took into our ranks on the same evening, Mr. Bailey, who is a man who stands high as a fraternity man, being a member of the Alpha Tau Omega literary fraternity. He is president of the freshman class and is, without doubt, one of the best men in the class. It is with pleasure that we introduce to all Psi Omegas Brother Edward F. Dean, M. D., of Denver, as an honorary member and Brother William C. Bailey, '09, of Adams Centre, N. Y., as an active member.

After these men were given the obligation we marched into the dining room where an elegant dinner awaited us. Brother Evans, Past J. M., and President of the senior class, acted as toastmaster. He delivered an enthusiastic and pleasing address and at eight o'clock proposed a splendid toast to which we all drank. Inspiring speeches from our alumni and older members followed, until the entire room seemed filled with that fraternal spirit which is characteristic of all Psi Omegas.

We were very glad indeed to have so many of our alumni and honorary members with us, to urge us on with words of encouragement and later as the banquet drew to a close to join with us in a silent toast to those who had left us.

We are also very sorry to state that two of our members, Drs. Brennen and Dolph, graduates of Denver University, on account of their not being ethical practitioners and refusing to become so, were expelled from Psi Omega ranks. These two men are with The Rex Dental Parlors in Denver. We state this in order that these men may never be recognized as Psi Omegas.

However, we are very glad to say that Mu has a bright future, although, until recently, things seemed to go against us. We now have three juniors pledged and one freshman, all of whom have the stamp of Psi Omega.. Besides these, we have two or three other men in view who say there is but one bunch for them, which is indeed very encouraging to us, as the Delta Sigs are working hard and are living up to their local reputation.

Brother Silverstein, M. D., of Denver, lecturer on physiology in Denver University, resigned on account of his practice. We were very sorry to have him leave us as a member of the faculty, but he is still a faithful Psi Omega.

Mu wishes all sister chapters continued success, and assures them that our latch string is always out to all Psi Omegas who may come this way.

NU—PITTSBURG DENTAL COLLEGE.

H. Boisseau, Editor.

January 18 was the gala day in Nu's history for the present year. On that date Nu descended on the quiet village of Millvale and proceeded to administer a physical degree to fifteen of her candidates, each of whom stood the tests to the complete satisfaction of all concerned and proved themselves worthy of membership in our order.

Since that date two new faces are seen in our mystic circle: Brother Rhodes, of the senior class, and Brother Myers, of the freshman class. In this connection it may not be amiss to mention a rather interesting little discussion which come up in regard to admitting members from the senior class this late in the year, as their history in connection with the school is so far advanced. Some claimed that it was hardly fair to the juniors and freshmen and others that if a man is fit to be a fraternity man he is "a man for a' that."

On February 12 we pulled off a dance at the Hotel Henry which will long be remembered in the history of the chapter as one of her most pleasant social events. Every one was "delighted" even though a balance of about $40 was left on the money side of the ledger.

On the night of February 15, Nu and Duquesne Alumni had a joint meeting at the fraternity house, which was very profitably spent. The early part of the evening was devoted to papers and discussions on the part of the alumni and the latter part to toasts to Psi Omega. At eleven o'clock, the hour set for the chapters in this meridian to respond to the toast, Supreme Councilor, Brother Friesell, arose and in a few appropriate and well selected words offered the toast at the end of which all present partook of an especial Psi Omega drink prepared for this occasion.

Nu sends greetings and best wishes to her sister chapters.

OMICRON—LOUISVILLE COLLEGE OF DENTAL SURGERY.

J. L. Selden, Editor.

On Friday evening, February 1, we had a very pleasant little theater party at the Hopkins. The lower boxes were secured for the occasion and, on that night, were occupied by honorary, alumni and active Psi Omegas. After having enjoyed the show, we all gathered at the frat hall, where refreshments and cigars were served. On November 20, Brother A. D. Wilhoit, '06, treasurer of our chapter last year, died from typhoid fever. Brother Wilhoit had located at Broadhead, Ky.

Brother McKee, who joined the fraternity here during his freshman year, and who has since been attending college in Denver, Col., died on January 9, while undergoing an operation for appendicitis. We mourn the loss of these departed brothers, whose prospects seemed so bright.

In honor of our Crystal Anniversary, our class poet, Brother Meredith, gave the following toast at the stipulated time:

Here is to Psi Omega, the grand old frat,
Which never, never wavers but always stands pat.
Our motto: Sincerity, Brotherhood and Trust,
To abide by which, brothers, we must.
May she continue to prosper and rapidly grow
To be the greatest fraternity the world shall ever know.

The efforts of the boys of Omicron for the welfare and advancement of our fraternity never cease.

We continue to add to our pledged list such men as will be a credit to Psi Omega. We take pleasure in introducing our recently initiated candidates:

Claude H. Bryan, '07 .... Nephi, Utah.
Newton B. French, '07 .... Clintwood, Va.
Harry E. Foster, '08 .... Owenton, Ky.

RHO—OHIO COLLEGE OF DENTAL SURGERY.

Edw. McCurdy, Editor.

In pursuance to the general plans adopted, Rho celebrated on the evening of February 15, the Crystal Anniversary of our fraternity.

At a previous meeting a committee had been appointed to arrange a program for the event. The program was carried out in a faultless manner, and in a way characteristic of anything Psi Omegan.

Dr. Burger, our genial Professor of Prosthetic Dentistry, opened the program with an exhaustive, and very excellent paper on "Value of Therapeutics and Preventative Measures in Prosthetic Dentistry."

To say that this paper was appreciated, is but mildly expressing it, for those of us who know Dr. Burger always expect the best from him and never yet have been disappointed.

Dr. Walton, '04, one of our demonstrators, followed with a very interesting paper on "Hints that are Essential to the Young Practitioner."

"My Idea of a Fraternity" was handled in a very able manner by W. F. Rule, '09.

The next paper had as its subject, "General and Local Anaesthetics" and was handled in a very scientific and instructive manner by Brother Paul Cassidy, '03, another of our Psi Omega demonstrators. Dr. Cassidy revealed that he possessed a deep knowledge of the subject.

At various points during the evening we were entertained with vocal and piano solos by Brother Cunningham, '09.

At promptly 10 o'clock, each brother, having been supplied with a glass of "punch," Dr. Burger arose and in a very impressive manner, and in a way calculated to arouse the enthusiasm of all loyal Psi Omegas proposed the following toast:

"Psi Omega, the path of your journey has been strewn with sweet flowers whose fragrance has penetrated the minds of your friends and left an impression of love and high regard. The light of your soaring star has been growing brighter, and, unlike the fabled Will o' the Wisp, does not flit about but has found abode in the hearts of those who know you best.

"Like the streamlet of the musing poet, your course has at times been strewn with rocks and forced into a narrow and roughened channel, but, after a few wild splashes you find yourself again at peace, widening at every turn.

"Here's to Psi Omega. May the future be as glorious as the past. May the love and good fellowship that ye bear toward each other find fruit in the good that we can do. Let harmony and not discord or strife be our watchword and it must follow as does night the day, that our cause will not suffer from the misjudgment of loyal hearts.

"May the Father of all Mercies be kind to us and to our friends, so that when our worldly cares are o'er, we may find eternal peace and happiness in the great unknown that is to come."

Brothers William, Cassidy, Miller, and Walton gave appropriate toasts during the evening.

Invitations are out for our annual dance, to be given at Walnut Hills Mansion February 27, '07.

The secrets of Psi Omega will be revealed to Fred R. Lauterbach, of Dayton, O., February 26.

Rho sends best wishes to all sister chapters.

CHI—NORTH PACIFIC DENTAL COLLEGE.

John E. Swanberg, Editor.

Our chapter has been strengthened very materially this year by the addition of a lot of good material from the various classes. When those who have been pledged become members, we will have one of the strongest chapters of the fraternity.

Due to the splendid entertainment committee, the members of Chi have had several treats, socially, and we hope the good work will continue in the future as it has in the past. One of the principal features was a social dance given by the chapter which was thoroughly enjoyed by the non-members who attended.

Our meetings have been helped wonderfully by the honorary members, especially Drs. Meyers and Drake. Their talks are interesting as well as instructive and we hope to have them with us more often in the future, as they are always ready to lend aid and advice which are especially appreciated by those who will soon graduate.

Sometime ago it was hinted that there was to be a new dental fraternity started in our college, but, due to unknown reasons to the writer, the matter seems to have been dropped.

A short time ago Brother O. H. Whaley received his transfer card from Beta Zeta, St. Louis, Mo., and he is now an active member of Chi.

PSI—OHIO MEDICAL UNIVERSITY.

S. E. Spangler, Editor.

On Wednesday, January 30, Psi gave one of her delightful dances at the U. T. C. Hall in this city. Nearly twenty-five couples attended and as usual, went away well pleased with the evening's entertainment.

Arrangements are now being made for our Annual Banquet. It will be held at the Hartman hotel on March 20. This is an event that is anticipated and looked forward to as the most important social gathering. Every effort is being made to make it the best one ever held. Supreme Councilor Friesell, of Pittsburg, promises to be with us then and we await his coming with pleasure. On February 15, Psi celebrated the Fifteenth Anniversary in fitting style. The chapter house was put in its best order and refreshments, together with other good things, were laid out for the occasion. The boys participated in a "smoker" until near the 10 p. m. hour and then all were served with ice cream, cake, and fruit punch. Promptly at ten p. m., Dr. Semans, acting as toastmaster, arose and offered the following toast to Psi Omega Fraternity:

"We are told that the cup of life is sweetest at the brim, and, as we drink, the flavor becomes impaired until the dregs are reached, the bitterness of which causes us to allow its removal from our lips without a struggle. But I quaff from a cup like Thor's unfailing cup of old, with its source from the sea itself, my lips are ever at the brim; because the supply is pure, copious, and unfailing like the everlasting fountains of brotherly love, bubbling with crystals, sparkling from the hearts of all true brothers of this fraternity. To Psi Omega—Drink."

In order that all readers of The Frater may know more about the men of this chapter who drank the toast to dear old Psi Omega, I close my editorial with the following horoscope of each active member:

NAME.	NICKNAME.	FAVORITE EXPRESSION.	STRIKING CHARACTERISTIC.	ULTIMATE END.
Paul Sherwood	"Sherry"	"I'll tell you fellows."	Beardless.	A man
V. W. Taylor	"Shug"	"Let me put you next."	A cigar for breakfast.	A stenographer.
J. H. Warner	"Warner"	"Come on, now."	A bean eater.	Owner and Dean of a dental college.
R. B. Wiltberger	"Wilty"	"Fast life is killing me."	Whistles Ragtime.	An "auto" fiend.
Paul Minton	"Scudge"	"Not so as you could notice it, Cappy."	Lefthanded.	A train caller.
E. D. Warner	"Big Kid"	"Saw some big queens."	Big grin.	A cobbler.
H. S. Shumway	"Shummy"	"Whoopee, out last night."	Looks over his glasses.	A society swell.
Wm. Warren	"Culp"	"Pass the potatoes."	Laughs continually.	An editor.
Roy Bode	"Bodie"	"Got a match?"	Beats the piano.	A second Paderewiski.
Geo. Moore	"Walla Walla"	"Ah, cut it out."	Eats continually.	A star boarder.
Harry Stewart	"Senior Stewart"	"That's what they told me."	Butts in.	A plate polisher.
Sperry Claypoole	"Midget"	"We can do it, can't we."	Plays euchre.	A champion.
E. E. Stewart	"Keeno"	"Smoke up, Moonshine."	Waits on table.	An office boy to a dentist.
Wm. Oann	"Ma"	"My bedbug!"	Talks over phone two hours at a time.	A football coach.
George Hawkins	"Hawk"	"Hair cut or shave?"	Shaver of little things.	A barber.
J. T. Williamson	"Joe"	"What can I sell you?"	Wears latest clothes.	A clothing clerk.
Harry Oliver	"Oliver"	"My Gracious!"	Easily embarrassed.	A reliable man.
Albert Soldner	"Sodder"	"Nothing like that in our family."	Shakes head when in earnest.	A minister's son-in-law.

NAME.	NICKNAME.	FAVORITE EXPRESSION.	STRIKING CHARACTERISTIC.	ULTIMATE END.
Wm. Carter	"Nick"	Saying cuss words.	Chews hard while working.	A tooth carpenter.
Amplius Galvin	"Moonshine"	"Keeno didn't say so."	Wears corduroy pants.	A distiller.
John Schaffer	"Schaffer"	"Oh, I've had the grippe."	"Wise scout."	A professor.
Harry Cowden	"Cowden"	"Got your Bonwill?"	Quiet all the time.	A dentist.
Carl Emmert	"Kid"	"Going home soon."	"Fiddles."	A musician.
Paul Gabel	"Gabe"	"All 'fussed' up."	Little but mighty.	A society man.
Earl Clark	"Clark"	"Oh! Oh! My!"	Takes life as it comes.	A man of knowledge.
Dennis Welch	"Welch"	"Ray White did so."	Gets excited easily.	A calmed man.
Arthur Knoderer	"Artie"	"Say kid."	Talks dance.	A dancing master.
S. E. Spangler	"Dr. Dippy"	"Heap big time."	Works all the time.	An inmate of the asylum.
Clyde Trumpower	"Trumpie"	"Hello Friendie."	Likes to be a committeeman.	A left-handed tinker.
John Barnett	"Jack"	"Hello Doctors."	Plays ball.	A professional ball player.
Craig Patton	"Pat"	"Me for that."	Likes the girls.	A dead game sport.
Clifford Schraeder	"Tramp"	"By Gosh Fellers."	Works hard.	A helper in a lab.
N. E. Rickey	"Rick"	"Where's Wehr?"	Always in a hurry.	An office assistant.
Andrew Fox	"Andy"	"Say, Vosper."	White headed.	A practioner of dentistry.
Elmer Wylie	"Dr. Wylie"	"Where did you get in?"	Getting acquainted.	A salve spreader.

BETA ALPHA—UNIVERSITY OF ILLINOIS.

G. W. Wheeler, Editor.

Beta Alpha sends greetings to all sister chapters and to all alumni members.

This has been a prosperous year for Beta Alpha. We are now at home at 406 Ogden avenue. We are all striving to make this the banner year for our chapter.

On January 23, we gave a smoker and invited several prospective members to enjoy the evening with us; there was present a nice crowd and several very good speeches from both honorary and active members added to the pleasure of the occasion. Refreshments and cigars were served, and it was a late hour when we disbanded for the night, each one feeling that the smoker had been a success. We pledged every one of the prospective members to Psi Omega that night.

We were unable to get a hall for February 15, and as our regular meeting came on the 13th, we held our celebration of our Anniversary then. A short session of business was held, ending in an open meeting. Refreshments and cigars were plentiful. Dr. Cigrand made the address of the evening, and, as he is a favorite with the boys, it is needless to say it was well appreciated. At the appointed hour the following toast was drunk:

> "Here's to our sweethearts,
>   May they sometime be our wives;
> Here's to our wives,
>   May they always be our sweethearts;
> Here's to Psi Omega,
>   May she live long and prosper."

We have four new members to introduce to the fraternity: Melvin E. Pontius, '08; Michael F. Hough, '08; Henry J. Kauffman, '08, and Chester W. Daye, '08.

We have a number of pledged men whom we expect to make full-fledged Psi Omegas in the near future.

Our Grand Master, B. F. Lockwood, has been confined to his room for the past two weeks with an attack of the mumps. We miss his smiling countenance very much and wish for him a speedy recovery.

We extend to all Psi Omegas an invitation to visit us at our meetings the 2nd and 4th Wednesday evenings of each month.

BETA GAMMA—GEORGE WASHINGTON UNIVERSITY.

W. H. Hildreth, Editor.

This is the season of the year when the student gets down to the real hard work that counts. Out door attractions are few; foot ball is only a memory; base ball is not even on the horizon; and the warm cozy den and a pipe are conducive to study. Some of ths mid-year exams have been safely weathered and a few are still to be encountered.

The all important event of the winter was the celebration of the quin-decennial of the founding of the Psi Omega fraterinty. On the evening of February 15, honorary, alumni, and undergraduate members united in one great effort to do honor to the fraternity.

Grand Master MacDonald called the members to order about an hour before the time designated for the toast to Psi Omega, and, in a few well chosen words, concerning the auspicious occasion, introduced Shirley W. Bowles, Eta, '98, Professor of Prosthetic Dentistry in the Georgetown University.

Brother Bowles gave a short history of the founding of the fraternity, our progress and achievements, closing his remarks with the following quotation as exemplifying true fraternity life: "The only reward of virtue is virtue, and the only way to have a friend is to be one."

Brother Henry C. Thompson, Professor of Operative Dentistry, spoke of the ideals of the fraternity as typified by friendship, mutual assistance and laudable emulation.

Brother Arthur B. Crane, Zeta, '99, in his inimitable manner, enlivened the occasion with his ready wit, closing his remarks by congratulating Beta Gamma on her fine contribution to the San Francisco relief fund, which fund, by the way, was inspired by Brother Crane himself.

Brother Constantini, Beta Gamma, '03, a charter member of Beta Gamma, reminded the brothers that the time selected for the celebration of the fraternity anniversary only lacked a few days of being the fourth birthday of our own chapter which, thereby, gave the occasion a greater significance.

Promptly as the clock chimed eleven, at a signal from the Grand Master, the brothers arose and stood with brimming wine glasses held high, while Brother Henry C. Thompson proposed the following toast: "Drink to Psi Omega Fraternity, which teaches us 'how good and pleasant it is for brethren to dwell together in unity' and eliminates unkind rivalry; which creates a spirit or emulation among the fraters as to who can best work and best agree. Drink to our chain of friendship around this broad land, each link of which is represented by a frater. Let us drink the toast and let the glass as it touches our lips, typify the chastened kiss of fraternal friendship."

The glasses were drained and the writer had a mental vision that he was in a glorious company with thousands of Psi Omegas, all doing honor to the great fraternity.

On the evening of January 26, Brother Allen S. Wolfe, of the faculty, entertained the brothers with a lecture or talk on Porcelain Inlays, illustrating his remarks with large plaster models. The seniors were especially appreciative of the doctor's kindness and all gave him a rousing vote of thanks. The newly initiated brothers sprung a surprise on us in the form of bountiful refreshments. Let all succeeding new members take notice, please.

After the regular meeting February 9, Mr. W. C. Jones, a relative of one of our brothers, kept us guessing for a couple of hours over his remarkably clever tricks of sleight of hand.

BETA DELTA—UNIVERSITY OF CALIFORNIA.

Leighton C. Brownton, Editor.

The Fifteenth or Crystal Anniversary of the birth of Psi Omega was fitly observed in San Francisco on the evening of February 15th. Beta Sigma and Beta Delta joined forces and in true Psi Omega fashion celebrated this historical occasion.

As the clock struck the hour of eight, there was gathered in the banquet room of Beta Sigma an enthusiastic crowd from each chapter.

Toastmaster E. Downs, G. M., Beta Sigma, introduced as the first speaker of the evening Dr. Winslow Anderson, who, after a short but impressive speech, proposed the toast to which we should drink.

L. E. Carter, G. M., Beta Delta, next spoke on the growth of Psi Omega during the past decade and a half, and of the position she holds to-day and will hold during the years to come.

In a neat and concise manner Brother John E. Gurley traced the life of a fraternity man in college, the benefits and assistance he receives from his brothers, and the fraternal training which is so valuable to him in after life. He impressed upon us the necessity of care in selecting new members, as it is to these men we look for the upholding of our principles and aims.

Brother L. E. Clay enlarged upon the thoughts presented by the former speakers and brought out several points which gave us good food for thought.

In an interesting manner Brother L. R. Packwood related the story of his trip to Oregon, following the fire of last April, and of the fine treatment accorded him by the boys of Chi.

Toastmaster Downs spoke at some length upon fraternity matters. He was especially enthusiastic about the feasibility of having the meeting of the Grand Chapter in 1913, during the World's Fair which will be held here at that time.

Following the toast and speeches a pleasant social time was enjoyed.

On the evening of February 8 we gave our individual attention to four anxious brothers, who, we are glad to say, made the acquaintance of the "lamb" without serious results. It is with pleasure we introduce to the fraternity:

B. J. Hoffman .... Tulare, Cal.
G. L. Talbot .... Lompoc, Cal.
F. W. Randol .... Angel Island, Cal.
F. L. Mordyke .... Berkeley, Cal.

BETA EPSILON—NEW ORLEANS COLLEGE OF DENTISTRY.

Leon Barnett, Editor.

The carnival now over, the boys have shaken off the dust and have begun their studies with renewed vigor.

Beta Epsilon held several meetings since and had a great attendance. On the 20th of March we hold our Annual Banquet. This will, hereafter, be known as Psi Omega Day in New Orleans and we hope to make it a great success.

Psi Omegas from all over the state will be invited to participate in this annual affair.

Psi Omega has been especially honored in having a number of her members elected to prominent offices in the Louisiana State Dental Society at its last meeting in this city, February 13-15.

Those elected were Dr. H. P. Magruder, first vice president; Dr. Leon Barnett, treasurer; Drs. J. C. Crimen was elected secretary and Paul De Verges, chairman of the executive committee; Drs. J. H. Landry and O. L. Brand were elected members of the executive committee.

It seems that the Psi Omegas are always in the front in New Orleans and I attribute it to the fact that each and every one is an earnest worker for the advancement of the profession.

At the Louisiana State meeting very interesting papers and clinics were rendered by Psi Omegas, as follows: "Who is and Who Should Be the Dictator?" by Dr. H. P. Magruder; "The Vagaries of a Dental Practice," by Dr. A. G. Friedrichs; "Treatment of Pulpless Teeth," by Dr. L. D. Archinard.

Among the clinics were: "The Use of Diatoric Teeth in Crown and Bridge Work," by Dr. J. C. Cremen, Jr.; "Non-Cohesive Gold," by Dr. A. G. Friedrichs; "Removable Bridges," by Dr. A. L. Ducasse.

The editor notes with regret the non-registering of Psi Omegas visiting our great city during the carnival festivities. It is hoped that we will have quite a few next year.

We had hoped that those attending the festivities would register as we intended giving a banquet and other entertainments, so that when they left the Carnival City, they would not forget the pleasant visit.

As the approach of the Fifth Triennial Convention is near at hand, Beta Epsilon extends a hearty invitation for the convention to convene in Greater New Orleans and assures all that a grand time will be awaiting their arrival.

In closing Beta Epsilon extends her heartiest wishes for the success of all sister chapters.

BETA ZETA—ST. LOUIS DENTAL COLLEGE.

S. A. Lusby, Editor.

Beta Zeta takes great pleasure in presenting to the fraternity nine men of good reputation and character; men who will help elevate the profession of dentistry to that high and lofty ideal which is the aim of Psi Omega and should be the aim of every good and true man in the profession.

It is very encouraging to us to go into the freshman laboratory and see seven of the best members of that class wearing Psi Omega pins, the only fraternity pin worn in that class up to the present writing.

We have the reins in our hands, and why not make them guide us to success?

At our last meeting, February 21, our goat had all he could attend to. The names of the new members are as follows, of whom the first three received their final degree at the meeting held previous to February 21:

Wm. Yount, '08	Pt. Pleasant, Mo.
E. M. Pitts, '09	Benton, Ill.
N. M. Eldridge, '09	Aikin, Ill.
Julius Boeker, '08	Mt. Olive, Ill.
C. A. Dames, '09	St. Paul, Mo.
H. A. Jacobi, '09	Martinsburg, Mo.
W. Hasselberg, '09	New York, N. Y.
P. J. Donnelly, '09	Parsons, Kan.
J. R. Conklin, '09	Arcadia, Kan.

We were glad to have two alumni brothers with us at this meeting, Dr. Plumpe and Dr. Kitchel, and to see Brother Shindler from Washington University present.

At the close of the evening we were favored with an intelligent paper written by Brother Mane for discussion. Subject, "Devitalization and Extirpation of the Dental Pulp." Brother Mane was highly complimented on his paper by all present, and we hope to have more papers read in future, especially by our senior brothers on account of their having had infirmary experience.

Our worthy Grand Master deserves credit for his work and influence in behalf of this fraternity this year, since he took advantage of the opportunity which presented itself of assisting Dr. Harper in part of his work with the freshman class. Brother Demko is a "good fellow" with all the boys of that class and we are glad to know that he is so well liked.

BETA ETA—KEOKUK DENTAL COLLEGE.

Geo. R. Narrley, Editor.

Again we greet our sister chapters and alumni brothers with the report that Beta Eta is alive and prospering. We have added to our roll a number of new members since the last issue of The Frater. Brothers Hurley and Ames will ever have occasion to remember their entry into fraternal ranks; placed in the hands of Brother Arnold, who is an artist when it comes to costuming, they were escorted through the business district of the city, one cold, dreary Saturday evening. After the candidates were introduced to all of their lady friends they were taken to one of the vaudeville houses where they bore the brunt of many a joke.

The Crystal Anniversary of the birth of our organization was celebrated in an informal way. After the regular business had been disposed of, the meeting was turned over to the committee having charge. At the mystic hour of ten, the following toast was given in the way that all good toasts should be given:

To Psi Omega:—The bright star of brotherhood as exemplified in true fraternity, whose smiles of brotherly love and sympathy have gone out to over four thousand brothers, whose principles and teachings are perpetuated through the lives of her members. To you, dear old Psi Omega, we drink."

Short talks were made by Brothers F. L. Ervay, O. L. Sohl, and A. B. Thompson, charter members of Beta Eta. This turned out to be one of the most enthusiastic meetings that we have had for a long time.

Brothers Ervay, Sohl, Thompson, and Crouch are sojournnig with us this winter. Brothers Thompson and Crouch are demonstrators in the Keokuk Dental College, Brother Ervay is studying medicine and Brother Sohl is connected with the O'Brien, Worthen Co.

We have the pleasure to introduce our new members: J. Bernard Hurley, '07; J. F. Ames, '08; F. J. Switzer, '08, and H. D. Stanwood, '07.

GAMMA KAPPA—UNIVERSITY OF MICHIGAN.

Le Vant R. Drake, Editor.

We are enjoying life to the fullest extent at present, our exams are over and only one siege is ahead, then some of us will be through. Our storage capacity was never greater, our consciences are clear and we are winning good men for the Psi Omega ranks. January was a bright month for us but February excels and we expect the succeeding months to assist in the strengthening of brotherly ties, the growth of our chapter, and the fame of the fraternity as a whole. We celebrated the Fifteenth Anniversary of our organization in the most enjoyable manner. The early part of the evening was taken up by music, games, etc. We have a chapter orchestra and it rendered fine music during the evening. At exactly 9:55 p. m. every member was at the banquet table. As it happened, our number was the lucky "skidoo" number and it is the same at present. When the city clock struck 10 p. m. every man was on his feet and drank to Psi Omega in response to the following paper and toasts delivered by Brother B. H. Masselink:

"This is a striking moment, indeed, from the raging Atlantic to the peaceful Pacific; from the frozen Inland Seas to the slumbering Gulf, Psi Omegas are drinking a toast to commemorate the Fifteenth Anniversary of their beloved Fraternity.

"No organization of a similar nature has had such a phenomenal growth or has attained an equal degree of honor and success in the dental profession as Psi Omega. The half hundred chapters stand as so many beacon lights casting beams of peace and principle into the profession; as it is being studied and practiced. Built upon Alpha's solid rock they picture a grand monument to the wisdom and courage of the men who wrought for Psi Omega. The true fraternal spirit encountered on every occasion bears witness to the character of the members of Psi Omega.

"That this selfsame wisdom and spirit may be continually fostered among all the chapters is the wish of Gamma Kappa.

As an expression of our earnest feelings let us arise, gentlemen, and drink to the welfare and love of all.

"First, here's to Psi Omega. May she become the greatest of all fraternities, not because of her strength in numbers, but by the force of good example. May she experience a new birth of consecrated brotherhood and assert at every opportunity in word and deed, the true principles upon which she was founded. May she ever be found keenly alive to the best interests of dental surgery and thus advance the profession beyond the scope of internal rivalry.

"Here's to the Supreme Councilors. May their examples be hard to emulate and their official acts be controlled with an eye single to the good of the whole.

"Here's to the individual chapters. May love and esteem perfume the atmosphere of each chapter's home. May scholarship and gentlemanly conduct be the guiding virtues in their selection of new members.

"Here's to the Grand Master of each chapter. May he display a deep appreciation of his official rights and great anxiety for the welfare of his chapter. May his words and actions conform to the principles of the order, thus leading others to aspire for the noblest in Psi Omega.

"Here's to Gamma Kappa, our own hope of joy and peace. May each brother become more and more endeared to her walls as they re-echo the songs and laughter of many a joyous hour.

"Here's to Willis W. Whipple, our leader. May Willie and all the willing little Willies to be, be as happy as the Whippoorwillies of the forest."

The Great Michigan locomotive yell was given substituting Psi Omega in the place of Michigan. When enthusiasm was at its height, the feed was brought on. After the eating part was over, everything was cleared away and a group photo was taken. Then a fire was made in the grate and we roasted marshmallows. Punch was brought in at this time, Brother Wurnt having charge of the canteen. Brother Auson camped alongside the punch bowl, and it was only after continued prayers and supplications that he was finally induced to change his position. Grand Master Whipple and Brother Auson had birthdays on the sixteenth and when the clock struck 12 p. m. we made them glad their birthdays came only once a year. At one o'clock the company broke up saying this had been the best ever. On the evening of February 22, we celebrated by giving the physical degree to several. We hope that date will be one that will always be remembered by them.

On that same evening the honorary obligation was given to Dr. D. M. Mackey, whom we take great pleasure in introducing to our fraternity. We introduce six other new and loyal Psi Omegas, as follows:

Harold M. Coss, '09 .... Cattaraugus, N. Y.
W. J. A. Wagner, '08 .... Ann Arbor, Mich.
Erwin L. Richardson, '09 .... Cattaraugus, N. Y.
R. C. Hall, 09 .... Pioneer, O.
H. B. Dunning, '09 .... Holloway, Mich.
Harry J. Fox, '08 .... Pigeon, Mich.

GAMMA LAMBDA—COLLEGE OF DENTAL AND ORAL SURGERY OF NEW YORK.

Gotthard E. Seyfarth, Editor.

Again we are permitted, by the kindness of our faculty, to breathe more freely—at least for a short time. Our mid-term examinations are over and we are glad to say that all of our boys stood the test. Our worthy Grand Master, McLeod, stands at the head of the senior class, while the other brothers all stand well in their respective classes. Let us hope that the final examinations will bring as satisfactory results as this last one, for then I may have the pleasant privilege to report that Gamma Lambda, again, as in former years, boasts of having the medal and honor men of the college.

While in the combats with science and art we have held our ground, certain members of the chapter have been vanquished by that mighty little soldier of the Goddess of Love, who travels under the name Cupid. Although the names of the fortunate "vanquished" are still generally unknown, or at least supposed to be, we send our heartiest congratulations to them; may success, happiness, and health be their constant companions for many years to come.

On February 15, Gamma Lambda, Beta, and the New York Alumni Chapter, united to celebrate the Fifteenth Anniversary of Psi Omega in a most magnificent manner at the Hotel Manhattan. The banquet, held in one of the finest hotels in New York, was a record breaker and it certainly was the most elaborate ever held by New York's Psi Omegas. A splendid program had been provided by the committee in charge. It included several vocal and instrumental selections by some of our active brothers. But let it suffice to mention only a few things regarding this grand time, for my brother editors of Beta and the New York Alumni Chapter will very likely give a more complete account.

The guest of honor was Dr. William Jarvie, one of the honorary members of Psi Omega, a grand and lovable old gentleman, who after fifty years of hard toil, is retiring from active dental practice to at last enjoy some of the fruits of his labors, and a well earned rest after so many years of unselfish and faithful service in behalf of his profession and fellow-men.

Among the speakers of the evening, who were introduced by our able Toastmaster, Dr. Ellison Hillyer, were: Dr. W. Jarvie, Dr. A. L. Northrop, Dr. W. W. Walker, Dr. S. G. Perry, Prof. J. Bond Littig, Prof. A. R. Starr, Prof. W. H. Haskin, and Dr. Colby, of London, all of whom are honorary members of Psi Omega, and you can be sure that their speeches were well received.

Following these honorary brothers the President, and Past Presidents of the Alumni Chapter were called upon; they, in turn, were followed by Grand Master Van Rinkle, of Beta, and Grand Master McLeod, of Gamma Lambda.

But the greatest event of the evening was undoubtedly the "Toast to Psi Omega" at eleven p. m., for we knew that at that precise moment thousands of brothers were drinking a toast to our great fraternity.

A great surprise still awaited Dr. Jarvie, for Dr. Hillyer again arose to congratulate him on his standing as a dentist, citizen and man. In ending his remarks Toastmaster Hillyer presented Dr. Jarvie in the name of Psi Omega with a solid gold seal ring surmounted by the Psi Omega crest, as a recognition or token of the great esteem in which he is held by all brothers who have the honor of knowing him.

Now, taking all in all, a most delightful evening had been passed, and, besides the pretty glass souvenir, every brother who had the good fortune to be present at this banquet, took with him the pleasant reminiscences of the evening of February Fifteenth, Nineteen Hundred and Seven.

GAMMA MU—UNIVERSITY OF IOWA.

A. R. Hamm, Editor.

Gamma Mu sends best wishes to the Supreme Council and to all chapters.

On the night of Friday, February 15, Gamma Mu called a special chapter meeting in place of the regular one for the following Tuesday. After all business had been disposed of, we held a smoker. A paper was read on "Anaesthetics," by Brother Heit. It was then discussed, Dr. Vollard answering all questions and explaining some things a little more in detail. At nine p. m. all members of Gamma Mu stood up and the following toast was proposed to Psi Omega and to all of her members, by our Grand Master, C. D. Bey:

"Here's hoping that all chapters of Psi Omega and all Psi Omegas may do even more good towards elevating the dental profession in the future than they have during the fifteen years of our life."

On the fourth and fifth of February the S. U. I. Alumni Clinic was held. There were 250 dentists here and Psi Omegas were among them. Some of whom we did not know were in the state. The morning of the fourth was taken up with getting ready and meeting old friends. The clinic started in the afternoon. In the evening papers on Orthodontia and Inlay Work were read and discussed. The fifth was taken up with clinic. In the evening a dance was held.

Walton is pledged.

Dr. Suma, our orthodontia instructor, is to be taken in as an honorary member.

--•◇•--

GAMMA NU—VANDERBILT UNIVERSITY.

E. Elwood Street, Editor.

On February 15 Gamma Nu celebrated the Crystal Anniversary of the fraternity by giving a combination banquet and smoker. Brother W. L. Merritt was chosen toastmaster for the occasion and he arranged a program which included almost every member. Although the youngest chapter in Psi Omega, none are more loyal or enthusiastic than Gamma Nu and the spirit manifested on this occasion speaks volumes for what our fraternity means to us.

Although we have given several highly successful dances, they could not compare with our celebration of the fifteenth.

GAMMA NU 1906-1907.

Brother Merritt made a splendid little talk in which he spoke of our celebration—its meaning—the spirit of Psi Omega which has grown, flourished and prospered for fifteen years. Brother Sledge then responded with a fitting toast on "Our Pin." Grand Master Fuller then gave a highly humorous talk during which he made a few predictions that were greatly applauded. "Our Fraternity" by Brother Noel followed, and then, as it was almost time for the toast of the evening, Brother Merritt called a halt and Brother Fuller spoke of the solemnity of the occasion, of the number of Psi Omegas all over the country, who, at that moment were vying with each other in commemorating an event which is so dear to the hearts and minds of us all. Brother Braly, the speaker of the evening, was introduced and spoke as follows:

"I appear before you on this auspicious occasion with feelings of pleasure and regret—pleasure that I have been accorded the honor of addressing you and regret that your compliment has fallen on one so unworthy to do the opportunity full justice. I beg to assure you, however, that any failure on my part to meet the measure of the moment will be from a lack of ability rather than from any lack of appreciation of your favor or the occasion which calls us together. As loyal members of Alpha Kappa Delta, we were not unconscious of the lofty ideals which made our association both agreeable and uplifting. It was not from any idea of disloyalty to those sentiments that we felt disposed to give that organization up, but because from it, as a basis, we were better able to appreciate a wider opportunity and a closer coming together in a fraternity. We felt the quickening within us of a desire to become members of another, and, as we believed, a better organization for the upholding of those ideals.

"We have taken no backward step but have gone forward, and are to be congratulated.

"We have united ourselves in the ties of a fraternity. We have by sacred bonds been admitted to one of the highest and best, if not the very best, fraternities in the profession which we look forward to joining. Psi Omega has thirty-eight chapters and some of these are situated in our dear Southland. We find our brethren in New Orleans, Atlanta, and Louisville, besides in many other prominent cities of this immediate section. Wherever duty or pleasure may call us, we shall be in the midst of loved ones and be greeted by the glad hand-clasp of Psi Omega. Indeed, brethren, we made no mistake in spreading our wings into the realm of the wider world of a professional fraternity. But my brethren, we must not lose sight of the fact that a wider range and greater opportunity bring larger responsibility. Such thoughts as have just been given tongue emphasize the importance of our "making good" under greater demands. We are in but the first stage of our association with a loyal fraternity. We have but recently assumed our sacred obligations, but having started right is only a very small part of our life long duty which is to continue right. Let each man appoint himself a rigid censor over his own conduct, to the end that our professional elevation shall continue and the standards of our profession shall suffer no hurt from our being in its ranks. The honor and integrity of all are in the hands of each and every one of us. It is said that no man liveth to himself, but whether this is true or not from now on no man can live to himself, lest he break the fraternal chain.

"Each man must act well his part, and, in a fraternity, the whole is no greater than any single part. We are all for each— each for all. In this sign, my brethren, let us uphold the standard of Psi Omega."

Experiences and stories were then told, the "spread" was demolished, each one present contributing something to the entertainment. Our quartet made a decided hit by rendering several clever songs. Just previous to our breaking up, our final toast "To our unknown brothers" was drunk, then came the adjournment and—the morning lecture.

We will soon initiate into honorary membership, Drs. R. Boyd Bogle, Professor of Anesthesia and Orthodontia, and L. G. Noel, Professor of Clinical Dentistry, men who are known throughout the country as eminent members of our profession. It is with much pleasure that we present them to the Psi Omega world.

Gamma Nu extends best wishes to all sister chapters and to each and every individual Psi Omega.

Alumni Chapters.

---◆---

PHILADELPHIA ALUMNI CHAPTER.

H. L. Chandler, Editor.

With a most flattering attendance Philadelphia Alumni Chapter held the initial meeting of 1907 at Boothby's Hotel on the evening of January 16.

Rarely in the history of our chapter has a meeting been marked by a greater display of good fellowship and brotherly love than was manifested at this meeting.

As is customary at the January meeting, the installation of new officers took place as follows: Grand Master, Victor Cochran; Secretary, R. E. Denney; Treasurer, Wm. C. Marsh; Inside Guardian, R. A. Zurbrigg; Editor, Henry L. Chandler.

Following this interesting ceremony, the members were ushered into the banqueting hall and amid a profusion of floral decorations, in which clusters of American Beauty roses interspersed with the colors emblematic of our order predominated, sat down to the following menu:

Oak Creeks
Olives   Gherkins
Cream of Celery
Chicken Cutlet
Roast Tenderloin Beef—Mushrooms
Potatoes   Peas
Lettuce and Celery Salad
Neapolitan Ice Cream
Cakes
Cafe Noir

Brother Cochran acted as toastmaster, and the members responded to his witticisms as follows:

"1906—A Retrospect"...............H. D. Winsmore.
"Ingenuity of the Modern Dentist"........J. G. Lane.
"Philadelphia as an Educational Center"..Alfred P. Lee.
"Dentistry in the Rural Districts".......R. E. Denney.
"The Future—What It Holds in Store for Us"....
.... J. A. Standen.
"The Ethical Dentist"..................C. F. Wilbur.
"Centralization of Modern Professional Men"....
.... J. E. Nyce.

A poem entitled "The Marksman" was recited in a touching manner by Brother Crooks, followed by responses from Wm. C. Marsh, Dr. A. Zurbrigg, A. M. Chandler, D. F. Davies, W. W. McClarren, J. L. Smith, J. R. Mallon, C. C. Mehler, a song by Brother Wetzell and a recitation entitled "Peaches" by Brother Cochran concluded the program.

Much credit is due the entertainment committee which consisted of Brothers Nyce and Standen.

With such an auspicious opening it is not presuming too much to look forward to the most successful year in our history.

With the echo of the mellow notes of cathedral chimes still resounding in the air, Philadelphia Alumni drank her toast to the past triumphs and future successes of Psi Omega Fraternity on Friday evening, February 15.

Gathering at the home of Brother Cochran, 1628 North Seventeenth street, almost the entire membership of our chapter spent the intervening time between eight and eleven p. m. recounting past events and pledging support in the growth and future prosperity of our order.

As the hour of eleven approached we gathered around the festive board and were treated to a most sumptuous repast, after which Supreme Councilor Nyce, the principal speaker of the evening, entertained us with a history of the order, recounting her modest beginning, early struggles, and, finally, her unparalleled triumph.

"Our order stands pre-eminent among her fellows," declared the speaker, "including among her members men who have achieved international reputation in the practice of dentistry." Continuing, the speaker admonished his hearers to be ever alert to further the interests of Psi Omega, declaring that with the co-operation of all her members our order would forever maintain her supremacy.

CLEVELAND ALUMNI CHAPTER.

Thomas J. McLernon, Editor.

A large and representative meeting for the purpose of reorganizing the Cleveland Alumni Chapter of the Psi Omega Dental Fraternity and election of officers was held Monday evening, March 11, 1907, at the Bangor building, 942 Prospect avenue, Cleveland, O., Brother A. L. Griffis presiding.

Brother H. E. Friesell, S. C., Dean of the Pittsburg Dental college, was present.

After discussion and full consideration of the whole matter it was decided that everything favored a successful future for the chapter.

The following officers were elected for the ensuing year: Dr. E. E. Belford, grand master; Dr. E. L. Pettibone, junior master; Dr. H. B. Rosenwasser, secretary; Dr. H. J. Friedman, treasurer; Dr. Thomas J. McLernon, editor, and Dr. L. M. Maples, inside guardian.

Brother Belford, in a neat speech, assured those present that, although, he was steadily assuming new responsibilities, he felt that his loyalty to Psi Omega compelled him to accept and assume the duties of office, which he did with the firm and steadfast resolution to perform the same to the best of his ability.

It was decided that the chapter meetings be held hereafter on the third Monday of each month. The executive committee will make arrangements for papers, discussions, and clinics on dental and general professional subjects, together with social features.

After some routine business had been transacted the meeting adjourned.

The next meeting will be held in the office of Brother Griffis, 728 Rose building, on the third Monday in April.

Editorial.

THE FIFTEENTH ANNIVERSARY.

The Fifteenth Anniversary of the birth of Psi Omega was joyously celebrated by active and alumni chapters. No event in the history of the organization has created so much interest and enthusiasm as did this celebration on the fifteenth of February. The enthusiasm and sincerity with which Psi Omegas renewed their pledges of loyalty to each other bespeaks a firmer, more closely united brotherhood. The stability, the usefulness and the aims of Psi Omega, after the vicissitudes of fifteen years of life, are now accepted and encouraged even by those who in former years, were inclined to belittle and retard the work and growth of the fraternity.

Psi Omega has not yet reached the great height to which she aspires, having distanced her contemporaries in the struggle for existence and stability, besides guarding laurels already won, she must steadfastly keep improving conditions under which candidates are received and must everlastingly strive for more chapter houses, and chapter ownership of the same, so that in fifteen years more of life, there will be as much for the betterment of the organization accomplished as has been accomplished during the past years

Our graduates must ever keep in mind and advocate the principles of Psi Omega. Upon graduation, when away from the influence of his fellow members, when the question of location and the manner in which he should attempt to establish his practice most occupies his mind, or, a little after hanging out his shingle, when funds run low and time passes slowly, because of lack of patients; then will the metal and true worth of the member be tested as a man and as a Psi Omegan. Some members(?) have not had sufficient stamina to go through the ordeal; others, a great number, had the necessary courage to sit patiently and await encouragement from the better members of the community. Fraternal history does not record that a member, possessed of qualities which enable him to adhere to his principles in the face of bankruptcy, failed to force the stamp of his worth upon the discerning public and in the end secured the esteem and patronage of the better class of people in his community.

In any one of the many dental journals published, do we ever read of anything good for the profession, in practice, in theory, or in research work, which came from the pen of a charlatan in the profession? Do any of them ever attain an honorable position in the social scheme of a community? Invariably they sink to, or are members of, the strata of society from which they draw their patients.

Psi Omega has been unfortunate in that some of her initiates have, during her fifteen years of life, not possessed those true qualities which would enable them to keep inviolate the obligations assumed and which qualities their sponsors felt sure they possessed. But these abandoned nonenties in the profession and in the community serve as forcible examples to those who might be tempted to disregard their obligations and sink their personalities into the oblivion of the charlatan. For, a man might as well be dead as not to be able to proudly take the place to which his profession and education entitle him in the community.

Psi Omega should take drastic measures and deal in no uncertain manner with those who are false to their obligation. Much against charlatanism has been accomplished during the past fifteen years. We feel sure that the next fifteen years will see Psi Omega especially honored because of the absence of these barnacles from her ranks.

With the unanimity of the pledges of good fellowship and brotherhood of our members as noted on the evening of the fifteenth of February and with the contemplation of what the labors of the Fifth Triennial Convention of the Grand Chapter will bring forth; we feel that Psi Omega is about to enter upon another epoch of even greater improvement and the more closely drawing together of her fraternal bonds.

GENERAL DIRECTORY.

The compilation of the general fraternity directory is proceeding as rapidly as can be expected; in most instances, the chapter secretaries have been prompt in rendering assistance, but the secretaries of a few of the larger chapters have not yet reported. The encouragement and services, rendered in the work by active and alumni members, have been most gratifying thus far. Prosecution of the work reveals that there was even a greater demand for this book than appeared on the surface. The Council aims to get out a work which will be a credit to Psi Omega, a work which will be interesting, not only because of the names of members of the fraternity and their addresses, but also because of the halftone illustrations of our chapters, as they appear in this the fifteenth year of the existence of our fraternity. The greater number of our chapters have already signified their willingness to furnish a cut for this purpose. The book will be handsomely and tastily bound, good paper will be used and there will probably be between one hundred and forty and one hundred and sixty pages.

Only a sufficient number of directories will be printed to supply those who have made or will make application for one by May 1.

We hope to have the directory ready for distribution by the end of May.

ALUMNI CLINIC OF THE ST. LOUIS DENTAL COLLEGE.

The Alumni Association of the St. Louis Dental College (formerly Marion-Sims) wishes to announce that its Annual Clinic will be held at the college building, Grand avenue and Caroline street on Tuesday and Wednesday, May 7 and 8, 1907.

All ethical members of the profession are cordially invited to come and enjoy the festival of good things being prepared, and every member of the Alumni is especially requested to show his allegiance to the Association by his presence.

Respectfully,
John Bernard O'Brien,
W. L. O'Neill,
Committee on Publicity.

Personal and Alumni Notes.

S. M. Crawford, Nu, is practicing at Kensington, O.

O. G. Latshaw, Nu, '06, is practicing at Rimersburg, Pa.

F. P. Hamilton, Tau, '05, is located at Clifton, S. C.

C. E. Norris, Gamma Iota, '06, is located at Warrenton, Ga.

C. C. Wood, Beta Epsilon, '06, is practicing at Bowie, La.

James H. Cardwell, Kappa, '05, is located at Minden, Neb.

Edw. J. Sammons, Gamma, '06, is located at Westfield, Mass.

A. A. Rounds, Theta, '05, is located at Philipsburg, Mont.

A. F. Schlappi, Alpha, '06, is now located at Curwensville, Pa.

A. H. Staples, Sigma, '06, is doing good work at Norway, Me.

W. M. Taylor, Tau, '03, has removed from Brunswick to Waycross, Ga.

Stanley S. Reynolds, Gamma, '06, is located at Rockville Center, N. Y.

E. O. Munson, Beta Epsilon, '06, is "making good" at Scranton, Miss.

H. M. Doudna, Xi, '05, is located in the Robbins block, Ishpeming, Mich.

Joe A. Jones, Pi, '05, is located at 114 Baltimore street, Cumberland, Md.

Henry A. White, Delta, '05, is located at 175 Tremont street, Boston, Mass.

W. B. Tyn, Beta Alpha, '06, occupies Suite 9, Johnston Block, Charleston, Ill.

Earle S. Harrison, Xi, '04, occupies Suite 30, Putney block, Waukesha, Wis.

H. I. Dowd, Delta, '05, is now located at 509 West Eleventh street, Pueblo, Col.

J. W. McMichaels, Beta Gamma, '04, is located at 14 Grand avenue, Portland, Ore.

Leon Barnett, Beta Epsilon, '05, has just recovered from a three weeks' attack of the grippe.

J. L. Wildberg, Kappa, '06, has his office over the Colgate National bank, Colgate, I. T.

W. W. Phillips, Omicron, '04, is located at Stearns, Ky., and has built up a splendid practice there.

O. J. Riess, Sigma, New Orleans, La., has been appointed representative of the Borine Mfg. Co., headquarters in New Orleans.

William C. Killinger, Alpha, '06, is making orthodontia a specialty. He is located at 602 Eleventh street, N. W., Washington, D. C.

John F. Curran, Kappa, '01, has removed his office from 1919 South Grand avenue to Suite 615 Auditorium building, Los Angeles, Cal.

The readers of The Frater are indebted to C. B. Gifford, Phi, '06' for the Pennsylvania State Board questions appearing in this issue of The Frater.

R. Chason, Gamma Iota, '06' is associated with his brother and is practicing at Columbus, Ga. Drs. Chason and Chason occupy rooms 220-222, Masonic Temple.

The readers of The Frater were indebted to A. A. Sherwood, Omicron, '06' for the set of Pennsylvania State Board questions which appeared in the November issue of The Frater.

William H. Gutelius, P. G. M., Beta, '06' will be pleased to have Psi Omegas drop in upon him at any time. He may be found at the Canton Christian College, Honglok, Canton, China.

The readers of The Frater are indebted to F. T. Daly for the set of Nebraska State Board questions which appears in this issue. Brother Daly has his office over the First National bank, Cambridge, Neb.

H. G. Davis, Phi, '04' is located at Williamsburg, Va. Brother Davis resides only seven miles from Jamestown, Va., and will be pleased to have Psi Omegas visiting the exposition call upon him.

Because of the efforts exerted by Drs. A .G. Friedrichs and L. D. Archinard, honorary members of Beta Epsilon, New Orleans was selected for the next meeting place of National Society of Dental Pedagogics.

Any graduate desiring to purchase a practice in a small town in Virginia can get into communication with the brother who desires to sell, by writing to the Editor-in-Chief of The Frater. Practice amounts to between $2,500 and $3,500 yearly. Reason for selling, brother desires to remove to Norfolk, Va.

Marriages.

SPEARS-MORGAN.

A. A. Spears, Omega, '03, Brazil, Ind., and Miss Laura Morgan were united in marriage on October 31, 1906. Brother Spears has been practicing in Brazil since graduation, likes Brazil and the people, and has secured an excellent practice.

BELFORD-KILLEN.

Edward E. Belford, P. G. M., Beta Gamma, '04, and Mrs. M. Selma Killen, of Columbus Grove, O., were united in marriage on February 13, 1907.

DALY-REED.

F. T. Daly, Gammu Mu, '06, Cambridge, Neb., and Miss Bessie Logan Reed, of Pulaski, Iowa, were united in marriage at the home of the bride on September 19, 1906. After an extended trip through the South and West, the happy couple is now at home in Cambridge, Neb.

BACKUS-BAILEY.

Wesley M. Backus, P. G. M., Theta, '04, and Miss Frances Amelia Bailey, of Buffalo, were united in marriage at Riverside Episcopal church, on August 20, 1906, Rector Ward Platt officiating. After the ceremony, a wedding supper was served at the home of the bride's sister, after which the happy couple started on a two weeks' honeymoon trip.

The ceremony was a distinctly Psi Omega affair in that the bridal party contained three graduate fellows: Brothers Cole, of Watertown, N. Y., who was best man, and St. John and Stiker, who were ushers. Dr. and Mrs. Backus are now at home at 104 Pooley Place, Buffalo, N. Y.

State Board Questions.

PENNSYLVANIA.

December, 1906.

Anesthesia, Materia Medica and Therapeutics.

1. In what class of cases is the administration of nitrous oxide gas contra-indicated? (b) Why? 2. How should the administration of an anesthetic be modified with reference to age, sex or temperament? 3. How is the muscular system affected in anesthesia? (a) Under ether? (b) Under nitrous-oxide. 4. What local effect have the following drugs on albumen? (a) Carbolic acid? (b) Creosote? (c) Mercuric chloride? 5. What is acetanilid? From what is it derived? State its physiologic action and dose. 6. What are alkaloids? Name three, stating from what each is derived and its dose. 7. What is an escharotic? Name three. 8. What drugs may cause ptyalism? (b) Write a prescription for the treatment of ptyalism. 9. State the composition of Dovers Powder, and give the proportion of each ingredient. 10. What is formaldehyde? State dental uses and strength of solutions that should be used for each purpose.

Special Dental Anatomy, Dental Histology and Dental Physiology.

1. Define alveolus. (b) Alveolar abscess. 2. Describe a lower cuspid tooth. 3. How many lobes has a deciduous upper second molar? (b) Name them. 4. Name and locate the ridges and grooves of the permanent upper second molar. 5. Describe the interglobular spaces. (b) What do they contain in their normal state? 6. Of what minute structures is the peridental membrane composed? 7. Give the approximate chemical analysis of dried dentin. 8. State the number of classes of teeth. (b) Give the functions of each class of teeth. 9. Describe the normal occlusion of the permanent teeth. 10. At

what age does calcification of a permanent cuspid begin? (b) At what age is it erupted? (c) At what age is calcification of the root completed?

Anatomy and Physiology.

1. Locate the sphenoid bone and state its articulations. 2. Name the muscles engaged in rotating the head. 3. Give the names and number of the cranial nerves. (b) Name the principal artery that conveys the blood to the interior of the cranium. 4. Describe the ribs. (b) How many are there? (c) What effect has inspiration on the diameter of the chest? 5. Describe the knee joint. (b) Name the ligaments connected with the joint. 6. State the functions of the special nerve centers in the spinal cord. 7. Describe the principal function of each constituent of the blood. (b) What causes the flow of blood in the veins? 8. What changes take place in the stomach caused by the introduction of food? 9. Describe the peristaltic action of the intestines. 10. Describe the function of the eustachian tube. (b) Function of the ciliary muscle.

Principles and Practice of Operative and Prosthetic Dentistry.

1. Describe systematic methods for examination of the teeth to discover and locate the cause of neuralgic pains. 2. Describe the preparation of a mesio-occlusal cavity with frail walls in a bicuspid to securely anchor a gold filling. (b) A porcelain inlay. 3. Describe the clinical appearance of pyorrhea alveolaris. (b) Give methods of treatment. 4. Name the conditions that would indicate the use of cement and gold in combination, to restore teeth to usefulness. 5. Describe a method of expanding a contracted arch and bringing protruding incisors into normal position. 6. Describe a method of constructing and retaining a removable bridge, to replace the lower incisors. 7. In a full upper metal base denture of single gum teeth, how is a perfectly fitting rim made and attached? 8. Describe the correct way of anatomically arranging and articulating teeth, for an edentulous mouth. 9. Describe the construction of a porcelain jacket crown. 10. Describe the method of making and using cores to obtain accurate dies, from models with deep under cuts.

Chemistry, Metallurgy and Oral Surgery.

1. Define the following chemical terms: Ozone, atom, anode, hydrate, molecule, acid, valence, gas, affinity, dialysis.

2. Write in chemical terms and indicate by formulae the following commercial names: Plaster of paris, table salt, water, lime, oil of vitriol. 3. Describe the preparation of nitrous oxid, and indicate the reaction by a chemical equation. 4. Give three forms in which the element carbon is found. 5. Define noble and base metals and give three examples of each. 6. Give the melting points of gold, lead, zinc, silver and tin. 7. What metals may enter into the composition of dental alloys? (b) Name the approximate proportion of each metal in a dental alloy. 8. Give indications, and describe the methods of operation for root amputation. 9. Define the method for reducing a dislocation of the mandible. 10. Describe the surgical operation for congenital cleft palate.

Dental Pathology and Bacteriology.

1. Distinguish between a ranula and epulis. 2. What is necrosis (b) What causes it? 4. Describe Hutchinson's teeth. (b) State the supposed cause. 4. Distinguish between abrasion, erosion and caries of the teeth. (b) State the probable cause of each. 5. Differentiate gingivitis, pericementitis, and pyorrhea alveolaris. 6. Name the classification of cocci, according to the number and order of arrangement of the cells. 7. What is a spore? Describe the process of spore formation. 8. Distinguish between parasitic and saprophytic bacteria. (b) How do saprophytic bacteria cause disease? 9. Describe the process of pus formation. (b) What class of bacteria are engaged? 10. Distinguish between an antiseptic and a germicide. (b) What is meant by sterilization?

NEBRASKA.

November, 1906.

Chemistry.

1. What effect do different proportions of calcium phosphate and calcium carbonate have on the structure of teeth? 2. Define organic and inorganic chemistry. Give example of each. 3. Give difference between mixture and chemical compound with an example in each case. 4. Give chemical description of the saliva. 5. Give process for making $N2O$, giving impurities some-

times found. Antidote. 6. Give chemical formula and antidotes for the following: carbolic acid, sulphuric acid, arsenic, copper sulphate, chloroform. 7. Name three general classes of dental cements and give ingredients. 8. Give a test for arsenic, gold. 9. Name solvent for gold and platinum. Of what is it composed? Give formula. 10. Describe preparation of plaster of paris. Explain action of H_2O_2 on putrescent pulps.

Metallurgy.

1. What are the noble metals? Base metals? An alloy? 2. What five metals are most useful in dentistry? Give fusing points of each. 3. Give formula for 18 K solder. 4. What is best metal for dies? Why? 5. Give best process for cleaning office scrap. 6. What is best metal for plates and why? 7. Give formula for an amalgam and state why chosen. 8. What properties should a counter die possess? 9. What is the use of flux? 10 . What properties are conferred to gold plate by adding silver.

Oral Surgery.

I. Define staphylorraphy. State the most favorable age for an operation. 2. State why alveolar abscess may cause suppurative inflammation of the maxillary sinus. 3. Mention the predisposing and the exciting causes, together with the local and constitutional symptoms of inflammation. 4. What treatment would you pursue in excessive hemorrhage after tooth extraction? 5. Give one of the causes of antral disease, its diagnosis and treatment. 6. How would you diagnose and treat hypertrophy of the gums? In what class of persons, as to age and mentality, does it occur? 7. Give etiology, pathology, and treatment of pericemental abscess. 8. State the causes of arrest of development of the maxillary bones. 9. Define asphyxia. Give treatment. 10. Define replantation of teeth, transplantation of teeth, and implantation of teeth.

Pathology.

1. Define pathology. 2. How may inflammation terminate? 3. Define sepsis and asepsis. 4. Differentiate thrombosis and embolism. 5. Differentiate hypertrophy and tumor. 6. Define plethora, hyperemia, anemia, ischemia. 7. State why the mouth is a favorable place for the development of bac-

teria. 8. State what is meant by (a) the predisposing cause of disease, (b) the exciting cause of disease. 9. What is sanguinary or serumal calculus? 10. What is the cause of apical alveolar abscess? Describe the process of its development.

Histology.

1. Name tissues that form a tooth. Give relative positions. Give functions of each. Has the pulp lymphatics? 2. Names of the different organs that go to form a tooth and give progress of development. 3. Osteo dentine, what is it? Where found? Give use. 4. What is a cell? Describe a tissue. Describe a blood vessel in and out of the dental pulp. 5. Describe the enamel and dentine organs. 6. What are lacunae? 7. Describe the blood supply to the dental pulp and pericementum. 8. Describe a dental pulp. Describe mucous membrane. 9. Describe the natural means by which the deciduous teeth are shed. 10. What is the function of the cementum? Describe osteoblasts, osteoclasts.

Physiology.

1. What is mastication? 2. What are the organs of mastication? 3. What is a tooth? Give number and period of eruption of the temporary teeth. Give number and period of eruption of the permanent teeth. 4. Briefly describe the development of a tooth. 5. What is the invariable course of a nerve fiber? Do nerve fibers ever unite? What is a plexus and give its function? What are the functions of the nerves of the teeth? 6. What is coagulation of the blood and its use? How may coagulation be aided? How may coagulation be retarded? 7. What is circulation of the blood, and why does it circulate? What are the organs of circulation? What is the normal pulse rate per minute? 8. Name the organs of respiration. What is respiration? Why is respiration necessary to life? What part does the blood play in respiration? Give number of respirations per minute, and relation to the pulse. 9. Give function of the fifth or trifacial nerve. What symptoms indicate an interference with the normal action of the fifth nerve? Give function of the seventh nerve. What results from the severing of the seventh nerve? 10. What is digestion? Name the organs of digestion. Can digestion be carried on without the stomach? If so, how? If not, why?

Anatomy.

1. Name the bones of the cranium. Name the bones of the face. 2. What sinus is in the superior maxilla? What canals or foramina are in the superior maxilla and what are they for? 3. What foramina are in the inferior maxilla? Where located and what are they for? 4. Name and locate the salivary glands, and tell where each discharges into the mouth. 5. Of what is the tongue mostly composed? What nerve supplies the tongue? 6. How many pairs of muscles are attached to the mandible? Name the muscles of mastication. 7. What vessels form the circulatory system? Briefly describe them. 8. How many coats have the arteries, and give function of each coat? Give blood supply of brain. Give blood supply of teeth. 9. How many pairs of cranial nerves? Name them. Give nerve supply of the teeth. 10. What organs are supplied by the pneumogastric nerve? What are its functions?

Materia Medica.

1. Describe how oil of cassia, oil of cloves, creosote and carbolic acid are obtained and used. 2. What agents are used to excite functional activity? (b) What to diminish? 3. In what forms are medicinal agents usually applied? 4. What are general anaesthetics? Name them. 5. What is the best antiseptic? How does it act? 6. What is cocaine? How obtained? Dose? Antidote? 7. What is arsenic? How obtained? Dose? Antidote? 8. What would you do in chloroform narcosis? 9. What is nitrous oxide? How administered? How does it act? What to do in case of asphyxiation from same? 10. Give hypodermic dose of cocaine, morphine, strychnine.

Prosthetic Dentistry.

1. What are the requisites for an impression material? 2. How should a plaster model be treated when a portion of the ridge is soft and the center of the mouth hard? 3. Describe the method of obtaining a correct bite for the full denture. 4. In full dentures are the upper or lower teeth first arranged on the models? Give general arrangement. 5. What muscles have a tendency to displace an upper denture and a lower denture? 7. Describe a Richmond crown and give method of preparing root for the same. 7. Describe the method of constructing a bridge to replace lost teeth between an upper cuspid and second

upper molar, both named teeth being in place and sound. 8. State a method of rotating a lateral incisor. 9. Describe an appliance for expanding or enlarging the arch. 10. Describe the method and material you would use to secure a perfect impression of the inferior maxilla when fractured.

Operative Dentistry.

1. Define dental caries. Give classes and treatment. Etiology. 2. Define abscess. Give different classes with full treatment in each case. 3. Give general rules for cavity preparation. Name classes of cavities and fill cavity in each class with material you advise. 4. Give treatment for exposed pulp, exostosis, conjestion and inflammation in pulp, pulp stones, root necrosis, hypersensitive dentine, erosion, abrasion. 5. Give kinds of materials used in filling teeth. Give examples of each material and the advantages of each. 6. Describe minutely the preparation and filling of a mesio-occlusal cavity of a lower front molar with non-cohesive and cohesive gold. Describe minutely the preparation and filling of a disto-occlusal cavity in upper second molar with amalgam. Give the anatomy of the cavities formed. 7. Give classes of dental irregularities. Give the causes in each class. What is the line of occlusion? What is normal occlusion? What is torso occlusion? What is intra occlusion? What is extra occlusion? 8. Make a gold inlay for mesio-occlusal cavity of a first molar. Insert a porcelain inlay in the gingival third, labial surface of a superior cuspid. Give technic of the two operations. 9. Where use separation in dental operations and why? Any difference in the cavity preparation for gold and amalgam? What difference in the bevel? What is the cavo surface angle? 10. What is the treatment in a case of eburnation or obliterated dentinal tubuli? How would you treat and fill root with blind abscess? How would you treat and fill root in putrescent condition? Differentiate pyorrhea alveolaris and calcic inflammation. How extract a lower third molar?

Antiphlogistine

(INFLAMMATION'S ANTIDOTE.)

Verbum Satis Sapientibus.

Inflammation in and about the buccal cavity does not differ in its nature from any other local inflammation.

Dentists say that Antiphlogistine has the same happy effect on peridental inflammation as it has on any other.

Use it externally and between the gum and cheek simultaneously.

The Denver Chemical Mfg. Co.,
NEW YORK.

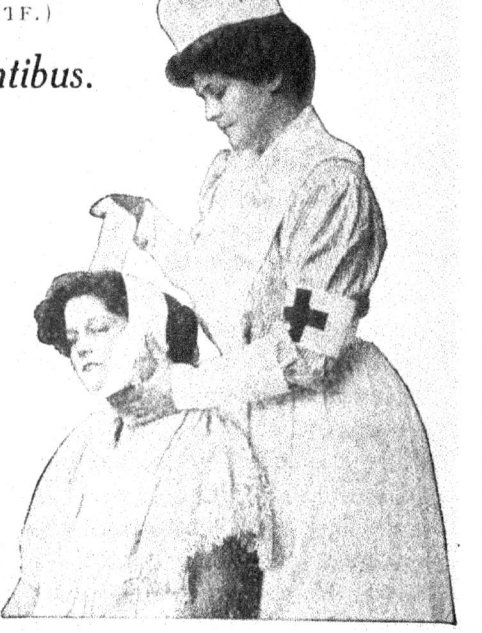

PHILLIPS' MILK OF MAGNESIA

"THE PERFECT ANTACID"

FOR LOCAL OR SYSTEMIC USE

| CARIES | SENSITIVENESS | STOMATITIS |
| EROSION | GINGIVITIS | PYORRHŒA |

Are successfully treated with it. As a mouth wash it neutralizes oral acidity.

PHILLIPS' PHOSPHO-MURIATE OF QUININE,

COMPOUND

TONIC, RECONSTRUCTIVE, AND ANTIPERIODIC

With marked beneficial action upon the nervous system. To be relied upon where a deficiency of the phosphates is evident.

The Chas. H. Phillips Chemical Co., New York and London.

HE
ATER

THE FRATER

Official Organ of The Psi Omega Fraternity.

PUBLISHED BY
THE SUPREME COUNCIL
In November, January, March and May,
AT TIFFIN, OHIO.

SUPREME COUNCIL

Dr. EDW. H. STING, 91 E. Perry St., Tiffin, Ohio.

Dr. J. E. NYCE, 1001 Witherspoon Bldg., Philadelphia, Pa.

Dr. H. E. FRIESELL, 6000 Penn Ave., Pittsburg, Pa.

BUSINESS MANAGER.

Dr. J. E. NYCE, 1001 Witherspoon Bldg., Philadelphia, Pa.

EDITOR-IN-CHIEF.

Dr. EDW. H. STING, Tiffin, Ohio.

SUBSCRIPTION.

One Dollar per year, payable in advance :: The Frater will be sent to all subscribers until ordered discontinued :: Send all communications to the Editor-in-Chief. :: Exchanges please send one copy to each of the Supreme Councilors.

Entered as second-class matter November 7, 1904, at the Post Office at Tiffin, Ohio.

FRATERNITY DIRECTORY.

Active Chapters.

ALPHA	Baltimore College of Dental Surgery.
BETA	New York College of Dentistry.
GAMMA	Pennsylvania Col. of Dental Surgery, Phila.
DELTA	Tufts Dental College, Boston, Mass.
EPSILON	Western Reserve University, Cleveland, O.
ZETA	University of Pennsylvania, Philadelphia.
ETA	Philadelphia Dental College.
THETA	University of Buffalo, Dental Department.
IOTA	Northwestern University, Chicago, Ill.
KAPPA	Chicago College of Dental Surgery.
LAMBDA	University of Minnesota, Minneapolis.
MU	University of Denver, Denver, Col.
NU	Pittsburg Dental College, Pittsburg, Pa.
XI	Milwaukee, Wis., Med. Col., Dental Dept.
MU DELTA	Harvard University, Dental Department.
OMICRON	Louisville College of Dental Surgery.
PI	Baltimore Medical College, Dental Dept.
BETA SIGMA	College of Physicians and Surgeons, Dental Department, San Francisco, Cal.
RHO	Ohio Col. of Dental Surgery, Cincinnati.
SIGMA	Medico-Chirurgical College, Philadelphia.
TAU	Atlanta Dental College, Atlanta, Ga.
UPSILON	University of Southern California, Dental Department, Los Angeles.
PHI	University of Maryland, Baltimore.
CHI	North Pacific Dental Col., Portland, Ore.
PSI	College of Dentistry, O. M. U., Columbus.
OMEGA	Indiana Dental College, Indianapolis, Ind.
BETA ALPHA	University of Illinois, Chicago.
BETA GAMMA	George Washington Uni., Washington, D.C.
BETA DELTA	University of California, San Francisco.
BETA EPSILON	New Orleans College of Dentistry.
BETA ZETA	St. Louis Dental College, St. Louis, Mo.
BETA ETA	Keokuk Dental College, Keokuk, Iowa.
BETA THETA	Georgetown University, Washington, D. C.
GAMMA IOTA	Southern Dental College, Atlanta, Ga.
GAMMA KAPPA	University of Michigan, Ann Arbor.
GAMMA LAMBDA	Col. of Dental and Oral Surg. of New York.
GAMMA MU	University of Iowa, Iowa City.
GAMMA NU	Vanderbilt Uni., Nashville, Tenn.

Alumni Chapters.

New York Alumni Chapter....................New York City.
Duquesne Alumni Chapter.....................Pittsburg, Pa.
Minnesota Alumni Chapter................Minneapolis, Minn.
Chicago Alumni Chapter.........................Chicago, Ill.
Boston Alumni Chapter........................ Boston, Mass.
Philadelphia Alumni Chapter...............Philadelphia, Pa.
New Orleans Alumni Chapter...............New Orleans, La.
Los Angeles Alumni Chapter...............Los Angeles, Cal.
Cleveland Alumni Chapter...................Cleveland, Ohio.
Sealth Alumni Chapter.........................Seattle, Wash.
Portsmouth Alumni Chapter................Portsmouth, Ohio.
Buffalo Alumni Chapter.......................Buffalo, N. Y.

ALUMNI DIRECTORY.

Allegheny, Pa.—
F. H. Deterding, Nu, '05,
417 Third street.
Reynolds M. Sleppy, Nu, '04,
1915 Beaver avenue.
Altoona, Pa.—
Herbert R. Wehrle, Nu, '03,
Altoona Trust Bldg.
Arkadelphia, Ark.—
J. C. Settles, Omicron, '04.
Augusta, Ga.—
R. H. Calhoun, Tau, '04,
936 Broad street.
Brooklyn, N. Y.—
Ellison Hillyer, Beta, '93,
472 Greene avenue.
Winthrop W. Thompson,
Beta, '02,
383 Hancock street.
Horace P. Gould, Beta, '95,
193 Joralemon street.
Warrington G. Lewis,
Beta, '01,
162 Clinton street.
Walter S. Watson, Beta, '02,
270 Halsey street.
Bowling Green, O.—
E. J. Frowine, Psi, '04.
Buffalo, N. Y.—
Wes. M. Backus, Theta, '04,
485 Grant street.
Chihuahua, Mexico.—
M. F. Bauchert, Beta, '96.
Chico, Cal.—
J. R. Young, Beta Delta, '03.
Box 515.
Columbus, O.—
H. M. Semans, Beta, '97,
289 East State street.
Cleveland, O.—
E. E. Belford,
Beta Gamma, '04,
E. 90 Place and Superior avenue.
Delhi, La.—
T. K. McLemore,
Gamma Iota, '06.
Edgefield, S. C.—
Augustus H. Corley, Tau, '04.
Florisant, Mo.—
G. S. Steinmesch,
Beta Zeta, '04.
Fort Gaines, Ga.—
R. H. Saunders, Tau, '05.
Fort Leavenworth, Kan.—
J. D. Millikin, Beta Sigma,
Dental Surgeon, U.S.A.

Fredericksburg, Tex.—
F. Keidel, Alpha, '04.
Gallitzin, Pa.—
J. L. Paul, Alpha, '01.
Gonzales, Tex.—
S. C. Patton, Tau, '03.
Hancock, Mich.—
Ralph W. DeMass,
Beta Gamma, '05,
Funkey Block.
Hull, Ill.—
L. H. Wolfe, Beta Eta, '05.
Iager, W. Va.—
G. E. Dennis, Phi, '05.
Ithaca, N. Y.—
A. M. MacGachen,
Theta, '03,
218 East State street.
Johnsonburg, Pa.—
H. C. Coleman, Nu, '03.
Johnstown, Pa.—
Owen Morgan, Alpha, '95.
Jolo Jolo, (Sulu Islands) P.I.
O. M. Sorber, Nu, '97,
Dental Surgeon, U. S. A.
Knox, Pa.—
A. J. Rose, Rho, '03,
Lafayette, Ind.—
A. R. Ross, Gamma, '03.
Lewistown, Pa.—
Curtis H. Marsh,
Gamma, '06.
14 E. Market street.
Liberty, N. Y.—
W. A. Duckley, Beta, '00.
Logansport, Ind.—
H. G. Stalnaker, Omega, '03.
Los Angeles, Cal.—
J. F. Curran, Kappa, '01,
Suite 615,
Auditorium Bldg.
C. C. Jarvis, Upsilon, '04,
302 Severance Bldg.
S. W. Clapp, Upsilon, '06,
24 Muskegon Bldg.
Malone, N. Y.—
R. N. Porter, Gamma, '01.
Mansfield, La.—
G. J. Griffiths, Tau, '03.
Ada, O.—
C. W. Brecheisen, Psi, '02.
Aiken, S. C.—
G. A. Milner, Tau, '05.
McKeesport, Pa.—
W. D. Fawcett, Nu, '99,
508½ Fifth avenue.

Milwaukee, Wis.—
  E. J. Schlief, Xi, '97,
    417 Wells Bldg.
  J. E. Callaway, Xi, '06,
    Suite 306, Stumpf and Langhoff Bldg.
Morganfield, Ky.—
  W. S. Green, Omicron,' 04.
New York City.—
  A. S. Walker, Beta, '97,
    295 Central Park, West.
  E. W. Burckhardt, Beta,'04,
    Van Corlear Place, Kingsbridge.
  S. W. Van Saun, Beta, '00,
    Broadway and 74th St. The Ansonia.
New Orleans, La.—
  A. J. Cohn, Alpha, '99,
    703 Morris Bldg.
  Leon Barnett, Beta Epsilon, '05,
    703 Macheca Bldg.
  Rene Esnard, Beta Epsilon, '05,
    612 Macheca Bldg.
Norristown, Pa.—
  D. H. Wetzel, Zeta, '02.
Oakland, Cal.—
  C. H. Merritt, Alpha, '98,
    308-9 Union Savings Bank Bldg.
Oroville, Cal.—
  L. H. Marks, B. Sigma, '04.
Paso Robles, Cal.—
  W. G. Gates, Kappa, '05.
Paterson, N. J.—
  A. Dewitt Payne, Beta, '99,
    160 Broadway.
Pikesville, Ky.—
  J. M. Williams, Rho, '05.
Pittsburg, Pa.—
  W. Emmory Ferree, Alpha, '00, 7138 Hamilton ave., East End.
  C. L. McChesney, Nu, '99,
    98 Washington avenue.
  H. E. Friesell, Gamma, '95,
    6000 Penn avenue.
Philadelphia, Pa.—
  A. F. Goddard, Gamma,'01,
    15th and Chestnut Sts., 1302 Pennsylvania Bldg.
  A. P. Lee, Zeta, '00,
    3403 Chestnut street.
  J. E. Nyce, Gamma, '02,
    1001 Witherspoon Bldg.
Roby, Tex.—
  J. N. Platt, Pi, '02.
Rowland, N. C.—
  C. H. Lennan, Tau, '03.
San Francisco, Cal.—
  C. W. Knowles, M.D., D.D.S., Beta Sigma, '99,
    2417 Washington St.

Thos. R. Morffew, Beta Sigma, Examiner Bldg.
Seattle, Wash.—
  Geo. T. Williams, Nu, '04,
    Snoqualmie Hotel.
  F. W. Hergert, Chi, '03,
    651 Colman Block.
  C. P. Poston, Chi,
    218 Lumber Exchange.
Springfield, Mass.—
  H. Everton Hosley, Gamma, '95,
    Phoenix Bldg.
St. Joseph, Ill.—
  H. E. Davis, Rho, '03.
St. Louis, Mo.—
  H. J. Braun, Beta Zeta, '04,
    2850 St. Louis avenue.
  H. V. Pfaff, Iota, '99,
    2217 St. Louis avenue.
Tiffin, O.—
  W. H. Holtz, Rho, '03.
  E. H. Sting, Alpha, '95.
  E. C. West, Psi, '02.
Topsham, Maine.—
  H. Q. Mariner, Sigma, '05.
Tuscaloosa, Ala.—
  H. Clay Hassell, Omicron, '98.
Upland, Ind.—
  J. A. Loughry, Psi, '04.
Union, S. C.—
  Jas. M. Wallace, Phi, '04.
Vinton, Iowa.—
  B. F. Schwartz, Iota, '04.
Washington, D. C.—
  Shirley W. Bowles, Eta,'98,
    825 Vermont Ave.
  C. L. Constantini, Beta Gamma, '03,
    814 14th St., N. W.
  Ralph Stuart Clinton, Beta Gamma, '06,
    The Carolina, 706 11th St., N. W.
  Marion Edwyn Harrison, Beta Gamma, '06,
    The Newberne, 12th St. and Mass.av.
Washington, Pa.—
  Howard R. Smith, Nu, '03,
    17 West Chestnut street.
Waynesboro, Miss.—
  C. H. Gray, Tau, '04.
Winchester, Ky.—
  George S. Brooks, Rho, '02.
Westfield, N. J.—
  Theo. R. Harvey, Gamma, '94, 245 Broad street.
Williamson, W. Va.—
  Wm. S. Rosenheim, Pi, '05.
Wellsburg, W. Va.—
  K. C. Brashear, Psi, '02,

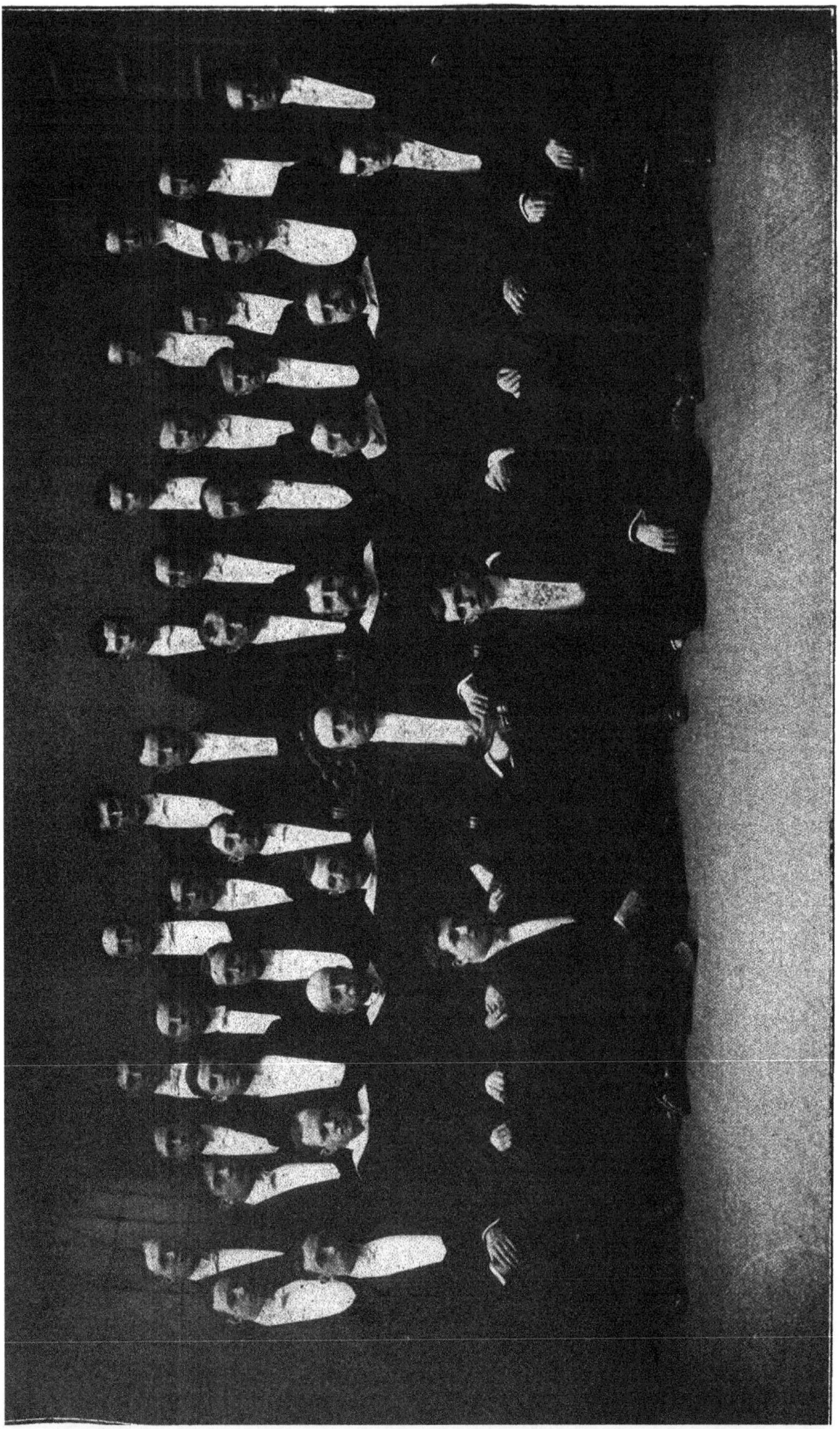

THE FRATER.

Vol. 6.   May, 1907.   No. 4.

BUFFALO ALUMNI CHAPTER.

A. G. Stiker, Theta, '07· Editor.

Organized on March 19, 1907, Buffalo, N. Y.

The Crystal Anniversary banquet brought out nearly all the Psi Omega alumni members residing in Buffalo. At this banquet preliminary steps were taken and on March 19, the organization of the Buffalo Alumni Chapter was successfully effected and the following officers were elected:

```
Grand Master...................G. A. St. John.
Junior Master..................W. M. Backus.
Secretary......................A. G. Stiker.
Treasurer......................F. H. Jelley.
Inside Guardian................J. D. Dixon.
```

Dr. St. John read an interesting paper on the "Care and Treatment of Children's Teeth" which caused a lengthy discussion.

The chapter will meet monthly, on the fourth Tuesday. Visiting Psi Omegas will please communicate with Amos G. Stiker, 669 Main street, in regard to place of meeting.

PROSELYTING.

Elison Hillyer, P. S. C., Beta, '95.

A genuine surprise is a rarity to the average individual in these "hustling" days and we are apparently ready to accept as perfectly natural the incidents which combine to make up our more or less eventful careers. Such has been my experience, as a layman, professional man and fraternity member. I acknowledge that within the last few days, I have as a fraternity man, received one of the greatest surprises I have ever experienced. A good Psi Omega brother recently wrote me that his relations—family and professional—had brought him in close touch with ——— Dental Fraternity and that he had received a pressing invitation to join that fraternity; much as he regretted severing ties with Psi Omega, he asked me if I would see that his resignation, as a member of Psi Omega, was presented to the proper authorities.

Now, primarily, let me say, that I have the highest personal regard for this particular brother and also for those who were the instigators of his desire to "change his colors." Nay, more; I hold the closest friendships with many fraternity men—other than Psi Omegas—and men for whom everyone has the highest esteem and whatever I may say here has no atom of personality behind it.

The surprise of this letter led me to reply to the writer indicating my feelings regarding the matter and referring him to the Supreme Council. It also led me to investigate somewhat and I found that a system (shall I call it) of proselytizing existed, with what results I do not know. Think of it! Ponder for a moment upon the initiation vow and then tell me how any true Psi Omega could even think of severing his ties. Is that vow of such light importance? Or could a man, breaking one vow, be a good candidate or loyal brother of any other fraternity?

And what of the fraternity which would use such means of furthering its membership? Surely nothing beyond this could be its object. If power or influence are desired let it be exerted as individuals—not as a fraternity. What is it that makes us figuratively—if not actually—"take off our hats" when "Fraternity" is even mentioned? It means that deep down under the superficial glamor the truest ethics lie, no matter what the name of the fraternity may be.

Has, then, our idea of "ethics" been so prostituted by our narrow conceptions, professionally, that we fail to comprehend the underlying basic principle? Let no Psi Omega ever fail to look deep into his sub-conscience, as it were, and make sure that his aims are as true and his heart as loyal as appearances would indicate upon the surface.

I am awaiting with interest the development of this new phase, which is to me a great surprise; for among all my experiences among literary fraternities, never has such a condition presented itself, to my knowledge. To assume and lay aside at will those closest of ties—other than blood and sometimes even more binding—would be a thing unthought of among such "brotherhoods." Have we so little appreciation of the life-long value of our associations as to think that they may be considered so lightly?

I would that this might catch the eye of every dental fraternity man and cause him to pause—though but for a moment—and re-pledge himself to whichever fraternity he may belong—for I know of none whose objects are not the best. Let fraternal rivalry, if such exists, cease and let us each following the paths prescribed by the environment of each, press forward for the good of each individual and the "uplift" of the profession at large.

PSI OMEGA INFLUENCE.

Howard Williamson, Omicron,' 97.

Delivered at the Fifteenth Anniversary Banquet Given by the Portsmouth Alumni Chapter.

The Portsmouth has just completed a successful year. We have passed safely through the ordeal of the formative period. We have convened with only two members to answer to roll call; we have listened to papers with less than half our members present; we have at several meetings had a full attendance. There have been times when enthusism flowed high, and times when enthusiasm was at a low tide; but to-night I am pleased to state that the enthusiasm and attendance assure us that we have weathered our storm period. It was not because your grand master made an active strenuous effort in the performance of his duties; it was not because any member of this chapter made a strenuous effort for permanent organization, although each member did his work and did it well; it was not because any member of this chapter set his head and his teeth, determined that it should be permanent that we have succeeded, but because our organization is founded on principles that cannot fail; on principles of right, and whatever is right must, if not immediately, eventually prevail.

I have seen times in this town when professional spirit had sunk to a low ebb, and it seemed that quackery had taken the wings of the morning and had infected the populace with a germ that caused it to think dentistry a profession which sold fillings by the job lot. I have seen the time when it seemed that each man was of necessity drawing the atmosphere of his office closer and was not permitted to partake of free intercourse with his fellow practitioners. But in the past year, while I have seen a few things that were not entirely up to the standard, yet again I have heard kind words and have seen acts that have made me feel that our profession in this town has been snatched from the depths and placed on a shrine around which we can all safely worship with pride. Much of this, my dear brothers, is due to you, due to your concerted efforts; dut to your loyalty in the trust Psi Omega gave you when it honored you with the pledge it imposed upon you. I have seen your concerted effort drive from your midst and from this town a member who violated this sacred trust which he had promised to keep inviolate. I have seen you benefited by associating with one another. I have seen you lend the helping hand. I have seen all the good results of fraternalism; out of this I have seen grow an institution which is a credit to you, to your profession, and to Psi Omega.

Does the dentist ever stop to think how much of his life is spent at the dental chair and in his office, does he realize the fact that a majority of the dental profession die with their shoulders to the wheel? If so, can he fail to know that unless his work is a pleasure, his life is, in a measure, a failure?

He can on a balmy spring day wander through green fields, over beautiful hills, along shady brooks viewing the landscape and see the sparkling of river and lake in the distance, rejoice with all nature and be glad, yes, even happy. He may sit down on the fresh green grass and fall into a reverie of contentment, but if his work is not interesting, if his profession is a bore, he may suddenly be called from the reverie by the thought of the irksome toil on the morrow.

He may attend the concert, or opera, and hear music express the deepest, highest, tenderest longings of the human heart; he may hear the soft murmur of a nocturne, the faint caressing diminuendo of the lullaby, the wailing harmony of the dirge, or music that bridges the vast distances and interprets to heaven the prayers of man. He can be wrought upon by these exquisite sounds and can lose himself in this beautiful entertainment and think divine thoughts only to be suddenly brought back to earth because of the thought of the morrow and the toil which he does not enjoy.

Brothers, we need this Psi Omega organization; you need it; I need it, and the dental profession of Portsmouth needs it. Most lives are filled with half finished tasks which were begun with enthusiasm but which were dropped because the enthusiastic beginner did not have enough grit to carry them to the conclusion.

How easy it is to start a thing when the mind is aglow with zeal before disappointment has dulled ambition; it does not take much ability to begin a thing, but it takes persistence and grit to carry a thing when ambition begins to lag.

The ability to hold on is one of the rarest of human virtues. There are plenty who will go with the crowd and who will work hard as long as they can hear the music, but when the majority have dropped out, when others have turned back and a man feels himself alone fighting for a principle, it takes a very different order of ability to persist, but there is not one member of this organization who has not the grit; therefore the Portsmouth Alumni chapter will live and as the town grows larger and better the dental profession of this city will be more ideal.

Every man of this chapter is self-made, which makes this a self-made chapter. Our future is an uncut block of marble. Let us beware how we smite it lest we ruin the model we have in our mind's eye for an ideal organization.

We have chosen for our grand master for the coming year Peter Young. Now this Peter is young only in name and appearance. In experience and judgment he is old, but in activity and vitality he is young, again. Since the chapter was first organized he has been a very energetic member. Since the name Peter is derived from the Greek word meaning "rock," with Peter Young at the head of our Portsmouth chapter for this year, we have an organization founded on a rock. And, while our grand master is made of this good material, he is made of no better material than each member of this chapter and I hope I will be practicing dentistry in Portsmouth long enough to see each one of you grand master of this organization.

Have you ever stopped to think that civilization, culture, and refinement are all due to association, organization and society where man meets his fellow man and fellow craftsman and has a free exchange of ideas, and do you ever stop to think, on the other hand, that ignorance and narrow mindedness are due ofttimes to seclusion? A child incarcerated from infancy will become lower than the lowest animals, yet take the same child, educate him, throw him in contact with brilliant minds, he will absorb and become so completely saturated with thoughts and ideas that he will be able to say as Victor Hugo said in his declining years: "I am like a forest once cut down, the new shoots are stronger and livelier than ever, sunshine is on my head, the earth gives me her generous sap and nature lightens me with things beyond. History, philosophy, romance, tradition, ode and song, I have tried it all and feel that I have not uttered a thousandth part of that which is in me."

There never was in the history of civilization a more thorough development of friendship between men than in Greek life, and this is the basis of idea of the men who founded Psi Omega.

When a lad goes through his college career without making friends and a fraternity, you may put it down he is going through life alone, undeveloped. When a lad becomes a member of Psi Omega, he, at that moment, receives his inspiration to be worthy of his society. He feels the confidence and support of her friendships. He realizes that it is not all of life to live for himself alone, but the best of life is to do for others. And what must become of Psi Omegas who affiliate with the advertising quacks, The Boston Dental Parlours, The Philadelphia Dental Parlours, the very scum of the profession? Far better be it for a human being to have a millstone tied round his neck and be dropped to the depths of the deep, than to take the sacred vows of Psi Omega and then affiliate with these outcasts of the dental profession who should also be the outcasts of society.

The twelve Apostles had their Judas, Caesar had his Brutus, Washington had his Arnold, the Masons had their Morgan, and occasionally there will creep into the ranks of Psi Omega a traitor.

TO ALL FRAT MEN.

Angus P. Rose, Eta, '07.

I was told:
    To hastily prepare
      For things that made my blood run cold,
    When witnessed anywhere.
    My heart was filled with misery
    And plaster filled my throat,
      A thousand night mares rode on me ..
    Before I rode the goat.

The Dream:
    The previous night while thinking o'er
      The goat that I must ride,
    Strong hands had bound me to the floor,
      And to my threats defied.
    A host of corpses rose in view
      That seemed in air to float,
    And scrutched that boiling lead;
      Now then bring in the goat.

    They dipped me in the boiling lead
      And stretched me out on ice,
    Then one great Achilles came and said:
      "Now skin him quick and nice."
    This done they put me in salt brine
      Then placed me in a boat
    To cross the equatorial line
      Towed by that blooming goat.

    The goat he frequently squeezed my hand
      Then spilt me in the sea
    But when I reached Matt Casey's land
      I struggled and got free
    The spell of fright at once was broke
      And to my aching head
    I quickly raised my hand and awoke
      To find myself in bed.

Anticipation.
    The horror of that dream next day
      Yet filled me with affright.
    Yet bravely finishing the day

I rode the goat that night.
But whether he was tired or weak
I took no time to cite.
Before they'd time to think or speak
I had thrown that goat all right.

Realization.
Then up came many a smiling friend,
Who grasped me by the hand,
And made me quickly comprehend,
That help I could command.
And, now, while sailing down life's stream,
To gain such friendship and esteem
I'd ride ten thousand goats.

SOME DENTAL FORMULAS. WHY AND HOW I USE THEM.

D. A. Zurbrigg, Sigma.

Arsenic. This drug I use very seldom, and then only when time to properly make use of pressure anesthesia is not available. I use it in cases of almost inaccessible cavity approach. This can only occur in molars or sometimes in malposed bicuspids. As we all know, arsenic is an irritant poison, therefore extraordinary precautions must be taken in handling it.

The formula in which I use it is this:

Cotton—carefully cut into short fibers.
Arsenic Trioxide.
Cocaine Hydrochloride.
Thymol.   Of each 30 grains.
Oil Cinnamon.   10 minims.

Triturate, in a glass mortar, the last four ingredients until a creamy paste results, then gradually add the cotton until uniformly distributed by further trituration.

On cotton, because I can handle it safely and place it exactly where wanted. With paste and powder preparations you cannot be sure but some has dropped or been smeared on the cavity margins or elsewhere, and you later wonder "how that arsenic got out." After placing over the spot wanted, take another small pellet of absorbent cotton, let it absorb a trifle of creosote, place, and seal all with gutta percha as hot as the patient can stand it, or with creamy cement.

Dismiss the patient assured that that pulp will be dead in twenty-four to forty-eight hours, if arsenic will do it, without having caused any pain whatever.

On removing that cotton pellet you are positive of removing all of the arsenic. This may be done as long as a week or a month after insertion without fear of any bad results because the thymol and creosote assure aseptic conditions.

The cocaine deadens first irritation and is much superior to morphine of the older formulas. Oil of cinnamon acts as a vehicle, is pleasant and a solvent for thymol.

Formaldehyde Solution, Formalin. A forty per cent. solution of the gas in water. In this strength I do not use it except to disinfect extracted teeth on which I want to perform an autopsy, or with tricresol to sterilize a root canal. Do not use it as a sterilizing agent on your steel pointed instruments, chisels, excavators, etc., unless very carefully dried after a short immersion. Almost any strength solution will rust them. Besides, there are better and safer ways of sterilization.

Cocaine Hydrochloride. From arsenic to cocaine is an easy step because of related uses. Here is a formula used for several things:

Cocaine Hydrochloride—36 grains.
Alcohol (95 per cent.)—3 fluid drams.
Dissolve by the aid of a water bath and add: ether—1 fluid dram.

This is a fifteen per cent. solution, resembling a marketed preparation which some of you may be familiar with. I use it altogether for pressure anesthesia in preference to crystals or tablets of cocaine, for anesthetizing in crown fitting or preparing, for touching gums previous to lancing, for placing the rubber dam for cervical fillings. For these purposes, use a little one-sixteenth inch square of spunk, this being less wasteful of my liquid and more easily handled. Adrenalin or adnepherin chloride (1-1000) added at the time of using above, offers almost bloodless operations, and is not physiologically incompatible.

Local Anesthetic.
　　Cocaine hydrochloride .... 12 grains.
　　Distilled water .... 1-2 fl. oz.

　　Carbolic acid .... 5 minims.
　　Glycerin .... 1 fl. oz.

　　Tr. iodine .... 4 minims.
　　Potassium iodide .... 2 grains.
　　Water .... 1-2 fl. oz.
　　Dist. Ext. Witchazel .... 1 fl. oz.

　　　Make three separate solutions as indicated and, when dissolved, mix all together, set aside one or two days, decant and filter, when it will be ready for use. This is a solution of less than one per cent. cocaine, never deteriorates and does not cause sloughing. It renders the extraction of teeth as painless as can be done with a local anesthetic.

　　　Paraformaldehyde, Paraform. A polymeric form obtained by heating the above aqueous solution until the solid form remains. It occurs in commerce as a white powder, insoluble in water, with a very pungent odor of formaldehyde. Also in solid form as a proprietary article. In my opinion it is a specific for the disinfection of root canals, in fact, the entire root with surrounding tissues, and, therefore, incidentally the cure of chronic abscesses. For on the thorough disinfection of the whole tooth structure with surrounding tissues, and later filling the canal with whatever you prefer, depends your permanent cure. This paraform does by slowly evolving formic aldehyde gas, which, being confined by gutta percha, penetrates "everything in sight" so to speak. Of course your canal, and fistula if any, has been physically cleansed beforehand. Closely allied to this treatment is the combination of tricresol and formalin after Dr. J. C. Buckley.

　　　Tricresol—Is a concentrated preparation of three cresols, ortho, meta, and para, free of all impurities. Obtained by the fractional distillation of that portion of coal tar oil coming over between 190 and 210 degrees C. It is a clear, brownish liquid, colorless when fresh, its chief drawback being its slight solubility in water, only two and one-half per cent. This justifies the many saponaceous preparations of it on the market.

　　　Creolin (Merch), Lysol (L. & F.), Cresylone (P. D. & Co.), etc.

　　　These are from thirty to fifty per cent. solutions of tricresol, are practically non-poisonous, entirely soluble in water in any proportion, and exceed carbolic acid in disinfecting powers three to five times.

Lysol and Cresylone.—Used as a two per cent. solution for instrument sterilization. In this strength it is equal to a five per cent. carbolic acid solution. Half hour immersion being sufficient on authority of W. D. Miller.

Broaches and hypodermic needle points are kept in twenty to twenty-five per cent. solutions. They will not rust and are always sterile.

Thymophen.—Equal parts phenol crystals and thymol, recently brought out by E. C. Kirk. It is the dressing after pulp extirpation when immediate root canal filling is for some reason contradicted. Campho-phenique has been used for the same purpose though it is not as good. Made in the same way, the two solids on trituration soon form a clear liquid.

Menthol, 20 grains; chloroform, 1 fl. dr.; ether, 3 fl. drs. may be used for post operative pains of tooth extraction; sensitive cavity preparation, or quieting those little nerve filaments which refuse to be comforted or removed after pressure anesthesia has been attempted.

Tincture Iodine, U. S. P., is a seven per cent. solution in alcohol.

Tincture Iodine, Dental—simply a saturated solution in alcohol, amounting to ten per cent.

Tincture Iodine, Churchills, N. F., stronger yet, made so by the addition of potassium iodide which also permits of the addition of twenty-five per cent. water. It is a ten and one-half per cent. solution.

Solution Iodine, Churchill's Caustic, N. F., is a twenty-five per cent. solution in a fifty per cent. potassium iodide aqueous menstrum.

Both the latter are useful in treatment of erupting third molars.

Soldering Fluid.
    Boric Acid .... 1-2 oz.
    Borax .... 1-2 oz.
    Ammon. Chlor. .... 12 grs.
    Potassium Carb. .... 5 grs.
    Water .... 4 fl. ozs.

Liquid Soap—(German Hospital.)
    Cottonseed Oil .... 33 C. C.
    Alcohol .... 300 C. C.

Water .... 325 C. C.
Sodium Hydrate .... 45 gm.
Potassium Carbonate .... 10 gm.
Ether Sulphuric .... 15 C. C.
Carbolic Acid .... 25 C. C.

To the oil in a flask add 100 C. C. water and 200 C. C. alcohol. Add the sodium hydrate, shake until the latter is dissolved, and set aside until the oil is saponified. Add the remainder of the alcohol and the potassium carbonate dissolved in the remainder of the waer. Lastly add the carbolic acid and shake, may be used as above antiseptic soap or for toilet uses by substituting some perfume or essential oil and omitting the ether.

Alkaline Antiseptic Solution.
A.
Sodium Bicarbonate .... 4 ozs.
Acid Boric .... 1 oz.
Acid Benzoic .... 1 oz.
Acid Salicylic .... 40 grs.

B.
Eucalyptol .... 40 minims.
Oil Pine Needles .... 20 minims.
Thymol .... 20 grains.
Menthol .... 10 grains.
Oil Wintergreen .... 10 minims.

Glycerin .... 30 fl. ozs.
Alcohol .... 40 fl. ozs.
Water .... q. s. to make one gallon.

Dissolve A in the water and add the glycerin slowly. Dissolve B in the alcohol and add to A when all effervescence has ceased. Shake well, and, after a few days, filter. May be used as above straw-colored solution, or solution carmine, N. F., 3 parts, tinct. budbear, N. F., 1 part, may be added to give it a deep wine color.

Excellent as a general mouth wash and for bracket table use. Stronger than most marketed solutions and very much cheaper.

Abscess Cures.—Nearly all take after this general formula and cannot do more than the following:

For the Powder:
Thymol .... 10 grains.
Exsic. Alum .... 25 grains.
Zinc Oxide .... 40 grains.

For the Liquid:
Formalin .... 1 fl. dr.
Creosote .... 1 fl. dr.
  or
Tricresol.

These are all working formulas, your druggist will be glad to fill them for you, and they can be depended on to do the work they are intended for.

FURTHER EXPERIENCES IN THE PHILIPPINES.

O. M. Sorber, Nu, '98.

In November, 1905, orders were received to proceed to Camp Darago, Albay Province, Luzon, for duty, where a stay of two months was made.

On December 17, an attempt was made to ascend Mount Mayon, the great volcano a few miles from the post. This mountain is very steep, especially the upper two thirds, and as it is about eight thousand, five hundred (8,500) feet high and rises at the edge of the sea, it presents a tremendously imposing appearance. Some months previously a party from the post had accomplished the ascent and the route followed at that time was chosen by our party, consisting of Lt. M——, myself, one private of the Hospital Corps, and a native boy who was taken to care for the horses.

We left the post at four-thirty in the morning and after riding through rough country for about eight miles, dismounted at seven-thirty, at approximately fifteen hundred feet elevation.

We commenced the ascent immediately, carrying canteens, a camera, a barometer, some packages of lunch, and stout sticks.

For the next thousand feet of ascent the course lay through grass knee high.

This was followed by thickets of low bushes which gradually grew smaller as we ascended and were finally succeeded by a short grass. Above this for a few hundred yards there was a belt of moss and lichens then we encountered a waste of sand and rocks without a trace of vegetation. All signs of life ceased at about thirty-five hundred feet.

Many interesting things were seen in the belt of vegetation, including great tree ferns, some of them twenty feet high and very beautiful.

Near the upper part of this belt we found a few raspberries, blueberries, and a variety of wintergreen (gaultheria) differing greatly, however, from the variety found in the Allegheny mountains.

The hard gray-black rock of this mountain is known as "Andesite" and the sand is very black.

Above vegetation we entered the clouds and a fine drizzling rain served to modify the heat which had caused us considerable distress.

Progress could be made only on the ridges of rock with which the mountain is ribbed from top to bottom, the intervals being sand slides down which stones and rocks came bounding like cannon shots.

Our way lay along the edge of a watercourse, thirty to fifty feet deep, with perpendicular walls. At this time, this watercourse contained no running water as the rock and sand absorb all moisture except from the heaviest rainfalls.

The ascent of the upper two thirds was much like going up a ladder. At any time we could touch the ground ahead by slightly leaning forward and the exertion of the climb proved to be extremely exhausting. There were no serious obstacles, however, until we neared the top where an immense gorge appeared to bar all progress and we were unable to find a way around owing to the dense mass of clouds and the pelting rain which made it impossible to see more than a few yards.

At this time we were among huge rocks, loosely poised and apparently ready, at a moment's notice, to give us a ride to the bottom. This did not serve to make us feel much at ease as earthquake shocks are extremely common in this neighborhood.

While I was recovering from that down-an-out-feeling Lt. M—— went up and to the right in search of a way out of the difficulty. He was soon out of sight of course and not long after we heard faint calls for help.

I was unable to cross an intervening sand slide, but the corps man found better footing and was soon on his way up. He soon met the Lieutenant returning with a couple of fingers badly skinned. It appears he was making his way around a particularly bad point of rocks, hanging on by fingers and toes, when a large rock above toppled over and caught his hand and, for some time, held him suspended between heaven and earth. With his free hand he at last secured a wedge shaped stone and using it as a lever managed to free himself.

This experience caused him to change his mind about going up and after a consultation it was decided that we would return.

At this point, as we learned later from members of the party that made the ascent before, we were about eight thousand feet above sea level.

We were soon chilled through by the cold wind and rain and getting on the nearest sand slide we started for the base at a great rate of speed.

The descent, for about five thousand feet, was made by a compromise between walking and skating, using our sticks as a kind of third support projecting backward, and working our feet as if walking. No effort was required to propel us but at intervals it was necessary to sit down and rest as the tendons of our knees felt very much as if they were about to pull from their supports.

We accomplished the five thousand feet in about thirty minutes, and, as we neared the lower slopes, we found we were obliged to shout to make ourselves heard. Our ears could not at once accommodate themselves to the rapid increase of air pressure.

The sand slides terminated at the belt of vegetation, then our progress was pretty slow. In order to find better ground we diverged to the right from the path of ascent and thereby made a great blunder but did not realize it until too late to turn back.

We got into an immense area of grass which was almost like a cane brake in character, the stems being about as thick as one's finger, hard, stiff and dry. It appears that this grass does not die down yearly but sheds its lower leaves as it puts on new ones above. This grass jungle appeared to lean in one direction and that in a direction which led us farther away from the trail at each step.

Eventually we were obliged to give up the attempt to get through by following the course easiest to pursue, as it bid fair to carry us miles out of our course. From this time our strength and endurance were taxed to their utmost. It was impossible to break a way through the mass of matted grass stems and we were compelled to crush them down which was no easy task—for three or four of them will support the weight of a man. How difficult this was may be imagined when you are informed that the whole mass was matted down to a depth of about three feet, the stems of the grass from nine to twelve feet in length, and the ground beneath covered with a yielding mass of rotting vegetable matter, resting upon a wet, slippery, spongy soil.

To add to our misery the saw-like edges of the leaves of the grass soon cut our hands into a crazy-quilt pattern causing them to bleed freely.

Matters were made still worse by a number of deep ravines, with perpendicular walls forty to fifty feet high, which were encountered at intervals and which had to be crossed somehow. Fortunately the walls were covered with vines, roots and brushes which made it possible to cross but our state of exhaustion was such that we believed each one was more than we could manage —until we tried. It was what is sometimes called "a groundhog case"—we were obliged to cross.

About three hours were consumed in fighting our way through this miserable jungle and when at last we emerged in short grass we could scarcely stand.

It developed later that we were, at this point, about three miles from our horses and the grass was still deep enough to much impede our weary feet, but no trolley car was at hand and there was only one thing to do and we did it.

Your correspondent was in a half comatose condition and has not a clear recollection of anything but numerous falls, another unexpected ravine too deep to cross necessitating a weary climb to find a crossing near its head, and the further fact that he was trailing along about a mile behind the rest of the party.

Somehow the horses were at last found and after we had absorbed numerous bottles of Tansan (Japanese mineral water) we managed to mount.

We rode furiously in the attempt to get clear of the forest before black darkness should overtake us, but failed, and were obliged to hire a native guide.

Most of the male inhabitants of the little village, where we picked up the guide, accompanied us out of curiosity, apparently.

Next day a count disclosed fifty-six cuts on my hands, besides a sufficiency of bruises.

My interest in mountains has declined to almost zero and the next one I ascend will have to have either a railway or an elevator.

Our clothes were almost reduced to rags. My camera, though protected by a sole leather case, wrapped in heavy oilcloth, was soaked; all of the botanical specimens in my pockets were reduced to fragments, and black sand was ground into the soles of my feet so deeply that Sapolio would not remove it.

While we were above the clouds on this trip, the scenery was generally restricted to a "topside" view of them with an occasional peep through an opening.

A stratum of clouds seems to be about as sharply defined on its upper as on its lower surface but of course appears very white and fleecy because of the strong light. Once, while near the summit, a few minutes' view of land and sea was permitted us and the sight will never be forgotten. Not many places in the world can furnish such a diversity of ocean, river, gulf, mountain and island.

After many hours spent upon the steep slope of the mountain we seemed to lose all ability to recognize level ground and when a sudden lift of the clouds revealed the plain at the base it appeared to us as another slope rising at an angle to the one we were on.

As we roosted high, among tumbled masses of broken rock, whirling masses of clouds driven by roaring gusts of wind, up, then down; from right to left; then back again, while rain soaked us through and through, we felt that we had witnessed what may well have been the state of things before "The Heavens and Earth rose out of Chaos."

Some months after my departure from Camp Darago information reached me that Lt. M———had, later, succeeded in reaching the summit.

This volcano has erupted at intervals of five or six years for some time and is about due for another one.

During my stay there we were treated to an earthquake one night but no damage resulted.

Many years ago an eruption destroyed the original town of Darago. The remains of the old stone church and two other stone buildings may still be seen projecting through the debris thrown out at the time. The last eruption was not long after the American occupation and several persons who witnessed it have described it to me.

There is a hot spring near the town of Legaspi, within two miles of the post.

All Philippine coins bear a profile of this mountain and the twenty-Peso bills have a fine engraving of it.

Active Chapters.

ALPHA—BALTIMORE COLLEGE OF DENTAL SURGERY.

C. P. Freeman, Editor.

Alpha sends greetings to all Psi Omegas wishing them a successful termination of their college year.

Alpha takes pleasure in presenting the following new members:

H. L. Desmarais, '09............North Grafton, Mass.
H. E. Foil, '08..................Mt. Pleasant, N. C.
B. L. Warner, '08....................Baltimore, Md.
C. W. Leps, '09......................Keyser, W. Va.

We are beginning to get the spring feeling which usually precedes the final examinations.

This time of the year brings its joys and its sorrows. We are finishing another good year and sending out many good men to battle with the world; yet we are also losing a number of bright lights from around our camp-fire. Although Psi Omegas complete the college course in three years, we often see some of them returning the following year with their brides to show them where they learned the mysteries of dentistry and where they made their first acquaintance with the plaster barrel.

Our retiring Grand Master Parks, of whom we cannot speak too highly, installed the following officers for the year 1907-08:

Grand Master..........................E. F. Mason.
Junior Master........................H. L. Fisher.

Secretary..........................M. L. Freeman.
Treasurer..........................A. E. Hennan.
Inside Guard......................D. H. Fleming.
Outside Guard....................F. E. Fraser.
Chief Inquisitor...................H. L. Desmarais.
Chief Interrogator................D. E. Fennesy.
Editor and Historian.............C. P. Freeman.

Before examination we wound up our frolics by having a theater party which was a success if the number of encores was any guide. I am pleased to report that every one arrived home safely before morning.

We hope to have the pleasure of meeting our brothers at the coming dental exhibition at Jamestown and have one of those good times in which all Psi Omegas know how to participate.

May all of the graduates go out in the world and enjoy prosperity and bring honor upon themselves and Psi Omega.

BETA—NEW YORK COLLEGE OF DENTISTRY.

George R. Christian, Editor.

Beta takes pleasure in presenting to the fraternity the following new members:

Roger C. Brush, '09................Huntington, L. I.
John C. Ellis, '09....................New York City.
Wm. L. Hildebrandt, '09...........Drakestown, N. J.
Wm. H. Kerr, '09...................Union Hill, N. J.
Thos. F. Matrustry, '08.............New York City.
Wm. L. Croll, Hony.......................England.

We pause in the whirl of excitement due to approaching examinations to send our greetings to the Supreme Council and all brothers of Psi Omega. As this most vital time draws near we are filled with a feeling of both happiness and regret, for we realize that it means that a large number of our brothers will enter upon their life's work and that their days of examinations will be past and also that the brothers of the active chapters are to be deprived of their company. Of course this is a necessary stage in evolution and we endure it as such, sending our fellow members on their various careers with true feeling for their happiness and ultimate success.

To strengthen their physical systems while the midnight oil's season is at hand, several of our more nimble brothers indulge in the game of hand ball. It is seldom that one can look from the window across the "campus" and see the court vacant. The "giant" team (Jurka and Teed) can scarcely find space enough to accommodate their mighty bodies in our small court, still they play, occasionally kicking themselves or ending a game minus a "two-bit" piece. If any of our neighbor chapters care to play a game or two we will send our champion team to their courts or invite their team to ours.

This reminds us that a little challenge to a whist tournament is still unsettled. We will cheerfully meet the challengers after exams. or in the fall of the year. Let them rest easy till then.

GAMMA—PENNSYLVANIA COLLEGE OF DENTAL SURGERY.

J. J. Durkin, Editor.

Gamma takes pleasure in introducing two new members:

Arthur P. Brown, '07..................Hazelton, Pa.
Augustine A. Gill, '07...............Philadelphia, Pa.

On the evening of March 5, in the beautiful banquet hall of the Hotel Bingham, Gamma held her Annual Banquet. The members of the faculty and Brother J. E. Nyce, of the Supreme Council, were guests of honor.

Grand Master Bonnick, acting as toastmaster, called upon the following to respond to toasts:

Faculty............................J. Bird Moyer.
Psi Omega..........................A. B. Carey.

Class of '07...................W. F. Luffbarry.
Ladies.........................G. P. McCall.
Class of '08...................L. H. Blose.
Alumni.........................J. E. Nyce.
Class of '09...................W. G. Sherwood.

Drs. Roe and Loeper, of the faculty, also responded to toasts.

The toasts were intermingled with beautiful selections from the orchestra and with Psi Omega songs.

The menu was as follows:

Martini Cocktail

Celery   Olives

Green Turtle Fanglaise

Rock Bass a la Menniers

Straw Potatoes   Sauterne

Fillet of Beef Surprise

Psi Omega Punch   Cigarettes

Roast Phila. Duckling   Apple Sauce

St. Julien

Romain Salad

Neapolitaine Ice Cream   Fancy Cakes

Cafe   Cheese

Perfectos

The souvenirs were beautiful menus, book form, with Psi Omega emblem engraved upon the corner in blue and white.

At midnight one of Gamma's most successful banquets came to a close.

At our recent election the following were elected officers for the next year:

Grand Master..........................L. H. Blose
Junior Master.........................A. D. Smith.
Secretary.............................A. L. V. Sharon.
Treasurer.............................H. A. Rall.
Chief Interrogator....................A. L. Buddinger.
Chief Inquisitor......................E. L. Smith.
Historian.............................F. T. McGinnies.
Editor................................E. F. Everett.
Inside Guardian.......................J. H. Boskoren.

Outside Guardian....................A. D. Stevens.
Senator.......................Dr. E. A. Kutchman.

Gamma sends best wishes to Supreme Council and all sister chapters.

DELTA—TUFTS DENTAL COLLEGE.

C. P. Haven, Editor.

Delta takes pleasure in introducing to the fraternity the following new members:

Frederic M. Briggs, Hony..........Brookline, Mass.
Alfred G. Richburg, '09............Winchester, Mass.
Rupert S. Lovejoy, '09.................Portland, Me.

EPSILON—WESTERN RESERVE UNIVERSITY.

C. C. Rogers, Editor.

Epsilon sends greetings to all sister chapters and congratulations upon the near approach of the close of another year. We feel that the present year has been a very profitable one with us and hope other chapters have been equally fortunate.

Since the last issue of The Frater we held a dance, to which were invited the Cleveland Alumni Chapter and the local chapter of the Delta Sigma Delta fraternity.

All present reported a very enjoyable time and voted the affair a success.

The month of April has been an uneventful one with us, nothing exciting happening to cause any special mention; all seemingly being intent upon preparing for approaching examinations.

ZETA—UNIVERSITY OF PENNSYLVANIA.

S. F. Williams, Editor.

Zeta takes pleasure in introducing to the fraternity three new members:

John W. Jones, '09.....................Scranton, Pa.
Sydney S. Warner, '09..............Wilkes Barre, Pa.
Edward R. Flatley, '07...............Philadelphia, Pa.

—•◇•—

ETA—PHILADELPHIA DENTAL COLLEGE.

Lewis B. Duffield, Editor.

Once more, and for the last time of our college term, we greet our sister chapters. This is a time when we all look back and see what good has been accomplished in the past nine months; I am sure that every member of Eta feels proud of our year's work, both from a business and social stand-point, especially we might say from a business point of view, as during the last year Eta has taken great strides toward purchasing her house and furniture. We hope that the good work will continue in the future so that in a few years our present senior brothers can come back and know that their untiring efforts were ably seconded by their successors.

Eta congratulates herself on the good men she initiated during the past term, they all are students of the staunchest character and have proven their worth as true Psi Omegas.

At our last initiation, held on April 13, the following men were taken in:

Alson L. Stone, '09..................Philadelphia, Pa.
Charles A. Fielder, '09..............Philadelphia, Pa.
John W. O'Connell, '09.............Wilmerding, Pa.

On Friday evening, April 19, the annual election of officers took place. The officers for the ensuing year are as follows:

Grand Master......................M. A. Buck.
Junior Master......................T. L. Wilcox.
Secretary..........................C. A. Lewis.
Treasurer.........................C. F. Kellerher.
Senator...........................C. J. Hollister.
Chief Inquisitor...................J. W. O'Connell.
Chief Interrogator.................R. F. Witz.
Editor............................J. A. Reddan.
Inside Guardian...................H. F. Somers.
Outside Guardian..................Wm. Sherer.
Executive Committee..L. L. Wilcox, W. W. Carson, W. P. Burns.

Eta regrets to say that she loses twenty-four brothers by graduation this year, and, as they enter the ranks of the profession the best that we can wish is that success, health and prosperity may be theirs and that the uplifting of Psi Omega may ever prevail in their ranks. To our departing brothers we extend this little toast:

> You human souls who in this world,
>   With health and strength have entered;
> Have for your living occupation
>   The study of dentistry tendered.
>
> So honor and distinction to you may come,
>   While your loved ones may pass away,
> But during such trials and tribulations,
>   Psi Omega will ever stay.
>
> So let her Royal Banner,
>   Be adorned in every land;
> And this your watchword ever be,
>   An "Honorable Psi Omega Man."

It is with profound regret that Eta chronicles the death of Brother Richard A. Aichele, who was a member of the senior class and just about to graduate after three years of earnest and painstaking work.

Brother Aichele was stricken with typhoid fever about three weeks ago and despite the ministration of physicians he sank gradually until the end.

The members of Eta marched in a body to the late home of Brother Aichele, to attend the funeral services which were held on the 26th of April.

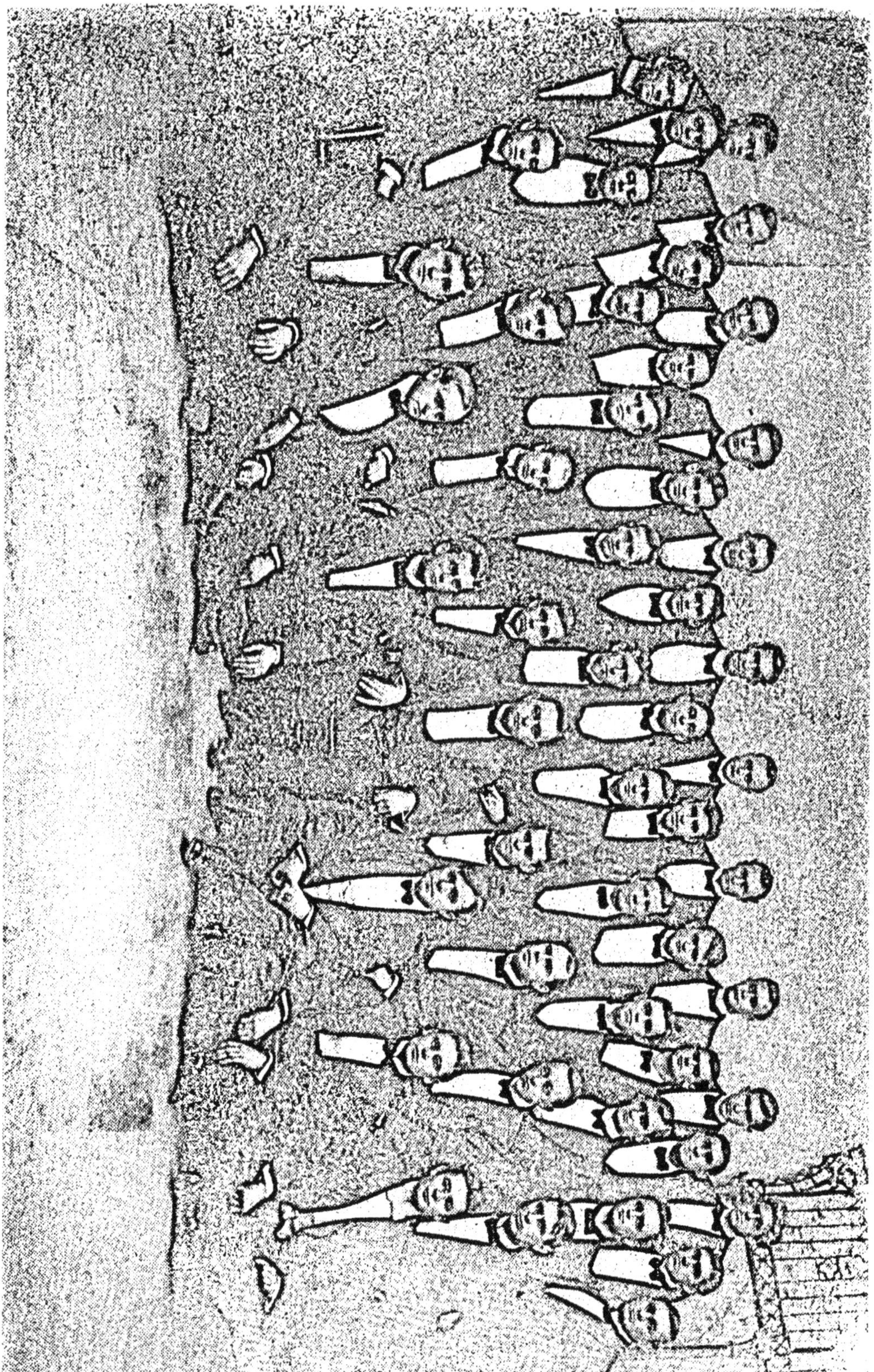

A floral design, a counterpart of the Psi Omega emblem, made up of blue and white flowers, was sent by the chapter.

The following resolutions were framed and sent to the family of the deceased brother:

Whereas: Richard A. Aichele departed this life in the month of April, 1907.

Whereas: Eta Chapter of the Psi Omega Fraternity, in a special meeting assembled, unanimously, adopted a motion appointing a committee to prepare suitable resolutions touching this sad and lamentable event, therefore, your committee recommends that it be

Resolved: That in the life of Richard A. Aichele, he exemplified all the graces and virtues of an upright Christian gentleman, the fidelity and affection of a loving brother in the truest and broadest sense of the word, and through the inherent force of his firm and manly character, his courteous and kindly nature and his sympathetic and affectionate disposition he enjoyed the confidence, respect, and esteem of all those with whom he came in contact.

Resolved: That in his death his sorrowing family lost a devoted, unselfish, and affectionate member, at whose untimely demise we mingle our tears with theirs, and this Fraternity has suffered an irreparable loss in that it has been deprived of the benefit of his untiring and unremitting interest and work in all that made for the uplifting of the Fraternity.

Resolved: That these resolutions be spread in full upon the minutes of this meeting and a copy thereof be sent to the bereaved family.

    Eta Chapter,
     Psi Omega Fraternity.
      Thomas A. Crowley,
      Oscar D. Glick,
      David I. White,
      Mathias H. Casey,
        Committee.

THETA—UNIVERSITY OF BUFFALO.

H. E. Marshall, G. M., Editor.

College year which is now drawing to a close has not been a very prosperous one for Theta, but we are glad to see that most of our sister chapters have had a very successful year.

Theta next year will be aided in every possible way by the new Alumni Chapter which is now in a very flourishing condition.

Our last meeting was held in conjunction with the Alumni and various ways and means were discussed for the coming year. We hope to be able to report greater progress in Theta at the end of next year.

Theta loses one member by graduation, but we hope to have back with us next year Brother Harry Tyler, who was taken seriously ill and was compelled to abandon his college work. The latest report shows a good change in his condition.

The officers for the ensuing year have not yet been elected.

Wishing all college brothers the greatest success in their exams and a very pleasant vacation we bid them adieu for the year.

IOTA—NORTHWESTERN UNIVERSITY.

C. S. Savage, Editor.

Another school year is near its end, when friends and brothers must part, some for a few months, others for time indefinite, as they start upon their careers as dentists.

But this parting ought not to be a sad one because there are good men going out into the field with the latest and best ideas to assist in bearing high the standard of the profession, while there are others who will continue their studies only to follow a little later.

Iota has been under good management during the past year, her Grand Master being an able ambitious leader. She has enjoyed the home comforts of the frat house and has had the interest of Psi Omega at heart.

One evening in January, at the frat house, just before the mid-term exams, the boys were greatly benefited by a quiz on Prosthetic Dentistry by Brother Shuttleworth, who demonstrates in this department at the college.

On March 9 the "round-up" committee changed its place and manner of confering degrees upon worthy stalwarts by lining them up in the street, in front of the house, in clothing of a peculiar gender and with faces painted to make identity uncertain, the victims being Harry Ross, Chas. A. McLean, Geo. T. Reed, and Arthur N. Wilen.

232   THE FRATER.

After a long march and many stunts for the amusement of the bystanders, they returned to the house, where items of vital importance were introduced to the worthy gentlemen. Throughout the ordeal the boys showed metal, now Psi Omega finished. On the night of April 24 the boys and honorary members gathered round the banquet table at the Sherman House to eat and drink to the health of Psi Omega and to celebrate the Annual Love Feast of Iota.

After the flavors of the feast, the occasion was elaborately finished as the program will indicate:

Thomas Shuttleworth, toastmaster.

Miscellaneous......................Dr. W. E. Harper.
Management of Financial Affairs...Dr. C. R. E. Koch.
Relation Between Dentist and Physician..Dr. C. L. Mix.
Advice to Young Men Starting in Dentistry......
    ....Dr. T. B. Wiggin.
History of Dentistry...............Dr. B. J. Cigrand.
Anything You Like.................Dr. W. T. Eckley.
Selections...........................W. S. Kennedy.
Past History of School Life and the Fraternity
    House...............Grand Master W. B. Power.
Social Affairs in Practice Building......Dr. Van Tuyl.
Piano Selections by Jno. L. Wehrheim and Jno.
    McLean.
Vocal Selections by W. B. Power, W. S. Kennedy,
    A. B. Linne, R. E. Pfouts, Rich and
    Walther.

Friday night, April 26, we had a farewell gathering at the House, and our lady friends were present to cheer us up.

Saturday evening, April 27, 1907, the following officers were elected with best wishes for a successful year, 1907-08:

Grand Master....................James E. Beck, '08.
Junior Master....................Walter Moore, '09.
Secretary........................Roscoe Stout, '09.
Treasurer....................Arthur D. Closson, '08.
Senator......................Arthur M. Wilen, '08.
Chief Inquisitor................Frank Desmond, '09.
Chief Interrogator..............James H. Ross, '09.
Historian....................Robert W. Reed, '09.
Editor.......................Thomas E. Butler, '08.

Inside Guardian.....................Fred Brown, '08.
Outside Guardian....................Paul Fridd, '09.

At a recent meeting another strong link was made fast to the Psi Omega chain in the person of Fred Brown, Mendota, Ill., whom we take great pleasure in presenting to the fraternity.

KAPPA—CHICAGO COLLEGE OF DENTAL SURGERY.

E. L. Harrison, Editor.

We are near the close of another college year, and shortly the class of '07 will be leaving us and with it nearly twenty Psi Omegas. The present year has been a record breaking one in cases of sickness among the boys. The following members of Kappa having been in the hospital: Hoye, Nourie, Meyers, Shinn, McCarthy and Goldberg on account of appendicitis, and Mortinson and Russel on account of pneumonia. However, all are with us again, except Russel who is still on the hospital list.

Kappa takes pleasure in presenting to the fraternity the following new members:

John C. Purdie, '08...................Mumford, N. Y.
Ed. H. Norrie, '07..................... Beverville, Ill.
W. E. Russell, '07....................Westfield, Wis.
Harry L. Spinney, '09...............Ellsworth, Wis.
Michael J. Sheeran, '08...............Waseca, Minn.
J. Chester Kintzer, '09....................Peoria, Ill.
Carl Van Sant, '09....................Findlay, Ohio.
Harvey H. Hay, '09....................Shannon, Ill.
Wm. A. Quinlan, '07.................Whitefish, Mont.
D. H. Woodward, '07....................Enson, Kan.
Thos L. Goldburg, '07............Spring Grove, Minn.
Richard M. Hubeny, '09.................Chicago, Ill.
Arthur Hall, '08.....................Valparaiso, Ind.
Emil F. Roegmen, '09...................Chicago, Ill.

NU—PITTSBURG DENTAL COLLEGE.

H. Boisseau, Editor.

Nu takes pleasure in presenting to the fraternity the following new members:

E. M. Donaldson, '09	Washington, Pa.
W. C. Horner, '07	Avalon, Pa.
J. F. Campbell, '09	North Adams, Mass.
D. P. Husler, '07	Finleyville, Pa.
W. P. Carson, '09	Pittsburg, Pa.

Nu is just now at the beginning of the finish of one of her most successful years. The present year has witnessed at Nu some of the greatest improvements possible in a fraternal organization. Starting the year with a membership of twenty-four we have increased until at the present time the enrollment is forty-three, and, it seems to me that no better men than those who have added their names to our roll during the present year could possibly be gotten together by any organization. We have among our members the leaders in all the branches of our school work.

Another improvement noticeable is this: At the beginning of the present year our meetings were held in two rooms on the second floor of a private dwelling down in the neighborhood of the college; now we reside in a more fashionable district of the city and have a whole house in which to meet and live.

Everything in connection with the chapter is running along in the usual manner and not much of importance has happened since the last issue of The Frater.

On Monday night, May 6, our annual election of officers will be held.

Friday night, May 17, is the date set for the Annual Banquet which will be held at the Nixon Cafe. Preparations are now under way to make it an event memorable to those who are fortunate enough to be present. This is the last big event on Nu's program each year and always serves as a fitting climax for the college year.

Nu will suffer the loss of fourteen members by graduation in June.

Nu sends best wishes to all brothers for a happy and prosperous vacation and to those who graduate we offer Rip Van Winkle's famous toast, "May you live long and prosper."

XI—MILWAUKEE MEDICAL COLLEGE.

I. B. Thackray, Editor.

Xi takes pleasure in presenting to the fraternity two new members, namely:

Russell F. Jones, '08..............Oconomowoc, Wis.
Alvin E. Bleck, '09................New London, Wis.

OMICRON—LOUISVILLE COLLEGE OF DENTAL SURGERY.

J. L. Selden, Editor.

Omicron takes pleasure in presenting to the fraternity the following new members:

Walter P. Claxton, '09................Stanton, Tenn.
Manning Hudson, '09..............Chalybiate, Miss.
Jacob T. Robertson, '09................Calhoun, Ky.
Fred L. Koontz, Hony..............Louisville, Ky.
Adolph O. Pfingst, Hony.............Louisville, Ky.

PI—BALTIMORE MEDICAL COLLEGE.

H. H. Kiniry, Editor.

Brother Lend successfully passed the Massachusetts State Board.

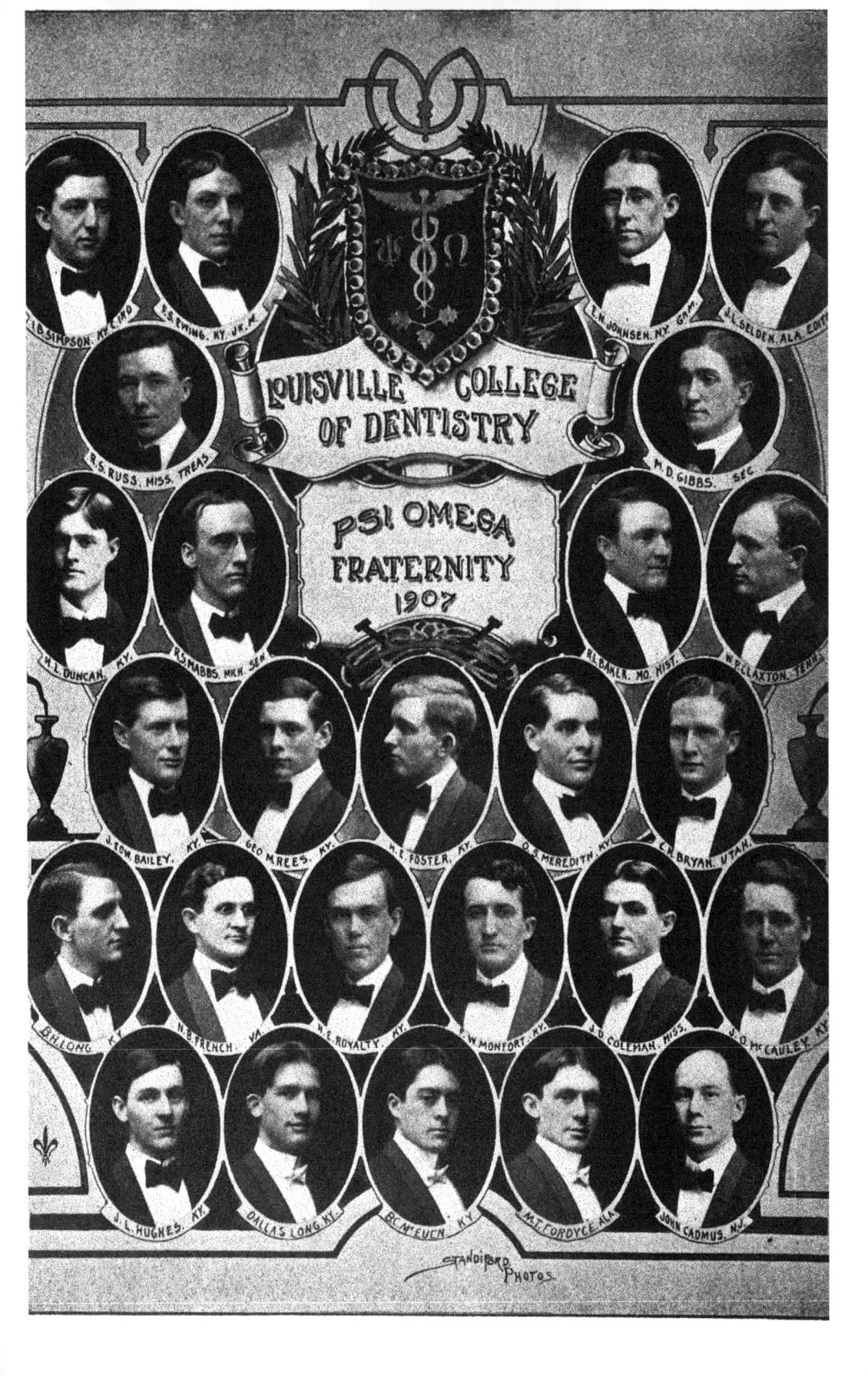

Louisville College of Dentistry

Psi Omega Fraternity
1907

Pi introduces to the fraternity F. A. Heefernan, '09, Providence, R. I.

Cards are out announcing the engagement of Brother E. L. Major, '06, Greenfield, Mass., and Miss K. Ryan, of the same city.

Pi held her annual banquet April 13, at "The Suburban." Brother Stanley was toastmaster, and, though a freshman, he is a hard one to beat. Remarks were made by P. G. M. McGee on The Progress of the Chapter. Brother Gregg replied to The Duties of Brothers to Each Other. Brother Powers, who has been the faithful chairman of the house committee, responded to The Prospects of Psi Omega; he also sang a very pretty solo, "Little Sammy Murphey."

Brother Botts, '04, the best friend Psi Omega has in B. M. C., made very fitting remarks and expressed appreciation of the courteous behavior of the boys. A number of other brothers made little talks. Brother Donahue was the soloist of the evening.

—MENU—

Ginger Ale	Schlitz	Mount Vernon
Celery	Blue Points	Olives
Sword Fish	Green Peas	Mashed Potatoes
Vermont Turkey	Gregg's Tomato Salad	Ring's Corn
Cheese		Boston Crackers
Suburban Ice Cream		Baltimore Cake
	Black Coffee	
Cigarettes		Perfectos

At the last meeting the following officers were elected for the coming year:

Grand Master.....................J. H. Kiniry, '08,
Junior Master....................W. E. Jenkins, '08,
Secretary........................A. D. Elkins, '08,
Treasurer.......................F. A. Hefferman, '09,
Senator.........................H. W. Williams.
Chief Inquisitor.................A. P. McGovern.
Inside Guardian..................C. H. Green.
Outside Guardian.................J. E. Harden.
Chief Interrogator...............E. T. Gill.
Historian.......................E. E. Sherwood.

BETA SIGMA—COLLEGE OF PHYSICIANS AND SURGEONS.

L. R. Packwood, Editor.

Beta Sigma has been a very busy chapter since the last editorial in The Frater. A fraternity dance was given some time ago and all enjoyed themselves. A dance and reception was given in honor of the rehabitation of our college and about one hundred couples were present. The affair was a grand success. On January 27, Brother McCormick and Miss Eillem Smith, of Redwood City, were maried. We wish the happy couple a long and blissful life and congratulate McCormick upon winning the heart of such an estimable young lady.

At 8 p. m., February 23, Beta Delta met with us and we drank a toast to Psi Omega's fifteenth birthday. Dr. Anderson gave a toast which was very appropriate. A few remarks were made by Grand Master L. E. Carter and J. E. Creeley of Beta Delta and Grand Master Downes and L. E. Cloy, of Beta Sigma.

A smoker was given March 14, every member being present. All thoughts of college work were thrown aside and all entered into the jovial spirit which made the affair a success. I wish we could hold more of these social affairs, but it is getting late in the season.

Our last initiation was a great success. The candidates were dressed in outlandish costumes and were paraded through the college during the afternoon. This caused a great deal of excitement in the different clinics which were full of patients. A banquet was given in the evening and at the close we were all happy, but, to our sorrow, Policeman 670 was looking for trouble and took the liberty of testing Brother Moon's skull. In the excitement and scramble Brother Conroy was the unlucky victim "jerked" to spend a few hours in the police station. The case was brought up in the police court and was immediately dismissed, as we had done nothing disorderly.

Our course this year has been a good one and I can see nothing but success ahead for all that take the State Board.

In 1913 a World's Fair will be held in San Francisco which promises to be a grand success and I do not see any reason why Psi Omega should not hold a reunion here at that time. It will be Psi Omega's twentieth birthday. Most of the chapters are in the

East but there are four strong chapters on this coast and if we can get the convention, I know that all visiting brothers will enjoy themselves. There would be nothing to mar their pleasure during their stay here in the Golden State where we have nothing but sunshine and flowers, and a quake every fifty years.

We would like to hear from sister chapters in regard to the matter. I know this is a little premature but we want to be sure so that all our energies may be applied to bring as many brothers as possible to the coast. I believe there is a movement under headway to form an Alumni Chapter on the coast and hope that all brothers will be with us.

Our new members are:

James A. Biggs, '07.................Folsom City, Cal.
Eugene C. Clendenin, '07..............Campbell, Cal.

RHO—OHIO COLLEGE OF DENTAL SURGERY.

Edw. McCurdy, Editor.

Rho introduces to the fraternity one new member; namely: Frederick R. Lauterbach, '09, of Dayton, O.

SIGMA—MEDICO CHIRURGICAL COLLEGE.

H. M. Walters, Editor.

Since the last issue of The Frater two members of our faculty, Professors R. Walter Starr and L. Ashley Faught, have been initiated as honorary members. On this occasion Professor T. N. Broomell, our Dean, who is also an honorary member, was present and addressed the brothers in an impressive manner. Our chapter is progressing this year as never before, and is continuing to draw into her fold some of the best material in the Department of Dentistry. The fraternity spirit is growing and interest maintained, special encouragement being given by the instructors who are Psi Omega men and who have gladly responded to our invitations to be present at our meetings from time to time.

Sigma takes pleasure in presenting to the fraternity her new active members, namely:

    Wm. E. Hoffman, '08...............Philadelphia, Pa.
    John R. Smith, '08..................Norristown, Pa.
    Isidore D. Magill, '07..............Philadelphia, Pa.
    Robert P. Slough, '09...................Easton, Pa.
    George W. Watson, '09.............Shenandoah, Pa.
    Harry G. Pollard, '09..........Oriskany Falls, N. Y.
    Paul H. Smith, '08..................Philadelphia, Pa.

Our annual banquet was held at the Windsor Hotel, April 4, at which time the installation of officers took place. Also, Supreme Councilor Nyce administered the honorary degree to Prof. Geo. H. Meeker, M. S., Phar. D., Ph. D., LL. D. In society work Dr. Meeker has done much good and we recognize in him a desire to do the same for our chapter. After these services the brothers gathered at a beautifully decorated table, where they were favored with the "dainties" of life and by some splendid addresses by Profs. Broomell, Faught, Starr, and by Brothers J. E. Nyce, S. C.; Byrne; Davies; Crooks; Zurbrigg; Barclay, G. M., and Caist, G. M. The affair was a grand success.

The graduating members of Sigma wish to their fellow brothers abundant success.

TAU—ATLANTA DENTAL COLLEGE.

C. G. Butt, Editor.

Tau takes pleasure in presenting to the fraternity the following new members:

    Sydney Atkinson, '07...............Jacksonville, Fla.
    Lester L. Bennett, '07..................Waycross, Ga.
    Marvin A. Connally, '08................Kershan, S. C.

Edward W. Durant, '08.................Rome, S. C.
Marion S. Whitehead, '09............Kingstree, S. C.
Esta S. Furr, '09·....................Pontotoc, Miss.
Worth M. Laurence, '09.................Ruston, La.
Don M. Meadors, '09............Junction City, Ark.
Samuel M. Long, '09.................St. Marys, Ga.
Sam J. Ware, '08......................Windsor, Ga.
Wm. P. McMeekin, '08..............Monticello, S. C.
Neallie E. Ross, '09....................Carthage, Tex.
George V. Cannon, '09................Venters, S. C.
Frank K. Boland, Hony.................Atlanta, Ga.

UPSILON—UNIVERSITY OF SOUTHERN CALIFORNIA

F. L. Osenburg, Editor.

The regular editor being occupied with other duties, the present writer will try to fulfill his obligations to The Frater in this, the last issue of the year.

In looking back over the last few months of college history, we feel that Upsilon has made an uphill fight, but has been decidedly successful. She began the college year with only seven members, and in view of the fact that there were two other fraternities to fight against, the outlook was somewhat gloomy. But by dint of hard work, and an exhibition of some hustle and vim, the very cream of the under classes was landed in our ranks. Instead of a membership of seven to start with next year, Upsilon will have double that number. They will have a struggle to maintain the present quality of the membership, but I feel certain that they will be ready to make a good fight next year. Upsilon is to be congratulated on her quota of new members this year, for without exception, the initiates are men of true fraternal instincts.

February 26 was a date long to be remembered by Upsilon, as the occasion of our annual hop. It was held as usual at "Kraemers," and was a signal success in every way. The boys worked hard in the matter of decoration and the committee received many compliments for the taste displayed in the profuse decoration of the hall.

UPSILON CHAPTER
1907

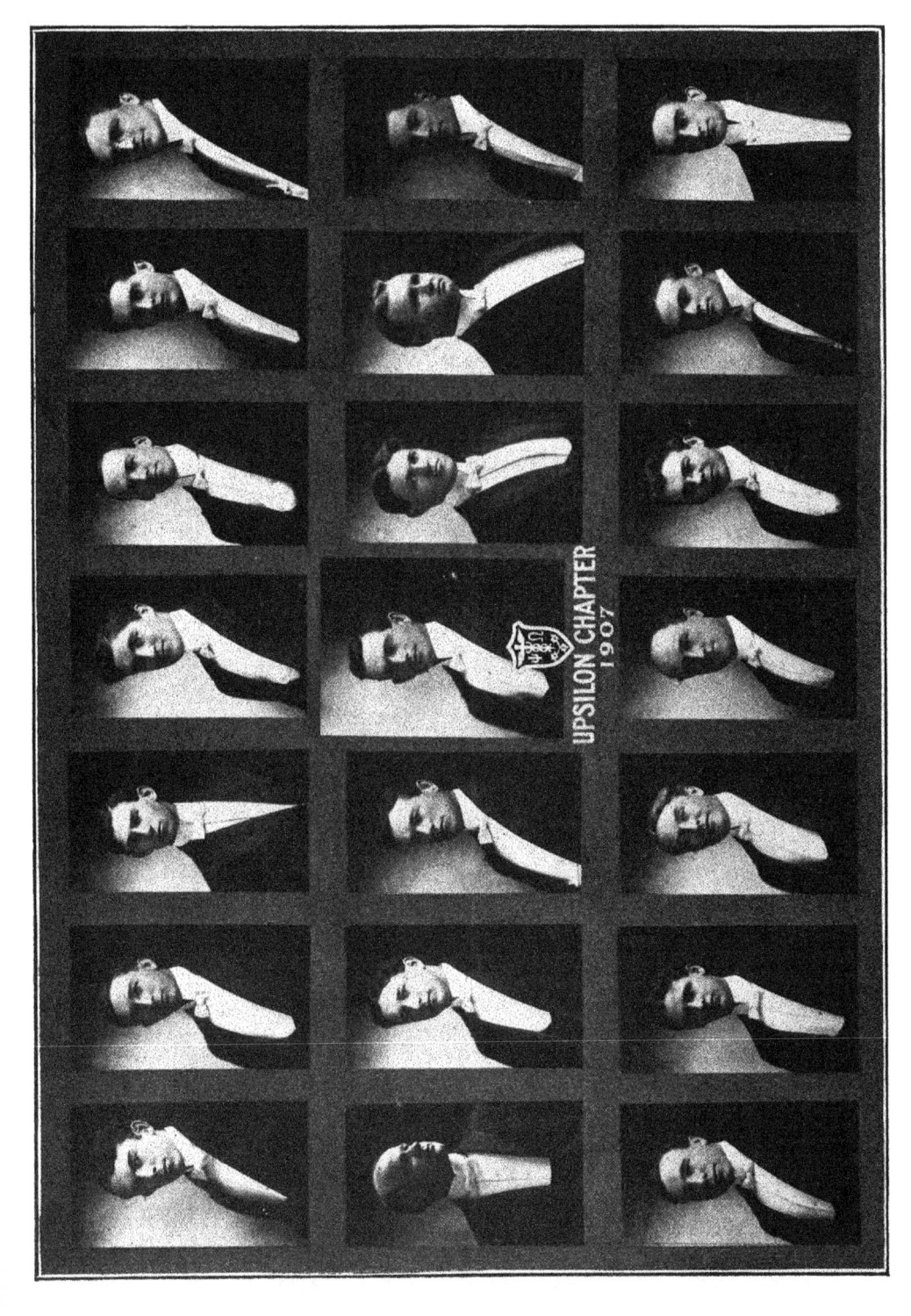

The annual banquet was given at "Levys'," a couple of weeks previous to the hop.

A number of smokers have been given during the year, especially on the night of initiation, and we have tried to make the new members feel entirely at home after their perilous journey.

Upsilon will lose eight members through graduation this year and although their presence and assistance will be missed, still the remaining members feel glad with them that they are about to receive their reward for their three years of faithful work.

In conclusion I will venture the hope that all sister chapters will receive their full measure of success in the next college year, and that each succeeding year will find them and their members closer together until we have attained that for which all Psi Omegas strive.

PHI—UNIVERSITY OF MARYLAND.

Phi takes pleasure in presenting to the fraternity the following new members:

Edward H. Bachman, '09..............Baltimore, Md.
Chas. J. Price, '09..................Hyattstown, Md.
George C. Weighart, '07...............Buffalo, N. Y.
John T. Underwood, '08.........Newton Grove, N. C.

CHI—NORTH PACIFIC DENTAL COLLEGE.

John E. Swanberg, Editor.

On April 19, Chi held her seventh annual banquet in the Green Room at the Hotel Sargent, and, needless to say, it was a thorough success. The honorary, alumni and active members were all represented.

It was not until the small hours of morning that any one seemed inclined to leave and it was not because they themselves wanted to leave, but because certain ones expected them to be home at a certain hour. The banquet room and tables were decorated with flowers. The menu was as follows:

Martini Cocktail
Canape a la Lorenzo
Toke Point Oysters on Deep-shell
Santa Anna Celery
Liebfraumilch
Essence of Fresh Tomatoes en Tasse
Salted Almonds
Filet of English Sole a la Meyerbeer
Pommes Julienne   Cucumbers
Spring Lamb Chops a la Maison d'Orr
New Garden Peas in Casses
Chateau Margaux
Roast Young Capon, Chestnut Dressing
Browned Sweet Potatoes
Salad a la Waldorf
Neapolitaine Ice Cream
Assorted Fancy Cakes
Imported Stilton Cheese
Bent's Wafers
Cafe Noir

Our Grand Master, T. Jones, acted as toastmaster, and the following was the program:

Selection	Orchestra.
The Fraternity	Dr. H. C. Fixott.
Our Absent Brothers	A. E. George.
Selection	Quartet.

Burrows, Boyd, Barton and Ferrier.

Our Chapter	A. T. Murdy.
Graduating Brothers	F. E. Casey.
Violin Solo	A. T. McMillan.
Incoming Seniors	W. C. Ketchum.
Physical Degree	R. B. Brandon.
Selection	W. A. Short.
Honorary Members	J. Swanburg.

Response..........................Dr. J. F. Drake.
Solo...............................G. E. Barton.
The Alumni.........................M. Y. Lucas.
Response..........................Dr. G. Larkins.
Selection .... Orchestra.

Besides the regular program, talks from other honorary members were enjoyed.

In this our last letter to The Frater for this college year, we are proud to state that Chi has made some magnificent strides toward making the chapter what it ought to be and will close the year in excellent condition. It is true that a number will be lost by graduation, but the interest manifested by those who will return is sufficient guarantee that the good work will be continued next year.

Chi takes pleasure in introducing the following new members:

Charles C. Burrow, '08..............Ridgefield, Wash.
Robt. B. Brandon, '09................Portland, Ore.
Huber V. Guiberson, '08................Kent, Wash.
Jas. H. Winstanley, '09..................Salem, Ore.
J. C. Reasoner, '09.....................Ashland, Ore.
Wm. J. McMillan, '09.............Walla Walla, Wash.
Ira R. Boyd, '09.....................Moscow, Idaho.

We wish as a closing remark, to extend our best wishes to all chapters, active and alumni, and especially to the graduating brothers, wishing them financial and professional success.

---◆---

PSI—OHIO MEDICAL UNIVERSITY.

P. E. Gabcl, Editor.

Psi sends greetings to all sister chapters and alumni members.

The present scholastic year closes, with the boys very busy, preparing for final examinations, and with the chapter in a very prosperous condition. Although we lose twelve active members in this year's class, we shall still number twenty-five, who will take care of Psi's interests here next year.

Arrangements have been made to retain the present chapter house during the vacation months, so that everything will be in readiness when we return, next fall, to take up the perplexing studies of another year.

At the last meeting the following officers were elected for '08:

Grand Master	H. L. Oliver.
Junior Master	J. L. Barnett.
Secretary	W. C. Warren.
Treasurer	C. Trumpower.
Chief Inquisitor	G. Moore.
Inside Guardian	A. T. Knoderer.
Outside Guardian	A. Galvin.
Interrogator	Earl Clark.
Senator	J. A. Shaffer.
Editor	P. E. Gabel.

On Wednesday evening, March 20, the biggest event of the season took place at the Hartman Hotel, the occasion being our Annual Banquet, which was the most successful and most eventful we have ever had.

The chapter was honored by having with us Doctors H. E. Friesell and E. H. Sting of the Supreme Council.

The following toasts were heartily responded to, J. Nelson Brown acting as toastmaster:

What is This Psi Omega?	Dr. H. M. Semans.
How a Busy Dentist May Find Pleasure	Dr. K. C. Brashear.
How to Economize in Time	Dr. H. V. Cottrell.
Psi Omega's Ambition	Dr. H. E. Friesell.
The Alumni	Dr. T. E. Sonnanstine.
The Beneficial Effects Dentistry Has on Its Practitioners	R. B. Wiltberger.
Roasts and Toasts	Paul E. Gable.
History and Horoscope of Class of '09	Arthur T. Knoderer.

Others responded to the call of the toastmaster and it was long past the midnight hour when the assemblage left the banquet hall.

BETA ALPHA—UNIVERSITY OF ILLINOIS.

G. W. Wheeler, Editor.

Beta Alpha takes pleasure in presenting to the fraternity the following new members:

Nelson R. Abbott, Hony..................Chicago, Ill.
Harry M. Korshak, '08...................Chicago, Ill.
O. C. Bailey, '09......................Leesburg, Ohio.
Richard F. Feiok, '09..................Freeman, S. D.
Herbert S. Hanson, '09...... ....Chicago, Ill.

BETA GAMMA—GEORGE WASHINGTON UNIVERSITY.

W. H. Hildreth, Editor.

With the writing of this last chapter letter comes the consciousness that the collegiate year 1907 is about over. Mingled feelings of pleasure and regret possess us and I fear that the regrets are badly crowded in the hearts of most of us. To every brother the keenest regret comes with the severing of fraternity ties and the intimate friendships that can only exist among men who have worked, played, studied, and lived together in the closest companionship.

However, we all feel pleasure upon the drawing near of the close of this successful and profitable year for Beta Gamma.

Of the four senior brothers who expect to graduate early in June, three will locate permanently here in Washington, while the fourth will practice here awhile before seeking a favorable location in the West.

Four new brothers have been welcomed during the year which will offset the equal number of brothers who are graduating. Thus with numbers undiminished we look forward to another

BETA GAMMA CHAPTER, 1906-7.

year with prospects of not only holding our own numerically, but of gaining more new men than we will lose by graduation.

We would consider the past year most successful if we had accomplished nothing beyond silencing adverse criticism by unsuccessful aspirants, and this we have done so well that we can count several of the traducers among our admirers.

The annual dance was held at Mrs. Dyer's parlors on March 26 and this affair did not suffer in comparison with any of the social functions given here this winter. The Psi Omega dance has become a synonym of a glorious good time and already plans are making for next winter's dance.

Brother R. S. Clinton, '06' has just received notice that he passed the Minnesota State Board successfully last month. By the way, Brother Clinton's practice here is growing so fast that he may be persuaded to remain in Washington.

I take pleasure in announcing the pledging of Casper F. Helmig, '08' who will have been initiated into all the mysteries of Psi Omega before the brothers will read these pages.

Beta Gamma bids farewell to all other chapters and wishes all graduates success.

BETA DELTA—UNIVERSITY OF CALIFORNIA.

Leighton C. Brownton, Editor.

A few short weeks separate us from the end of this semester, then we must break the bonds which have held us together during the past nine months and scatter to the four winds—some of us to launch into the sterner atmosphere of professional life to practice that which has been learned during the past three years—others of us to take a few brief months of recreation and return with renewed vigor for the ensuing year's work.

This has been a year of readjustment and new conditions, but it has all been for the best interests of our college and therefore our fraternity.

A year ago our work was brought to a sudden close and much uncertainty existed as to the future; to-day we find ourselves surrounded with every convenience known to an up-to-date college.

Our annual banquet was held on the evening of April 26, and more than made up for the one we were on the eve of celebrating last year when the trembler interfered. The "doings" began at 8:30 and lasted into the wee hours. Several alumni were present and added their wit and eloquence to the genial flow of merriment around the hickory board.

One of the events of the evening, as has been our custom, was to install officers for the ensuing year.

The following are the officers who will guide Beta Delta during 1907-08:

Grand Master................Leighton C. Brownton.
Junior Master.........................F. A. Leslie.
Recording Secretary................Chas. E. Harper.
Treasurer...........................Wm. H. Bliss.
Senator.............................Gordon S. Rodda.
Chief Inquisitor....................Jas. C. McManus.
Chief Interrogator......................F. A. Ross.
Editor..............................John E. Gurley.
Historian.......................Hermann A. Eggert.
Inside Guardian.....................F. L. Nordyke.
Outside Guardian....................F. W. Randol.

In the early part of May, immediately after the senior exams, we will give a Farewell Dance in honor of out ten graduating brothers. Though regretting the loss of so many, we wish to give them, as they stand on the threshold of life's work, our heartiest wishes for success.

Dr. W. W. Leslie, P. G. M., Beta Delta, '04, and Miss Florence A. James were united in marriage, April 17, '07, at Porterville, Cal. Dr. and Mrs. Leslie have the best wishes of the boys.

Beta Delta in closing the last letter to The Frater this semester, extends to all Brother Greeks, graduate, graduating and undergraduates, sincerest wishes for a profitable summer.

BETA EPSILON—NEW ORLEANS COLLEGE OF DENTISTRY.

Leon Barnett, Editor.

Beta Epsilon takes pleasure in presenting to the fraternity the following new members:

Charles S. Prosser, '08..............Alexandria, La.
Barney M. Gibson, '09..............New Orleans, La.
Nelson H. Williams, '08............New Orleans, La.
D. C. Herbert, '09....................Lafourch, La.

BETA ETA—KEOKUK DENTAL COLLEGE.

Geo. R. Narrley, Editor.

The time is fast approaching when graduating brothers will sever the ties which have bound us together for so many weeks, and, it is with regret that I write this my last letter to The Frater. The last few months have been very active ones for Beta Eta. We have taken in a number of new members and gladly present them to the fraternity:

E. E. Courtright, Hony...............Keokuk, Iowa.
John S. Gault, '08....................Centerville, Iowa.
Claud R. Thomas, '09.................Keokuk, Iowa.
James S. Sullivan, '09................Detroit, Mich.
Jesse E. Scott, '08...................Farson, Iowa.

At our last meeting the following officers were elected for the ensuing year:

Grand Master..........................N. C. Hargis.
Junior Master.........................F. D. Switzer.
Secretary.............................J. E. Scott.
Treasurer.............................J. S. Sullivan.
Historian.............................J. F. Eames.
Chief Interrogator....................C. R. Thomas.
Inside Guardian.......................J. S. Gault.

Our annual banquet was held April 26 and was a grand success. We had Bros. Sohl, Thompson, Crouch, and Covell, Beta Eta, '05, with us, and letters of regret were read from Bros. Justice, '05, and Mitchell, '06, and from Bro. Nepper who is now located in India. It was indeed a late hour when we finally broke up.

GAMMA IOTA—SOUTHERN DENTAL COLLEGE.
GENERAL DIRECTORY.

Gamma Iota takes pleasure in presenting to the fraternity the following new members:

Wm. C. Smith, '09	Red Level, Ala.
Burt C. Williamson, '07	Knoxville, Tenn.
Wm. B. Henderson, '09	Shorter, Ala.
H. Leonidas Keith, '09	Currie, N. C.
Wm. A. Clardy, '08	Almond, Ala.
H. H. Sizemore, '09	Sizemore, Ala.
Amos O. Burnham, '09	Magee, Miss.
Clarence S. Petrey, '08	Petrey, Ala.
Herbert E. Woodward, '08	New Orleans, La.
Fred L. Huis, '07	Bowdon, Ga.
Robert E. Cunningham, '07	Pabahatchie, Miss.
Hilry H. Kendrick, '09	Commerce, Ala.
Cooper P. Bevil, '08	Kountze, Texas.
Wesley G. McAnally, '07	Richmond, Va.
G. B. Ash, '09	Oliver, Ga.
James R. Henley, '09	Dade City, Fla.

GAMMA KAPPA—UNIVERSITY OF MICHIGAN.

Le Vant R. Drake, Editor.

Gamma Kappa is still progressing, though we have not increased in numbers since the last issue of The Frater. All of the fellows went home during the spring vacation excepting Brother Whipple, who accompanied the varsity base ball team on its spring trip. Brother Whipple seems to be the most promising twirler on the pitching staff and we are expecting him to help materially in bringing the base ball championship again to Michigan.

About this time of the year the seniors commence thinking about what is going to become of them after June 20. The fellows that expect to practice outside the state of Michigan are beginning to tremble in fear of the State Boards.

Gamma Kappa expects to close this year in a very creditable manner. The great risk we thought we would run in starting a house this year has turned out to be no risk at all and we have something to show for our year's effort.

We will lose nine of our brothers by graduation but we expect to see a larger number than that come in next year to fill the vacancy. The standard that Psi Omega has set here is commanding attention so that we expect greater things from the brothers who will return to carry on the work. We have taken in exceptionally good men this year so the future of Gamma Kappa is safe.

Gamma Kappa extends greetings to all sister chapters and wishes for the brothers who graduate, success.

We wish undergraduate brothers an enjoyable summer and a profitable next year.

GAMMA LAMBDA—COLLEGE OF DENTAL AND ORAL SURGERY OF NEW YORK.

Gotthard E. Seyfarth, Editor.

Again a year has passed, and, before this number of The Frater reaches the hands of its readers, many of the colleges will have closed their doors for the year 1906-1907. Again some of our boys leave the active ranks of our chapter and go to fight life's sturdy battles alone, far away from their brothers at college and without the guiding supervision of their instructors and professors.

This year Gamma Lambda will lose eight brothers by graduation, but as the present junior and freshman brothers are our able successors, the control of the chapter remains in worthy and competent hands. Departing brothers will be missed, like those who left in former years, but good men will come and take their places, and, we hope, fill them even more worthily, to the great honor of our chapter and our beloved fraternity.

The brothers who are about to part from us are: G. B. Ellor, H. A. Kammerer, J. B. McGrath, J. J. McGrath, R. H. McLeod, F. E. Pierce, E. W. Toshack, and G. E. Seyfarth. The active brothers who remain wish them success in all that awaits them, and that health, happiness and prosperity be their constant companions in life's long and eventful journey.

The above brothers depart with sorrow, for while they have reached the goal for which they had so long been striving, they must sever the bonds of a most intimate companionship. This end had been anticipated, but still it makes our hearts throb when we realize that we must part, as it may be—forever.

They leave familiar scenes and faces, leave behind them the happy times of college life, but, no matter what may come, nothing can efface the impressions these have left upon their hearts. In later years, when the advancement of time has left its marks upon their brows, then the recollection of their college days will come back to them as bright sunbeams in many sad and dreary days.

But why dwell so long upon such a sentimental theme, since we all must leave when our time arrives? Let this be our parting greeting to the graduating brothers of our chapter and of all sister chapters: "Farewell, Brothers and Comrades; may God be with you and guide you, and may He grant you health, success and prosperity."

On March 15, Gamma Lambda received another new member into her fold. This new brother, George G. Starke, is fully deserving of the honor and it therefore gives me great pleasure to introduce him to all Psi Omegas.

The work of our chapter for this year is nearly over and only a few weeks remain before we hold our final meeting of the year. This has been a very busy year for us, and, while we have accomplished a great deal not all of our intentions have been realized. We trust that the coming year will show even better results.

As our final examinations were drawing near, we decided to hold our annual elections on the 19th of April instead of the first meeting in May. This was very easily accomplished with the following result:

Grand Master....................D. B. Thompson, '08.
Junior Master.....................F. L. Carey, '08.
Secretary..............................J. D. Street, '08.
Treasurer...........................E. A. Curtis, '08.
Senator................................O. Palmer, '08.
Editor and Historian.................G. G. Stark, '09.
Chief Inquisitor.....................F. L. Carey, '08.
Chief Interrogator.............M. F. McPhillips, '09.
Inside Guardian...................J. A. Robertson, '08.
Outside Guardian.................F. J. Doherty, '08.

All these brothers are sincere workers and we therefore expect much from them in the administration of the affairs of our chapter during the coming year. They are sure of the co-operation of all active members, as in every case the election was unanimous.

After the election and all other business of the evening had been transacted, Bro. Baldwin, one of our alumni brethren, gave a most interesting and instructive clinic on "The manipulation of soft or non-cohesive gold, the filling of teeth with cohesive gold without the use of a mallet, and last but not least, the method of combining oxyphosphate of zinc with amalgam to form a most excellent filling material which may be called cement-amalgam."

As this will be the last issue of this year, I employ this means of thanking the Supreme Council, particularly Supreme Councilor Friesell, for unselfish endeavors in our behalf. We hope that our successors will make liberal use of the advice of this honorable body, for, I am glad to say, it is cheerfully given whenever it may be desired.

Gamma Lambda again sends her greetings and wishes of good luck to all sister chapters. May all brothers enjoy a pleasant vacation after the hard labors of the year 1906-1907 which have now come to an end.

GAMMA MU—UNIVERSITY OF IOWA.

A. R. Hamm, Editor.

Gamma Mu takes pleasure in presenting to the fraternity three new members, as follows:

Wm. J. McGuire, '09.................Watkins, Iowa.
Max C. Frazier, '08.................Nevada, Iowa.
Dr. Richard Summa, Hony..........Iowa City, Iowa.

GAMMA NU—VANDERBILT UNIVERSITY.

E. Elwood Street, Editor.

As we write this our last editorial for The Frater, we are conscious of the emotions which are common among our seniors at this time. They are buoyant, though depressed; pleased, yet filled with regret. A feeling of good will and joy steals over them because of the near approach of the time when they will receive that long-sought "sheep-skin," earned by three years of hard toil. Yet there is sadness as they realize that their college life is spent and that the hand, which waves us a last farewell, may next greet us in the land beyond. They are about to step from the student to the professional ranks. They regret to think they can no longer be the former, they are glad to think that they can at last enter the latter. So they continue to walk "Old Vandy's Corridors" hilarious, depressed, complaining, but lastly "Delighted."

We men of Gamma Nu realize that we are young; that we have nothing to give but much to gain, yet our cup of brotherly love is bubbling over, and mistakes which we continually make may be credited to our enthusiasm over "Glorious Psi Omega."

Seemingly, little has been accomplished, since our organization, yet we feel proud of the advancement attained, for we are the thirty-eighth part of a grand brotherhood and with grim determination stand ready to advance Psi Omega's work.

It is with extreme pleasure that we present Dr. Wynne as an honorary member of Gamma Nu. Dr. Wynne belongs to that staunch body of men known as the Vanderbilt Faculty. We are also pleased to present Frank C. Wilson, '08.

At our meeting last week the officers elected for the ensuing year, were as follows:

Grand Master	A. C. Braly.
Junior Master	L. H. Wilson.
Secretary	E. L. Williams.
Senator	J. A. Byrd, Jr.
Treasurer	J. N. Sledge.
Chief Inquisitor	I. W. Noel.
Chief Interrogator	J. B. Jones.
Historian	W. E. Simms.
Inside Guardian	C. McCain.
Outside Guardian	H. R. Penny.
Editor	J. K. Williams.

We give a little promenade in honor of our seniors on the evening of May 10, and are anxiously awaiting this occasion. Please bear in mind that there goes out from Gamma Nu a feeling of love and hope that honors may heap themselves at the feet of all Psi Omegas; that a vacation filled with pleasure and success, may be the good fortune of all.

Alumni Chapters.

PHILADELPHIA ALUMNI CHAPTER.

H. L. Chandler, Editor.

The regular monthly meeting of Philadelphia Alumni Chapter was held in the office of Brother A. M. Chandler, 314 South 52nd street, West Philadelphia, on Wednesday evening, February 27, with fourteen members present. The meeting was opened with Brother Cochran in the chair.

After the opening ceremonies, a paper was read by Brother Marsh entitled, "Abscesses" and discussion was opened by Brother Love who was followed by Brothers Zurbrigg and Denny.

The exchange of ideas on this most imporatnt subject was productive of much good to those assembled.

That the interest manifested by the members of Philadelphia Alumni Chapter will not be permitted to flag, was attested on the evening of Wednesday, March 20, when fully three-fourths of the total membership attended the meeting. The meeting was held in the office of Brother Harry D. Winsmore, 1624 Walnut street.

With all of the officers present the meeting was opened promptly at 8 p. m. Grand Master Cochran congratulated the members of the chapter on their promptness in assembling and their evident interest in the work of the order.

The paper of the evening, "Some Dental Formulas—Why and How I Use Them" was read by Brother D. A. Zurbrigg.

The discussion which followed occupied the balance of the evening.

SEALTH ALUMNI CHAPTER.

Geo. P. Williams, Editor.

The March number of The Frater is at hand and we have very much enjoyed its perusal. The accounts of the Crystal Anniversary celebration were especially interesting. Our boys were scattered somewhat at the time so that a formal celebration could not be considered.

We, however, were with the boys in spirit and feel that these meetings all over this country have given the Psi Omega cause a great impetus, and the effect in the next ten years of the work of this aggregation of live, hustling young fellows, always striving to do the best they know, but always striving to know the best, can scarcely be estimated.

We have one meeting each month, and there is always something doing! Dr. Luithlen, G. M., has a program committee at work, composed of Drs. Osterberg, Poston and Alexander, which, evidently, has been threatened with some dire calamity by the G. M., because it always has a full program arranged.

Our meetings are not of the "mutual admiration" sort either. We are learning to accept criticism of the most cutting sort, with good nature and a desire to profit by it, and also to render criticism with a view to ferreting out error and guess work, and withall to be broadminded, ever helping to set our profession upon a sound, scientific basis.

What do you think of having a big P. O. meet here in 1909? During our Alaska Yukon Exposition? We may invite the National Dental to meet here then, and if they accept, what a fine chance for our P. O. boys to get together!

Editorial.

TRIENNIAL GRAND CHAPTER.

The Fifth Triennial Grand Chapter will probably convene at Minneapolis, Minn., in the latter part of July and just preceding the meeting of the National Dental Association thus giving Psi Omegas the advantage of the low railroad rates which will be in force at that time and an opportunity of attending the meeting of the National Dental Association, which promises to be one of the most interesting in the history of the society. It is hoped that there will be a large attendance of Psi Omegas, both at the Grand Chapter and at N. D. A. meeting. More definite arrangements will be announced later.

NEW SUBSCRIPTIONS.

Heretofore, it has been the practice of the Supreme Council to send The Frater to each graduate for one year, risking his making good the amount at the end of the year. While this plan proved satisfactory in a great number of instances, quite a few were found who assumed that there was no obligation upon their part. Hence financial difficulties fell to the lot of The Frater. The purpose of this little message is to urge each of you loyal graduates of Psi Omega, who have the good of the fraternity at heart and who are interested in the affairs of the fraternity, to send in your subscription for Volume Seven of The Frater as soon as you are permanently located.

If you have not the cost of the subscription at hand, send a line stating that you desire The Frater, and remit for it later. The former practice of sending The Frater promiscuously, to graduates, will be discontinued.

GENERAL FRATERNITY DIRECTORY.

The close of the school year is at hand, yet, notwithstanding continued urging, certain secretaries of certain chapters have not rendered the assistance in getting out the directory which the Fraternity had a right to expect. This gross neglect of duty of these officials is an obstacle which will be overcome, but at the expense of promptness in completing our directory.

When finished, the directory will be complete in every detail, but more time will be needed.

STATE BOARD QUESTIONS.

An important feature of The Frater is the publishing of various State Board Questions. Undoubtedly every active member appreciates this feature, especially if the state in which he hopes to practice requires an examination, so, we ask that those of you, who will soon "go against" a state board, procure for The Frater a set of the questions asked. Others coming after you will appreciate your kindness and forethought in helping to make less trying the taking of these examinations.

HALF TONES.

Chapter illustrations have been used in the order in which they have been received. Those not used in this issue will be used in the November issue of The Frater.

Personal and Alumni Notes.

Clyde Mount, Chi, '05' is located at Wallowa, Ore.

A. J. Rose, Rho., '03' has removed from New Kensington to Knox, Pa.

D. C. Davenny, Kappa, '05' Conneaut, O., will remove to Ritzville, Wash., about August 1.

Leland E. Phelps, Kappa, '05' has removed from Adrian, Mich., to The Browning, Toledo, O.

E. W. Moore, Delta, '98' has removed from Newport, N. H., to 118 Pleasant street, Malden, Mass.

For Sale—Dental practice and office fixtures in Delaware town of 3,000 population. Inventory furnished upon application. Other business demands entire attention.

H. Everton Hosley, Gamma, '95' has been elected Chairman of the Finance Committee, which will raise funds for the purpose of adding a dental library to the Springfield, Mass., city library.

M. J. Moran, Omega, '03' Deming, N. M., a member of the New Mexico legislature, and also of the dental examining board, recently succeeded in having a new dental law enacted by the legislature.

W. L. Barnett, Omicron, '06, has been traveling in southern Mexico and is now located at Rincon Antonio, Edo de Oaxaca, Mexico, where he is meeting with success in the practice of his profession.

The readers of The Frater are indebted to S. A. Lusby, Editor, Beta Eta chapter, for the set of Arkansas, and to J. E. Callaway, P. G. M., Xi, for the set of Wisconsin State Board questions which are published in this issue of The Frater.

H. D. Srigley, Psi, '03, Athens, O., spent the month of March at his old home in Canada. On March 18, while hunting, he accidentally shot himself through the left foot. We are pleased to state that Brother Srigley has about recovered from his mishap and will soon resume practice.

For Sale—Complete outfit, practice and house in small town. Center of finest farming district in Ohio. College town. Fine class of patients. Capable man should make $2,500 a year. Expenses very low. Terms can be arranged with reliable purchaser. Present owner going to far West. For further information apply to The Frater.

Marriages.

NEWCOMB-GEESEMAN.

Lewis J. Newcomb, Theta, and Miss Abbie Bell Geeseman were united in marriage at the home of the bride, Ansley, Neb., on Wednesday evening, May 1, 1907.

HASKIN-LANIER.

J. P. Haskin, Psi, '05, Gallipolis, O., and Miss Eva Lanier, Crown City, O., were united in marriage at the home of the bride on March 31, 1907. Brother Haskin has been practicing in Gallipolis since graduation and is enjoying a nice practice.

KNIGHT-McBRIEN.

A. W. Knight, Gamma, '05, and Miss Mabelle McBrien, of Ripley, Ontario, were united in marriage at the home of the bride on April 2, 1907. Brother Knight is practicing at Cadillac, Mich.

FORSYTH-BRIARD.

J. E. Forsyth, Iota, '07, and Miss Claudia Briard were united in marriage on April 27, 1907. The date first set for the happy event was June 4, 1907, but was finally changed to April 27. The Chicago Tribune of March 27, contains a very good likeness of the bride and the following:

"The prospect of a long ocean voyage and a home in Australia, thousands of miles away from parents and friends, was a matter of no consequence to a sixteen-year-old Oak Park girl when it came to a choice between that alternative and giving up the man she loved.

"Despite her youth and the objections of father and mother, Miss Claudia Zelia Briard, daughter of Mr. and Mrs. Benoit Briard, decided yesterday that she would marry J. Elder Forsyth, a student in the Chicago Dental College. So the engagement was announced and the date of the wedding was set for June 4.

"The young man heard Miss Briard sing one evening at a concert in Oak Park. He lost his heart to her immediately and sought her friendship. After the first introduction the two became almost inseparable. The parents of the girl frowned on the affair, because they considered their daughter too young for marriage, and when they saw the case was becoming serious they forbade the two keeping company.

"But the young people did not swerve from their course. Miss Briard made a strong appeal for her fiance and overcame the objections of the father and mother, who opposed the idea of the trip to Australia, where Forsyth proposes to hang out his shingle after his graduation in May. After the marriage at the Briard residence, 316 Home avenue, Oak Park, the young bride will accompany her husband to Sydney, Australia."

Necrology.

C. J. McDERMOTT, ZETA.

It is with sorrow that we announce the death of Brother C. J. McDermott, of Boston, Mass., who was a member of Zeta along in 1899. The funeral services were held at the residence of his parents, 201 South Forty-first street.

JAMES C. BINGHAM, NU, '05.

It is with sorrow that we announce the death of James C. Bingham, Nu, '05. which occurred at his home in Washington, Pa., on Tuesday, March 12, 1907. Brother Bingham had been afflicted with tuberculosis for some time. He was a quiet, square, unassuming young man and was a favorite among his acquaintances.

State Board Questions.

WISCONSIN.

January, 1907.

Chemistry.

1. What is alcohol? How is it formed and what are its properties? 2. Name a solvent for phenol. Gutta percha. 3. Give the most important properties of peroxide of hydrogen, and explain its chemical action when used for dental purposes. 4. What materials are used in making nitrous oxid gas? Describe the process. 5. Of what is plaster of paris composed? Explain the change which takes place when it sets. 6. What compound of zinc is used in oxyphosphate of zinc, and what is the liquid? 7. Give symbols of nitric acid, sulphuric acid, sodium chloride, calcium sulphate, gold, mercury, tin, zinc, copper. 8. (a) If H_2SO_4 is placed in a tooth chamber what is the effect? (b) How would you attempt to dissolve a broken broach in a root canal? 9. What will dissolve au? Fe? Rubber? Rosin? Gum sandarac? Camphor gum? Iodine? Ag? 10. (a) Name some substance that has a great affinity for H_2O. (b) How is it used, especially in dentistry?

Materia Medica.

1. Tell all you know about cocaine. 2. Tell all you know about chloroform. 3. Tell all you know about strychnine. 4. Tell all you know about atropine. 5. Tell all you know about carbolic acid. 6. Tell all you know about morphine. 7. Tell all you know about sulphuric acid. 8. Write a prescription containing any three of the above. 9. What are the differences between escharotic and astringent? 10. What are the differences between disinfectant, deodorant and antiseptic?

Anatomy.

1. Name the bones of the trunk. 2. What bones articulate with the temporal bone? 3. What bones articulate with the superior maxillary? 4. Give muscular attachments of inferior maxilla. 5. Describe the medulla oblongata. 6. How is the nervous system divided? 7. Describe the portal system. 8. Describe the structures of the nervous system. 9. Describe the thoracic duct. 10. Describe the pulmonary veins.

Histology.

1. What is histology? 2. Give difference between histology and pathology. 3. Give difference between histology and physiology. 4. Give histology of tongue. 5. Give histology of teeth.

Physiology.

1. What is the physiological action of the heart during the heart-beat? 2. Describe the heart sounds. 3. Upon what three things does arterial pressure depend? 4. What three forces assist the heart in circulation? 5. Describe the physiological process of secretion. 6. Give two sources of animal heat. 7. Describe pancreatic secretion. 8. What is the object of digestion? 9. Describe the spleen. 10. Describe the lung.

Orthodontia.

1. Give three local causes of irregularities of the teeth. 2. Which is more difficult to accomplish, forward or backward movement of upper incisors? 3. What is the difference between an ordinary appliance and a machine? 4. What is the first thing to do with a regulating case? 5. Name three pronounced evils of malocclusion.

Oral Surgery.

1. How would you treat a fracture of the superior maxillary? 2. How would you treat a fracture of the inferior maxillary? 3. Define ankylosis and give treatment. 4. Give treatment for facial neuralgia and operation for same. 5. What is a cyst? Give treatment. 6. What would you do in case of nonunion of inferior maxillary? 7. Describe the diagnosis of a frac-

ture. 8. How does an incised wound heal? Give treatment. 9. What prevents a wound from healing?

Operative Dentistry.

1. Give method of operating gold filling material into a cavity. 2. What should be shape of filling and why? 3. How protect margin of cavity when filling with gold? 4. State reason why cohesive gold should be annealed? 5. State method of exposing a cavity extending beneath margin of gum. How exclude moisture while filling? 6. When preparing a cavity for filling how direct bur and why? 7. What comprises examination of the mouth? 8. What is danger of forcible wedging of superior central incisors? 9. What is danger of making retaining points at apex of approximal cavity? 10. State method of preparing and filling an approximal surface cavity where both labial and palatal surfaces are involved.

Prosthetic Dentistry.

1. How take impression with wax and plaster? 2. When use modeling compound instead of plaster for impressions? 3. (a) How do you know when you have correct bite? (b) How judge distance of bite? 4. How should six anterior teeth be arranged? 5. What is the shape of a full case? 6. What is the longest and most prominent tooth in plate? 7. How know when lead is ready to pour? 8. How make metal cast from plaster impression? 9. Give objection to swaged rim on lower plate. 10. What are conditions of a successful soldering operation.

Pathology.

1. Explain difference between predisposing and exciting causes of disease. 2. What is inflammation? 3. Give effect eruptive diseases have on children's teeth. 4. Diagnose pyorrhoea alveolaris. 5. Explain symptoms of pulp calcification. 6. Give causes of periodontitis. 7. Give diagnosis and treatment of abscess of antrum. 8. What is exostosis? 9. Give theory of predisposing cause of caries. 10. Differentiate between caries and necrosis.

ARKANSAS.

Anatomy.

1. Give articulation of malar bone. 2. Give branches of facial nerve. 3. Describe superior maxillary. 4. Name muscles of mastication. 5. Give muscles that produce the lateral movement of jaw. 6. Give blood supply of palate. 7. Give blood supply of lips; gums. 8. Give blood and nerve supply of teeth. 9. Does necrosis occur most frequently in inferior or superior maxillary? 10. Give course of facial artery. 11. Name muscles attached to inferior maxillary and action of each. 12. What is the nerve of taste?

Histology.

1. What causes clotting of blood? 2. What is purpose of secondary dentine? How differ from dentine? 3. Describe enamel. Give composition. 4. What is the pulp composed of? 5. How does structure of an artery differ from structure of vein?

Pathology.

1. What is pathology? 2. What is inflammation? 3. How does a nerve enter a tooth? 4. What causes pain in inflammation? 5. What results may follow the premature extraction of temporary teeth? 6. What is erosion? 7. What is abrasion? 8. Give difference in caries of teeth and caries of bone.

Anesthesia.

1. How administer chloroform? Antidote, contra indications? 2. How administer ether? Antidote, contra indications? 3. How administer nitrous oxide? Antidote, contra indications? 4. How administer cocaine? Antidote, contra indications?

Materia Medica.

1. What is a counter irritant? Name two. 2. What is action of aconite? 3. Name two medicines that depress heart action. 4. When and how is capsicum used in dentistry? 5. What preparation of arsenic is used? 6. How treat cocaine poisoning? 7. How treat carbolic acid poisoning? 8. Give difference between narcotic and hypnotic. 9. Distinguish be-

tween stimulant and tonic. 10. How are medicines administered? 11. Define diuretic, diaphoretic and expectorant. 12. Give signs of mercurial poisoning. 13. How relieve tooth ache? 14. Define materia medica. 15. How administer medicines to obtain quickest result?

Therapeutics.

1. How diagnose pulpitis? Give treatment. 2. How diagnose pericementitis? Give treatment, 3. What is a counter irritant? Name two. 4. What preparation of iron is injurious to teeth? 5. What is the active principle of a drug? 6. What happens when H_2O_2 is applied to a tooth cavity? 7. Give action of phenol. 8. Give action of carbolic acid? 9. Define escharotic, name two.

Hygiene.

1. What is hygiene? 2. What is the best method of disinfecting instruments? 3. What hygienic measure should a dentist observe after operating? 5. State best method of disinfecting the room of a diphtheretic person.

Physiology.

1. How are digestion products taken up? 2. How is nourishment to tissues supplied? 3. Into what classes are muscles divided? 4. State function of salivary glands? 4. Name digestive fluids. 6. Tell where each is found and give ferment of each. 7. What causes discoloration of a tooth when the pulp is dead?

Chemistry and Metallurgy.

1. Mention three acids and give formula of each. 2. What is meant by analysis, synthesis? 3. Define atom, molecule. 4. Describe manufacture of H_2O. 5. What happens when plaster of paris and water are mixed? 6. What is an amalgam? 7. Does cohesive gold need ever be annealed? 8. What salt of silver is used in dentistry? Give formula. 9. What does each of the following stand for: Au, Ag, Pt, Zn, N, Ka, Fe, Pb? 10. How is arsenic obtained?

Operative Dentistry.

1. Give general rules for preparation of cavities. 2. Why are risks especially great in wedging superior central incisors? 3. Name different filling materials. 4. What are the desirable and undesirable points of gold as a filling material? 5. Why does tin arrest decay, when other fillings fail? 6. What is difference

between cohesive and non-cohesive gold? 7. Why are pt. and gold used together in a filling? 8. What causes gold to tarnish in the mouth? 9. What is treatment of fistulous abscess? 10. How treat a congested pulp? 11. When is extraction of teeth indicated? 12. Give treatment of excessive hemorrhage after extraction. 13. How treat decay in deciduous teeth? 14. What is use of sulphuric acid in dentistry?

Prosthetic Dentistry.

1. How would you make a full denture, from the time patient enters office until it is complete? 2. How construct a superior right bridge from cuspid to first molar, cuspid a Richmond crown and molar a shell, porcelain facings for dummies? 3. What is a plaster of paris formula? 4. Give ingredients of porcelain teeth. 5. When use gum section and when plain teeth? 6. How construct die and swage a gold plate for upper denture? 7. How repair a vulcanite plate with cracked central incisor? 8. Give formula for good fusible metal. 9. What guage and carat gold for crown? 10. What guage and carat gold for plates? 11. Why is flux used? 12. Why do we use a pickling solution?

PHILLIPS' MILK OF MAGNESIA

"THE PERFECT ANTACID"
FOR LOCAL OR SYSTEMIC USE

| CARIES | SENSITIVENESS | STOMATITIS |
| EROSION | GINGIVITIS | PYORRHŒA |

Are successfully treated with it. As a mouth wash it neutralizes oral acidity.

PHILLIPS' PHOSPHO-MURIATE OF QUININE,
COMPOUND
TONIC, RECONSTRUCTIVE, AND ANTIPERIODIC

With marked beneficial action upon the nervous system. To be relied upon where a deficiency of the phosphates is evident.

THE CHAS. H. PHILLIPS CHEMICAL CO., NEW YORK AND LONDON.

Lightning Source UK Ltd.
Milton Keynes UK
UKHW012328120119
335431UK00006B/339/P